# Canary Island Walks

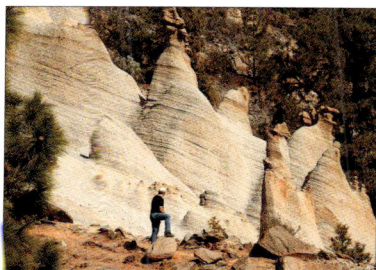

Noel Rochford
with additional notes by Sunflower Books

SUNFLOWER BOOKS

First edition © 2022
Sunflower Books™
PO Box 36160
London SW7 3WS, UK
www.sunflowerbooks.co.uk

ISBN 978-1-85691-544-1

*Margaritas del Teide (Tenerife)*

## Important note to the reader _____

We have tried to ensure that the descriptions and maps in this book are error-free at press date. The book will be updated, where necessary, in future editions. It will be very helpful for us to receive your comments (sent to info@sunflowerbooks.co.uk, please) for the updating of future editions.

We also rely on walkers to take along a good supply of common sense when they explore. Conditions can change fairly rapidly in the Canary Islands, and *storm damage or bulldozing may make a route unsafe at any time*. If the route is not as we outline it here, and your way ahead is not secure, return to the point of departure. *Never attempt to complete a tour or walk under hazardous conditions!* Please read carefully the notes on pages 8-18, and the introductory comments at the beginning of each walk about equipment, grade, distances, and timings. Explore *safely*, and at the same time respect the beauty of the countryside.

*Cover photograph and title page: the Paiaje Lunar on Tenerife (Walk 23)*

Photos: Peter Brož (Chmee2, CC BY-SA 3.0, via Wikimedia Commons): 38-9 (bottom); Shutterstock: cover, 1, 2, 14, 16, 17, 28-9, 30 (top), 37, 38 (middle), 42-3, 46, 48-9, 50, 54-5, 58, 62-3 (bottom), 65, 72-3, 77, 80, 83, 92-3, 96, 99, 102-3, 112-3 (both), 114-5, 122 (top), 124-5, 139, 141, 148, 156-7, 168 (top), 174-5, 181, 186, 188, 195, 196-7, 198; Conny Spelbrink: 4-5, 56, 72 (top), 123 (top), 132-3, 149, 183; John Underwood: 9, 15, 24-5, 26, 27 (top), 38 (top four), 39 (top), 44, 66, 70, 118, 119, 122 (bottom), 130 (middle); Ottilie Sefton: 191; all other photographs: Noel Rochford
Maps: Nick Hill for Sunflower Books. Base map data © OpenStreetMap contributors. Contour data made available under ODbL (opendatacommons.org/licenses/odbl/1.0)
Drawings of island flora (pages 18-19, 119): Sharon Rochford
Sunflower Books is a Registered Trademark
A CIP catalogue record for this book is available from the British Library.
Printed and bound in England: Short Run Press, Exeter

# 🌻 Contents

*The giant ferns (Woodwardia radicans, see panels on pages 125 and 151) at Los Tilos — one of the special reasons for walking on La Palma*

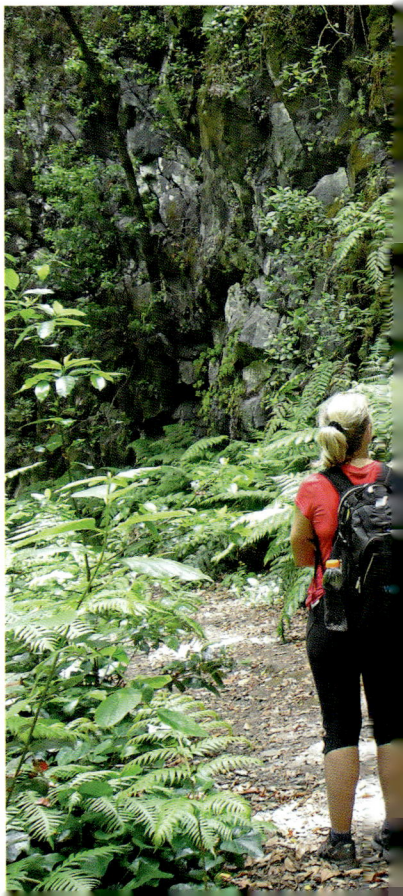

# ☀ Preface

Few places in the world can offer the kaleidoscope of natural beauty found in the Canary Islands. What one island lacks, another has in plenty. Each island has a personality of its own — as you will see when you use this book!

We at Sunflower are great enthusiasts of these islands and were the first publishers in Europe to bring them to the attention of walkers — thanks to the intrepid Noel Rochford who spent many, many years there tramping unmapped paths. Now, in the quiet of lockdown, while the international walking world has been put on pause, we thought it would be a good idea to put what Noel says in the first paragraph to the test: a book of walks covering *all* the islands.

This guide is a *taster* — a selection of mostly easy and moderate walks on each of the islands, designed to emphasise

their differing highlights. Once you've had a taste, perhaps you will go on to indulge yourself by taking a longer holiday on the island of your choice, using one of Noel's 'Landscapes' guides dedicated to that specific island or islands.

To Noel's walking notes we at Sunflower have incorporated 'Stories and snippets' in separate panels with each of the walks, something that struck us as 'special' or interesting — from water collection to World War Two gossip, the bravery of the original island inhabitants, the plant life, the many myths and legends…

One of the advantages of walking on the Canaries is the excellent public transport system. You do not have to rent a car. With very few exceptions, these walks are accessible by bus (or boat).

Another plus is the weather — perhaps the best in the world for walking all year round. Winters are mild, and summers are not swelteringly hot as they are in some destinations around the Med. Year-round temperatures are generally in the 20°sC (70°sF).

For most tourists in Britain, the Canary Islands mean Tenerife, Gran Canaria, Lanzarote and Fuerteventura. But there are actually seven islands in the archipelago (nine, if you're counting their offshoots of La Graciosa and Lobos). Lesser-known La Gomera, La Palma and El Hierro are still utopias for nature lovers. They are still quite unspoilt. They lack the fine glistening beaches of the more popular islands, and this may be their saving grace. Great news for those of us who seek peace and quiet. So if you want a holiday with razzmatazz, head for one of the 'big four'. But if you don't mind unrushed service, and if you want to return home more relaxed than when you left, perhaps you'll choose from one of the 'quiet three'.

— NOEL ROCHFORD AND SUNFLOWER BOOKS

## Recommended books and maps

If you can find it, we highly recommend *Wild Flowers of the Canary Islands,* written by David and Zoë Bramwell, dating from 1974. It's usually available from third party sellers via Amazon or one of the other online book suppliers.

If you have enjoyed the walks in this book and you would like to explore the islands in greater depth, Noel has written several 'Landscapes' guides for the Canaries. These contain both car tours and timetables for public transport, as well as plenty of walks. All are published by Sunflower Books.

*Lanzarote: 68 long and short walks, 3 car tours*
*Fuerteventura: 45 long and short walks, 4 car tours*
*Gran Canaria: 60 long and short walks, 6 car tours*
*Tenerife (Orotava • Anaga • Teno • Cañadas): 80 long and short walks, 5 car tours*
*La Gomera and Southern Tenerife: 70 long and short walks, 6 car tours*
*La Palma and El Hierro: 48 long and short walks, 4 car tours*

# 🌻 *Introduction*

This book covers some of the best walking on all seven Canary Islands, as well as the outlying islets of La Graciosa and Lobos. Enough ground is covered to keep most walkers exploring for a good week to 10 days — to have an enticing first taste of each of these islands.

*There are walks in this book for everyone.*

**Beginners:** Start on the walks graded 'easy', and be sure to look at the short and alternative walks — some are easy versions of longer hikes.

**Experienced walkers:** If you are used to rough terrain and have a head for heights, you can tackle any of the walks in this book. Of course, you must take into account the season and weather conditions. For example, in rainy weather some of the *barranco* walks will be unsuitable; in strong winds or snow do not plan excursions to the mountains! And always remember that **storm damage can make these routes unsafe at any time!** Remember, too: always follow the route as described in this book. If you have not reached one of the waypoints after a reasonable time, please go back to the last 'sure' point and start again.

**Experts:** There's nothing here to really *challenge* you. But if you fall in love with one of these islands and get the relevant 'Landscapes' guide, I can guarantee some will test your mettle!

**All walkers:** Be sure to check the update service described on the inside front cover of the book before you travel.

## Grading, waymarking, maps, GPS

There is a quick overview of each walk's **grade** in the Contents. But many of the walks have shorter and/or alternative versions. In the Contents we've only had space to show the *lowest grade of a main walk:* for full details of grading, see the introductory remarks about the walk itself. Here is a brief overview of the three gradings:

● very easy — more or less level (perhaps with a short climb to a viewpoint); good surfaces underfoot; easily followed

● easy-moderate — ascents/descents of no more than about 300-500m/1000-1800ft; good surfaces underfoot; easily followed

● moderate-strenuous — ascents/descents may be over 500m/1800ft; variable surfaces underfoot — you must be sure-footed and agile; possible route-finding problems in poor visibility

Any of the above grades may, if applicable, be followed by:

❗ *danger* of vertigo — you must have a very good head for heights

**Waymarking** and **signposting** have been brought up to 'Euro' standards on all of these islands, although the waymarking is often faded and specific signposting may vary. There are three types of waymarking:

- *Red and white* waymarks indicating GR routes ('Grandes Recorridos': long-distance footpaths);
- *Yellow and white* waymarks indicating PR routes ('Pequeños Recorridos': short trails of up to six hours);
- *Green and white* waymarks indicating SL routes ('Senderos Locales': local trails, up to about 10km long).
- For all these routes, two parallel stripes (=) mean 'continue this way'; right-angled stripes (⌐) indicate a 'change of direction'; an '**✗**' means 'wrong way'.

**Trail numbering** often differs in the national parks, and **trail maps** are usually available at their visitors' centres. We show trail numbers existing at the time of publication on our walking maps. But new trails are being cut all the time (and existing trails sometimes closed), so you may find some not on our maps — nor even on the maps from visitors' centres.

The **maps** in this book are based on Openstreetmap mapping (see page 2), but have been very heavily annotated from notes and GPS work in the field. It is a pity that we have to reproduce most of them at only 1:50,000 to keep the book to a manageable size; quite a few walkers buy both the paperback *and* our downloadable pdf files so that they can print the maps at a larger size in very sharp focus — but you can always enlarge them on a colour photocopier.

*Walkers' signposts at La Caldera on Tenerife (Walk 26): at the top is a standard GR sign; its wine-red livery is repeated on the signs below, where the GR131 coincides with the yellow/white PR trail to Mamio and the green/white SL La Orilla trail. You may also see orange stripes (not shown here): they are for mountain bikers.*

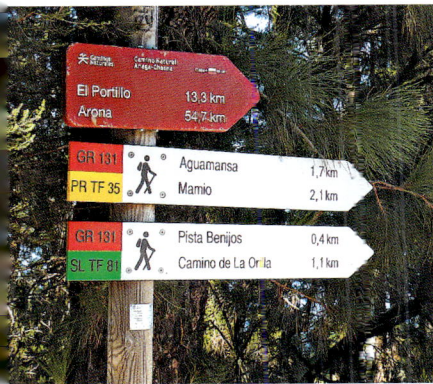

Free **GPS tracks** are available for all these walks: see the *Canary Island Walks* page on the Sunflower website. Please bear in mind, however, that GPS readings should *never* be relied upon as your sole reference point. Conditions can change at any time — especially on these islands, where mountainsides come down overnight from landslides … or eruptions! Those of you who cannot be bothered to use GPS on the ground might nevertheless enjoy opening the GPX files in Google Earth to preview the walks in advance.

## Where to stay and public transport

If you're visiting one of the islands for a general break, it's likely that you've already booked your accommodation — perhaps as part of a package deal. If you hire a car, it doesn't matter much where you stay. But if you've no car and you plan to do some walking, stay close to good bus connections!

Below are the websites of the bus companies serving the seven islands, where you can check timetables and routes (at the top of each walk the appropriate bus line is shown). Some of these websites have interactive maps where you can even find the nearest bus stop to your accommodation.

Lanzarote: www.intercitybus-lanzarote.es
Fuerteventura: www.tiadhe.com
Gran Canaria: www.globalsu.net
Tenerife: www.titsa.com
Gomera: www.guaguagomera.com
La Palma: www.tilp.com
El Hierro: www.transhierro.com

## Weather

Island weather is often unpredictable, but there are a few signs and weather patterns that may help you forecast a walking day. All these islands are blessed with year-round walking weather. Winters are warm, with temperatures of around 20°C/68°F, and summers — even July and August — generally not unbearably hot (unlike the southern European mainland or the Greek islands, for instance).

**Weather patterns** in the archipelago are influenced by two **winds**: the northeasterly trade winds (the *alisio*) and the easterly or southeasterly wind from the Sahara (the *calima*). Two other winds blow very infrequently: a northwesterly wind from the north Atlantic and a southwesterly wind from the tropics. Both carry heavy rains and storms. Rainfall varies: the westerly islands see the most rain, whereas Lanzarote and Fuerteventura, with no high mountains to catch the clouds, are much drier … but can be very windy.

The northeasterly trade wind, the *alisio,* which prevails for much of the year, is easily identified by low-lying fluffy clouds — which add so much character to your photographs …

unless you are trapped in them and can't see where you're going! These clouds hover over the north of Gran Canaria and the westerly islands for much of the year, sitting between 600m and 1500m (2000ft and 5000ft). The mountainous centres of these islands catch the clouds, with the result that in the north it tends to be misty and rainy, whereas the south soaks up the sun.

The *calima,* quite different, brings heat and dust. The temperature rises considerably, and the atmosphere is filled with very fine dust particles. This weather is more frequent in winter than in summer. It seldom lasts more than three or four days. These days are always good for walking (but in summer stay under tree cover!); even if it's a little warm, the sky is cloudless, although a bit hazy.

The only wind that could really spoil your day is the one from the tropics. It *always* brings heavy rains which cover the whole island. This wind is recognisable from its uniform cloud cover. Fortunately it rarely blows.

The winds bring fresh breezes off the sea, making the days very pleasant for walking. And remember, the clouds don't block out the sun altogether; especially on the heights, you will tan (or burn) due to the combination of sun and wind. Don't forget sun protection! On the other hand, when walking at higher altitudes, one must always be prepared for the *worst* as well: all seasons can be experienced in one day.

# What to take

The *minimum year-round equipment* is listed at the top of each walk. Where walking boots are required, there is no substitute: you will need to rely on the grip and ankle support they provide, as well as their waterproof qualities. All other walks should be done with stout lace-up shoes with thick rubber soles, to grip on wet, slippery surfaces.

You may find the following packing list useful:

walking boots, spare bootlaces
mobile/smartphone/gps
waterproof rain gear (outside
  summer months)
long-sleeved shirt (sun protection)
first-aid kit, including bandages
walking pole(s)
windproof (zip opening)
up-to-date island map
extra pair of socks
sunhat, sunglasses, suncream

up-to-date bus timetable
small rucksack
water bottle with purifying
  tablets
long trousers, tight at the ankles
insect repellent
knives and openers
lightweight fleece, warm fleece
swimming things
groundsheet
torch, whistle, compass

Please bear in mind that neither Noel nor the Sunflower team have done *every* walk in this book in *all* weathers. Use good judgement to modify our lists according to the season.

# Nuisances

**Dogs** aren't a problem in the Canaries. But if dogs make you nervous, you may wish to invest in a 'Dog Dazer', an ultrasonic device which frightens dogs off without harming them. These are available from various sources on the web. Usually, where there are goats and sheep, you find **ticks**. Keep arms and legs covered (good for sun protection too), and the problem is solved. Give **billy goats** a wide berth; they don't like intruders. During the hunting season (August to December), **hunters** blasting away on weekends and bank holidays may frighten you. Exercise your lungs if you think they're too close. **Jeep safaris** may make you eat dust on some walks. Fortunately, in their frenetic search for quick thrills, they never stay in one place for very long. That's it: there are *no* poisonous snakes or insects on the islands.

# Refreshments

There is almost always a place to get drinks or proper meals at the start or end of these walks, while it is rare to find something en route. At the top of each walk we highlight where you can find cafés or restaurants. On any but a short walk near villages, be sure to take some snacks or high-energy food — in case you are delayed. And plenty of water!

*This lovely orange track, lined with asphodels, leads through bucolic countryside to the Arbol Garoé, the Holy Tree (Walk 47).*

# Country code

A code for behaviour is very important on the Canaries, where the rugged terrain can lead to dangerous mistakes.

■ **Only light fires at** picnic areas with fireplaces.

■ **Do not frighten animals.** The goats and sheep you may encounter on your walks are not tame. By making loud noises or trying to touch or photograph them, you may cause them to run in fear and be hurt.

■ **Walk quietly** through all hamlets and villages, and take care not to provoke the dogs.

■ **Protect all wild and cultivated plants.** Don't try to pick wild flowers or uproot saplings. Leave them for other walkers to enjoy. Obviously fruit and other crops are someone's private property and should not be touched.

■ **Leave all gates just as you found them**, whether they are at farms or on the mountainside. Although you may not see any animals, the gates have a purpose: they are used to keep goats or sheep in (or out of) an area. Animals could be endangered by careless behaviour.

■ **Never walk over cultivated land.**

■ **Take your litter away with you.**

# Safety

The following points cannot be stressed too often:

■ **At any time a walk may become unsafe** due to storm damage, landslides, bulldozing — or even eruptions. If the route is not as described in this book, and your way ahead is not secure, do not attempt to go on.

■ **Never walk alone** and *always* tell a responsible person *exactly* where you are going and what time you plan to return. Remember, if you become lost or injure yourself, it may be a long time before you are found. Four is the best walking group: if someone is injured, two can go for help, and there will be no need for panic in an emergency.

■ **Do not overestimate your energies** — your speed will be determined by the slowest walker in your group.

■ **Transport connections** at the end of a walk may be vital.

■ **Proper shoes or boots** are a necessity.

■ **Mists** can suddenly appear on the higher elevations.

■ **Warm clothing** is needed in the mountains; even in summer take some along, in case you are delayed.

■ **Extra rations** must be taken on long walks.

■ **Mobile or smartphone, compass, whistle, torch, first-aid kit** weigh little, but might save your life.

■ **Always take a sunhat with you**, and a cover-up for your arms and legs as well (sun and tick protection).

- **A stout stick/walking pole** is a help on rough terrain and to discourage the rare unfriendly dog.
- *Do not take risks!* Some of the walks cross remote country and can be both ***very cold and potentially hazardous.*** Distances on these islands can be deceptive — perhaps with exhausting descents into and ascents out of hidden *barrancos* between you and your goal. We urge you to read through the entire walk description before setting off.

# Spanish for walkers

In the tourist centres most people speak English. But out in the countryside, a few words of Spanish come in handy, especially if you lose your way. Here's a way to communicate in Spanish that may be helpful. First, memorise the few short key questions and the possible answers below. When you have your 'mini-speech' memorised, always ask the many questions you can concoct from it **in such a way that you get a 'sí' (yes) or 'no' answer**. Never ask an open-ended question like 'Where is the main road?' Instead, ask the question and then *suggest the most likely answer yourself.* For instance: 'Good day, sir. Please — where is the path to Erjos? *Is it straight ahead?*' Unless you get a *'sí'* response, try: *'Is it to the left?'* Go through the answers to your own question until you get a *'sí'* reponse.

Following are the two most likely situations in which you may have to practice some Spanish.

The dots (...) show where to fill in the name of your destination.

*La Culata, backed by Roque Bentayga (Walk 16)*

*The Casa de Cultura in Yaiza, where you meet your guides for Walk 1 and the base for Walk 7*

## ■ Asking the way

### The key questions

| English | Spanish | pronounced as |
|---|---|---|
| Good day, | Buenos días | **Boo**-eh-nos **dee**-ahs |
| sir (madam, miss). | señor (señora, señorita). | sen-**yor** (sen-**yor**-ah sen-yor-**ee**-tah). |
| Please — | Por favor — | **Poor** fah-**voor** — |
| where is | dónde está | **dohn**-day es-**tah** |
| the road to ...? | la carretera a ...? | la cah-reh-**teh**-rah ah ...? |
| the footpath to ...? | la senda de ...? | lah **sen**-dah day ...? |
| the way to ...? | el camino a ...? | el cah-**mee**-noh ah ...? |
| the bus stop? | la parada? | lah par-**rah**-dah? |
| Many thanks. | Muchas gracias. | **Moo**-chas **gra**-thee-as. |

### Possible answers

| English | Spanish | pronounced as |
|---|---|---|
| is it here? | está aquí? | es-**tah** ah-**kee**? |
| straight ahead? | todo recto? | **toh**-doh **rec**-toh? |
| behind? | detrás? | day-**tras**? |
| to the right? | a la derecha? | ah lah day-**reh**-chah? |
| to the left? | a la izquierda? | ah lah eeth-kee-**er**-dah? |
| above/below? | arriba/abajo? | ah-**ree**-bah/ah-**bah**-hoh? |

### ■ Asking a taxi driver to return for you

| English | Spanish | pronounced as |
|---|---|---|
| Please | Por favor | **Poor** fah-**voor** |
| take us to ... | llévanos a ... | **Yay**-vah-nos ah ... |
| and return | y volver | ee vol-**vair** |
| for us at ... | para nosotros a ... | **pah**-rah nos-**oh**-tros ah ... |

*Point out the time when you wish him to return on your watch.*

An inexpensive phrase book will help you compose other 'key' phrases and answers. A CD or an app will help with pronunciation.

# Inter-island travel

You can travel between the islands by air or ferry but, unfortunately, not always in the most convenient manner — often you have to go via Tenerife or Gran Canaria. For instance, from the western Canaries you can't fly direct to Lanzarote or Fuerteventura; you have to go via Tenerife North or Las Palmas.

**Flights** are operated by Binter Canarias (**www.binter-canarias.com**), and flights can be booked online — or contact your travel agent *before you go* (flights may be full if you wait until you are on the islands to book). At time of writing, Binter is flying out of Las Palmas and the northern airport in Tenerife. From Las Palmas there are flights every half hour to Tenerife, every couple of hours to Lanzarote and Fuerteventura, twice a day to La Palma, and once a day to El Hierro. For La Gomera you have to change on Tenerife (Aeropuerto de Tenerife Norte). From Tenerife North there

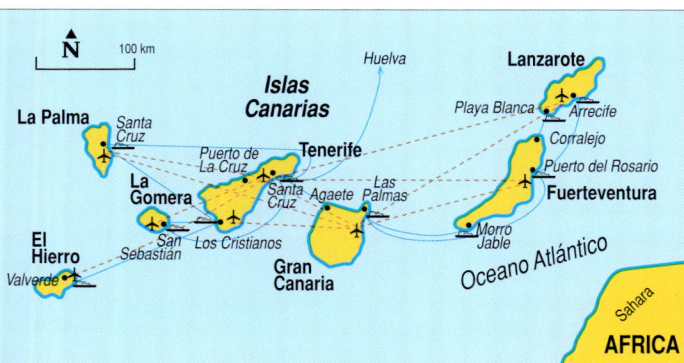

*Below: Fred Olsen fast car ferry to Corralejo on Fuerteventura at Playa Blanca on Lanzarote; opposite: Binter airlines coming in to land at Tenerife Norte*

a half-hourly flights to Las Palmas, and frequent flights to the westerly Canaries: every hour or two to La Palma, three times a day to El Hierro, and twice a day to La Gomera.

Two **ferry** companies currently serve the islands: Naviera Armas (**www.navieraarmas.com**) and Fred Olsen Lines (**www.fredolsen.es**). Ferry bookings can be made online, at travel agencies before you go or once you are on the islands themselves at the port ferry kiosks.

Here at Sunflower we've often used the really convenient ferry crossings between Lanzarote and Fuerteventura and southern Tenerife and La Gomera. You may want to use these yourselves; even if you are based on one of these islands, you could have a day out on the other to take in a walk.

# Organisation of the walks

There are 47 main walks in this book, and many short or alternative suggestions. We hope that the book is set out so that you can plan your walks easily — depending on how far you want to go, your abilities and equipment, and the season. You might begin by looking at the 'map of walk areas' at the start of each section. Here you can see at a glance the location of the walks on each island. Quickly flipping through the book, you'll see that there is at least one photo for every walk.

Having selected one or two potential excursions, turn to the relevant walk. At the top of the page you'll find planning information: distance/time, grade, equipment, and transport

details. It is assumed that you have a good map of the island
to help you if you are driving (or use your smartphone: we
give coordinates for all parking parking places at the start of
each walk).

When you are on your walk, you will find that the text
begins with an introduction to the overall landscape and then
quickly turns to a detailed description of the route itself. The
**large-scale maps** (see notes on page 9) have been annotated
to show key landmarks. **Times** are given for reaching certain
waypoints, based on an average walking rate of 4km/h, with
extra time allowed for ascents and steep descents. *It would be
a good idea to compare your own times with those in the book on
a short walk, before you set off on a long hike.* Remember that
Noel has included only *short stops* at viewpoints; allow ample
time for photography, picnicking, swimming and nature-
watching.

The following **symbols** are used on the walking maps:

| | | | | |
|---|---|---|---|---|
| motorway | | **❶❷** | walk start/waypoint | |
| main road/secondary road | | **A ⌂** | shelter; picnic tables | |
| minor road or lane | | 🎵 ∩ | *galería*, tap, spring/cave | |
| jeep track/motorable track | | ⫯ ⌂ | transmitter, pylon/rock formation | |
| path or steps | | 🚗 🚐 | car parking/bus stop | |
| main walk/alternative walk | | ❗ | danger! danger of vertigo! | |
| waymarked trail, number | | ✝ → | church/shrine/cemetery | |
| national park trail, number | | ▪ 📖 | specific building/best views | |
| other described route | | — 824 — | height (metres) | |
| watercourse *(canal)* | | ⸫ ◡ | AA lava/pahoehoe lava | |

# Plants you may see on the islands

Here are some of the plants mentioned on the walks,
drawn years ago by Noel's sister, Sharon. These drawings
should enable you to identify many of the plants you see, but
do try to get the Bramwell book referred to on page 6.

*Red-flowering
tabaiba*
(Euphorbia
atropurpurea)

*Vinagrera*
(Rumex
lunaria)

Ranunculus
cortusfolius

*Verode* (Kleinia
neriifolia)

Senecio sp.

Aeonium manriqueorum

*Taginaste* (Echium decaisnei)

Greenovia aurea

*Codeso* (Adenocarpus foliolosus)

*Prickly poppy*

*Cerrajón* (Sonchus ortunoi)

*Cardón* (Euphorbia canariensis)

*Margarita* (Argyranthemum)

*Rock rose* (Cistus)

*Palo sangre* (Sonchus tectifolius)

*Prickly pear* (Optunia ficus-indica)

*Valo* (Plocama pendula)

*Canary bellflower*

*Retama* (Spartocytisus supranubius)

*Sea fennel* (Astydamia latifolia)

Lavandula pinnata

*Peorera* (Andryala cheiranthifolia)

*Century plant* (Agave americana)

## Walks on
# Lanzarote & La Graciosa

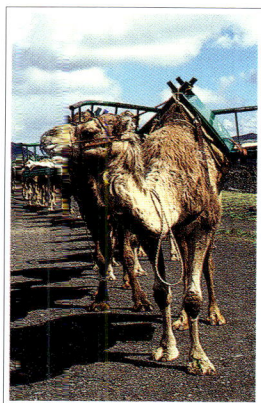

| **Lanzarote** | **La Graciosa** |
|---|---|
| AREA: 846/km² (327sq mi) | AREA: 29/km² (11sq mi) |
| LENGTH OF COAST: 191km (118mi) | LENGTH OF COAST: 30km (19mi) |
| HIGH POINT: Peñas del Chache (671m/2201ft) | HIGH POINT: Agujas Grandes (266m/872ft) |
| POPULATION: 154,530 (2020) | POPULATION: 734 (2018) |
| POPULATION DENSITY: 180/km² (466/sq mi) | POPULATION DENSITY: 25/km² (65/sq mi) |
| CAPITAL: Arrecife (pop 62,988) | 'CAPITAL': Caleta del Sebo (pop 730) |
| PROVINCE: Las Palmas | PROVINCE: Las Palmas |

In the early 1990s Lanzarote grew from a quiet, relatively unknown resort to an island buzzing with three million tourists annually these days — plus another 500,000 day trippers who arrive in cruise ships.

Fortunately, the island had one advantage when it followed Tenerife and Gran Canaria into mass tourism. It was the home of the well-known artist-designer — and, more importantly, conservationist — the late César Manrique. Together with his supporters, he worked to preserve the island's environmental heritage. Despite the tourist boom, they succeeded in orchestrating a well-pitched harmony

ISLA
GRACIOSA

Pedro Barba

2

Caleta del Sebo
*Salinas del Río*
Órzola

3

Guinate
4
Máguez
5
Haría

Arrieta

La
Santa
Los Valles
Mala

Tinajo
Teguise
Guatiza

Mancha
Blanca

PARQUE
NACIONAL
DE TIMANFAYA

1
Mozaga
San Bartolomé

El Golfo
Montaña
Blanca
Costa Teguise

LA
GERIA
6
Arrecife

La
Hoya
Uga
Tías
Playa
Honda

*Salinas de Janubio*
Yaiza
7
Puerto
del Carmen

Las
Breñas
Femés
Puerto
Calero
Playa
Quemada

LANZAROTE

Playa
Blanca

between man and the landscape. As a result, in 1994 Lanzarote was declared a 'World Reserve of the Biosphere' by UNESCO — the first such award ever given to an entire island.

This fascinating 797-square-kilometre island is truly extraordinary. Its fate was decided almost three centuries ago, when the largest volcanic eruption in recorded history took place, leaving a strange and alluring countryside in its wake — a landscape littered with volcanoes and dark streams of jagged lava. This is the backdrop to nearly every scene on the island, and intriguing sights abound.

If you were to suggest walking on Lanzarote to most visitors, they would think you mad. 'Where is there to walk?' But I can think of no better place in the Canary Islands for just strolling. No doubt 'serious' walkers will find Tenerife, La Palma and Gran Canaria, for example, more challenging, but ramblers will be in their element here on Lanzarote.

## Walk 1: TIMANFAYA — THE TREMESANA ROUTE

**Distance:** about 3km/2mi, 2h walking time (but allow about 4h)
**Grade:** ● easy, almost level walk
**Equipment:** stout shoes, fleece, raingear, sunhat, suncream
**Refreshments:** bars and restaurants in Yaiza
**Transport:** 🚌 to/from the 'Supermercado Yaiza' bus stop (Playa Blanca bus, Line 6), or 🚗: park in the car park west of the church (28° 57.114N, 13° 45.952W)
**Important:** This is a *free* guided walk limited to groups of eight, all of whom must be over 16 years of age and sensibly shod. The groups fill up quickly! *Before you travel,* log on to www.reservasparques nacionales.es (English pages) and *pay careful attention to the information given* or you may be unable to take part. When I took the walk years ago, the route was linear; these days a circular route is on offer (see map). It doesn't matter; both cover much the same ground.

*D*o take this walk — as early in your visit as possible. You will learn so much that will add to the pleasure of your stay on Lanzarote — after you have learned to 'read' the landscape. Not only are the guides schooled in vulcanology, but they can answer many more questions besides. *Book this walk before you travel; the places fill up very quickly!*

You may wonder why visitors are not allowed to walk freely in Timanfaya. There are several reasons. Firstly, some of the lava 'tunnels' have a very thin crust — your weight could collapse them, leading to a nasty accident, far from help. A second reason is a matter of aesthetics! The park is picture-postcard perfect: the rolling volcanic slopes all appear to be dusted with a smooth coating of caster sugar — a *patisserie* of pristine, freshly-iced cakes.

The rangers are very house-proud: they may well tell you that just one footprint in this sand changes its colour, and that it can take three years for a footprint to disappear, no less jeep tracks! But the single most important reason is conservation. It can take lichen, the first of the vegetation, on which all subsequent growth depends, *hundreds of years* to take hold.

Your day starts by assembling at the PLAZA IN FRONT OF YAIZA CHURCH at 09.15 (the time and venue may change; all details will

**Lichens — the 'pioneer' plants**
Timanfaya is one of the best areas in the world to study lichens: they can be seen evolving on the naked rock in extreme conditions of heat and cold, their only source of moisture the water in the rock itself and the humidity of the northeasterly trade winds.

In the absence of water to cause erosion, lichens break down the lava, helping to develop soil which can sustain more demanding forms of plant life. Lichens grow most readily on relatively flat surfaces (where they can trap the greatest amount of moisture; see bottom photo on page 26) and in crevices of northeast-facing slopes, where they catch the moisture off the trade winds.

Some tiny lichen which you might not even notice (so please keep to the designated path!) bear hairs that provide life-giving moisture to the animals and birds which survive in the park.

be given when you book). The maximum group size is eight people, and usually there are two groups. Each starts at one end of this linear trail, and the drivers exchange minibus keys halfway along. (Where there is only one group, probably you will do the circular walk shown on the map.)

Starting from Yaiza, your guide may point out two old houses that survived almost six years of eruptions beginning between nine and ten o'clock at night on September 1st, 1730. (See what the parish priest wrote about it in the panel 'Yaiza's Volcanic Gardens' on page 50.) Nearby is a raised water tank with a large tilted 'apron' surface to collect water — a *mareta*. The tank below is much smaller than the 'apron'. These are less common than *aljibes* — sunken water tanks with flat roofs.

How could some houses have survived and, more surprisingly, why was no one killed in the eruptions that obliterated 14 villages in what was once one of the most fertile areas on the island? Probably because the first material vomited out was 'AA' lava, which moves very slowly; families were able to load up their camels and get away. In an eruption, three types of lava spew out: *lapilli* (fine ash), *malpais* or AA-type lava (scoria), and 'bombs'. Bombs are solid and hard; they fly on average 30 to 300m away from the volcano. Bombs can be tiny (you'll be given one to examine) or huge — perhaps 5m/15ft high!

*It's exhilarating to enter the national park on a clear day, when the Fire Mountains glow red above the sea of jagged 'AA' lava. The park's emblem, the Timanfaya 'fire devil', was designed by César Manrique.*

When you **start the walk** ( **◉** ), **Tremesana** (also called *Ter*mesana) will be the first volcano you come to. You will see many fig trees here, most of them encircled by drystone lava walls. All this land was once private; now the national park has an arrangement with the farmers: the trees remain in private hands, but the farmers are obliged to use certain paths to reach their plots. Some of these venerable old fig trees have a circumference of 12m — 40ft!

A very strange construction stands near the fig trees: a scoria-walled enclosure with a 1m/3ft-high 'bed' of *lapilli* on top. What on earth could it be? Called a *pasero*, it's for drying the figs. Since scoria is full of holes, air can circulate all round the fruit. And on the subject of lava walls… those

*Map showing:* Montaña Quemada ▲149, Pedro Perico ▲25, Montaña Encantada ▲254, Caldera Rajada ▲225, Montaña Rajada ▲373, Montaña Hernández ▲238, Montaña ▲324 Termesana, Caldera del Islote de la Vega ▲135, EL GOLFO, 705, 704, LZ2, scale 1 km / 0.5 mi

in this part of the park were built over 100 years ago by the men who built the walls in the Salinas de Janubio — 'master stonemasons', who can build a fairly high drystone wall using just one thickness of rock. (Try it yourself on one of your other walks — goodness knows there are plenty of rocks around to play with...)

The colours in the rocks are dazzling. And they vary enormously depending on their mineral content. Red comes as no surprise, but the sapphire-blue to mauve hues are particularly striking. Look at an example, as in the photo overleaf: you're likely to see that one part of the rock has been formed beneath the earth and another after coming into contact with the air — this is often evident from the shape as well. The part that solidified underground comes out almost black, but the part that came into contact with the air is

*Left: the vivid colours in the rocks are due to oxidation. Below and opposite: it's easy to recognise the difference between jagged AA lava (shown on the preceding page) and smooth pahoehoe lava (opposite, top). The solidified lichen-splattered crusts of pahoehoe lava eventually break up into great blocks, sometimes revealing the underlying tubes, as in the photo below.*

more red from oxidisation. Some rocks are blue from cobalt mixing with oxygen and others gold from sulphur. (The guides know, from the colour of the hillsides, which way the wind was blowing during the eruption. They may point out a cone with yellow streaking on only one side — indicating both the wind direction *and* a second passage of sulphurous wind as the rock cooled, which makes the gold colour even paler.)

**Caldera Rajada** (❶; 'Split Mountain') lies north of Tremesana. If you thought volcanoes always 'blew their *tops*', then this one comes as a surprise. It split its *side*,

and the resulting volcanic tube (*jameo*) reaches out just to the edge of your path. When tongues of lava flow from the point of eruption, they drag along the surface of the ground. The surface lava cools rapidly and solidifies, but molten lava (magma) continues to flow beneath the crust. The magma sinks gradually (either because the eruption ceases or because the flow follows a natural depression). Thus a cavity or 'tube' sometimes forms beneath the crust and the depressed lava flow. Volcanic tubes vary in size — this tube from Rajada formed inside and over a *barranco* and is

*Right: one type of pahoehoe lava is called 'ropey' for obvious reasons. The liquid magma flowing beneath a thin crust wrinkles the still unsolidified surface into shapes resembling rope. The name 'pahoehoe' is Hawaiian. Bottom: after a long day carrying tourists, these camels are making their way home via Yaiza.*

very high. The ceilings of tubes vary greatly in thickness, too: some are very thick, while if you tap the tops of others, you'll hear how hollow they are. (At the end of the walk you'll climb inside a tube and see the 'stalactites', where the lava dripped as it cooled.) The famous tubes at Cueva de los Verdes and Jameos del Agua resulted from the eruptions of Monte Corona, a volcano north of Máguez.

Near the end of the walk you pass **Montaña Encantada** ('Enchanted Mountain') ... a cartographic misnomer. The fig farmers in the area paid a watchman to sit atop this mountain and sing out *('Canta!')* if anyone was stealing their fruit, so the mountain became known locally as Montaña Canta. But the map makers were from Madrid… Around here you will pass terrain where *malpais* and *pahoehoe* lava intermingle; their different surfaces make them instantly recognisable. There's a 'bubble' on show, too: called a *hornito*. The island of Lobos, off Fuerteventura (Walk 8) is famous for its *hornitos*.

The linear walk ends at **Pedro Perico** (❷); the circuit runs in a clockwise direction, back to **Tremesana**. Then it's all aboard the minibus, back to **Yaiza**.

## Walk 2: A DAY OUT ON LA GRACIOSA

**Distance/time:** See Walks a and b and the Short walk below

**Grade:** 🔵 easy ups and downs, but Walk b is long and you must be sure-footed for its coastal path. *Jeep safaris ply these tracks, raising dust.* Can be very hot; *no shade.*

**Equipment:** comfortable walking shoes, sunhat, light fleece, raingear, swimwear, suncream, picnic, water

**Refreshments:** at Caleta del Sebo

**Transport:** 🚌 to Órzola (Line 9), then ⛴ ferry to La Graciosa. *Note:* the sea can be choppy!

**Walk a: Playa de las Conchas** (🔵; 12km/7.4mi; 3h20min). *Special note:* This walk follows cycle/motor tracks throughout. You may want to cycle rather than walk; there are bicycle hire shops on the seafront.

**Walk b: Pedro Barba via the coast and inland route back.** (🔵; 11.5km/7.1mi; 3h30min). *Note:* On this walk, only the *return* track is a cycle route.

**Short walk: Bahía del Salado** (🟢; 3.8km/2.4mi; 1h). See overleaf.

A ll of you will have seen La Graciosa from the Mirador del Río. The vista is unsurpassed. For many people, this view from the *mirador* is sufficient. But this little desert island deserves a second look. Take a ferry over and see for yourself. Getting there is half the fun! The ferry sails through the straits of El Río in the shadow of the towering Famara cliffs. On *terra firma* you'll discover superb beaches, sand dunes, lopsided craters, and a lagoon. The 'capital', Caleta del Sebo, seems to be in perpetual slumber; a relaxing calm pervades.

All versions of your day out on La Graciosa start from the QUAY (🔴) at **Caleta del Sebo**. Once you've got your legs back on steady ground again, **start out** by heading along the waterfront to the left. The village is a simple fishing haven of small low-slung houses. There are no gardens and very few trees; the landscape is devoid of colour.

At the end of the promenade, **Walk a** veers inland up past the Restaurante Girasol and straight up Calle la Popa. Out of the houses you cross a sandy/gravelly flat area, veering slightly left to a 'Parque Natural' information board. The ground is covered in various species of drought- and salt-tolerant vegetation — spiny *aulaga, lechuga de mar* (shown in the photo opposite), *barilla* (the 'ice plant', see overleaf), *salado verde, balancón, lecheruela, verode.*

Looking back down the gravel road, you have a superb shot over the village clustered along the water's edge to the dramatic Risco de Famara and the striking Playa del Risco curving round the foot of the cliffs. The two volcanoes, **Agujas Grandes** (right) and **Montaña del Mojón** (left), rise up ahead on either side of the track. A third, **Montaña Clara** (an island), soon appears in the background, centred between the other two.

When you come to a three-way fork (🔴; **35min**), keep straight

ahead for 'PLAYA DE LAS CONCHAS';
Walk b comes in from the right here,
the inland route from Pedro Barba.
To the left is a track to Montaña
Amarilla in the south of the island,
via Montaña Mojón.

After an almost imperceptible
descent, the landscape fills with
**Montaña Bermeja**, the 'Red
Mountain'. Quite a steep path rises
to its summit. To its left, out to
sea, is Montaña Clara. You cross a
tongue of lava from the eruption
of Bermeja and come into a sandy
area of low dunes populated by
more salt-resistant plants —
including *espino de mar* and
*matabruscas*. Approaching the
beach, you come to a cycle 'car
park' beyond which no cycles or
4X4s are allowed. Now a path
takes you down to **Playa de las
Conchas** (❷; **1h30min**).

From the beach, return to the
wide main track (**1h40min**) and
keep ahead; retrace your steps,
gently ascending over the low col.
Heading between the two craters,
the Risco de Famara reappears like
a green curtain in a theatre,
bringing an end to the walk. When
you rejoin your outgoing track,
keep straight on to the port at
**Caleta del Sebo** (**3h20min**).

**Walk b** turns right in front of the
Restaurante Girasol on a paved
walkway, then joins a wide street
(Calle García Escámez) and passes
the village CHURCH on the left.
When this street turns left, keep

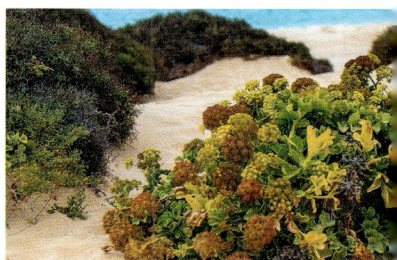

*Great clumps of* lechuga de mar
(Astydamia latifolia) *flourish in the
sand on the approach to Playa de las
Conchas. The strongly scented fleshy
leaves are sometimes eaten in salads or
soups — hence the name 'sea lettuce' or
'Canary samphire'. It has a high
vitamin C content— recognised by
sailors in antiquity, who collected it on
the shores of the Canaries to supplement
their poor diets.*

straight on — crossing a paved
area with a restaurant on the left —
and then continue on the sandy
seaside path, edged with stones.
On your left are the twin peaks of
**Agujas Grandes** and **Agujas
Chicas**, on your right the Famara
cliffs rise above the strait called El
Río. And in the immediate
surroundings are typical Canarian
coastal plants: the delicate mauve
and white florets of *culantrillo
salvaje*, the 'grapes' of *uvilla de mar*,
*cosconilla*, *balancón*, *lecheruela* and
swathes of *cosco*.

Beyond a bay (**Caleta del
Aguardiente**), there is a beautiful
small gold-sand beach at the foot
of the **Barranco de los Conejos**

*Playa de las Conchas rests at the foot of the maroon slopes of
Montaña Bermeja — a beautiful beach of golden sand.
Montaña Clara, an island out at sea to the left,
seems joined to the island.*

## Ice plants

There are about 1800 species in the sprawling, ground-hugging, salt-resistant ice plant (Aizoaceae) family, native to South Africa. All have a daisy-like flower and all are named for the bulbous water-conserving hairs on their leaves which sparkle in the sun like ice crystals.

The leaves and stems of *barrilla* (*Mesembryanthemum crystallinum;* middle) are eaten in salads and as chutneys in Africa and Asia, but haven't caught on in Europe. With its high soda content this plant was a money-spinner for the Canaries (especially Lanzarote and Fuerteventura) in the early 19th century, when it was used to make soap before the advent of commercially produced soaps. It is also used in skin creams, as an antiseptic, and to heal minor wounds.

*Cosco* (*Mesembryanthemum nodiflorum;* top) brightens up the tracks on Graciosa. It is often found growing next to barrilla. The Guanches (original inhabitants of the islands) ground up the seeds of *cosco* to make a flour or *gofio* substitute when crops failed.

A related species, *Carpobrotus edulis* (bottom), is commonly used as ground cover and spreads rapidly — sometimes becoming invasive. But its flowers can be spectacular.

(**❸**). Then watch your footing, as the narrow path runs some 20m/60ft above the sea at the foot of the **Morros Negros** cliffs. Your goal has been in sight for some time, and beyond its sandy cove you come into the beautifully kept seaside hamlet of **Caleta de Pedro Barba** (**❹**; **1h45min**). All the fishermen's old cottages here have been given glamourous 'facelifts'; gardens filled with palms and shrubs encircle them. The good-sized jetty, which encloses a pool,

points to the fact that this is no ordinary weekend retreat — it's a serene spot with a good outlook over the cliffs and to Órzola.

Leave the hamlet on the access track. In 10 minutes, at a junction (**❺**), go left for 'CALETA DEL SEBO'. Heading along the base of the Agujas, be sure to look behind you for the view stretching beyond the wall of cliffs to the Jable plain and the distant volcanoes of Timanfaya. You're crossing a plain edged by short, abrupt hills. Soon you cross

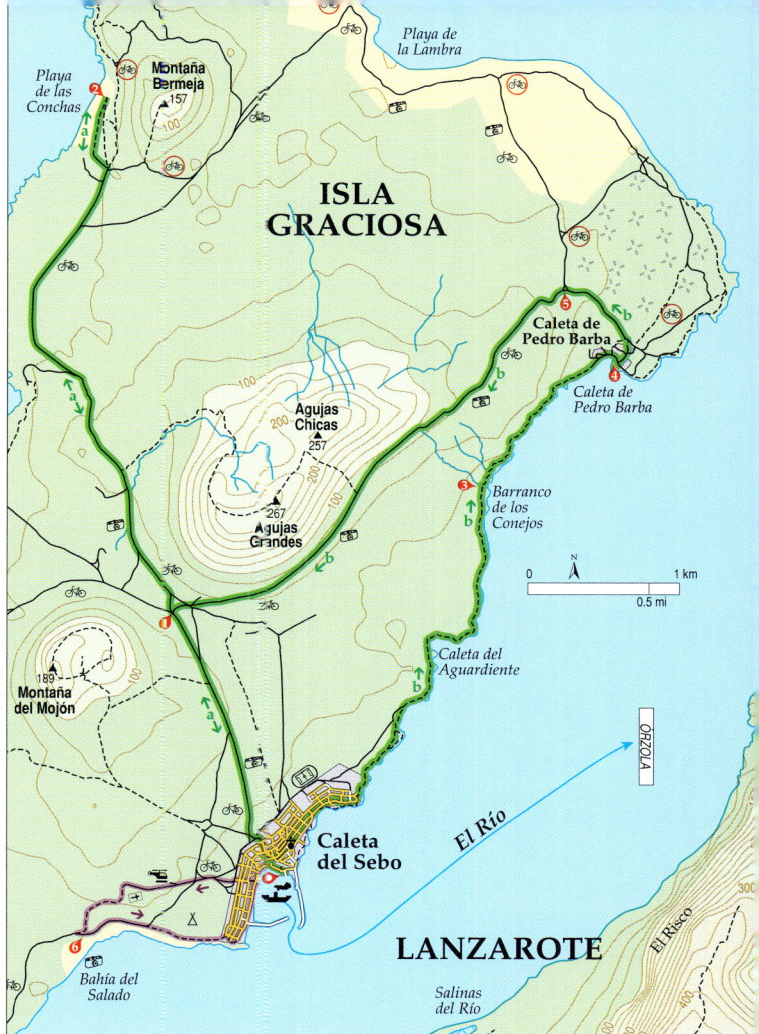

*Playa de la Lambra*

**ISLA GRACIOSA**

*Playa de las Conchas*

**Montaña Bermeja**
157

**Caleta de Pedro Barba**

*Caleta de Pedro Barba*

**Agujas Chicas**
257

*Barranco de los Conejos*

**Agujas Grandes**
267

N

0                          1 km

0.5 mi

*Caleta del Aguardiente*

**189**
**Montaña del Mojón**

ORZOLA

*El Río*

**Caleta del Sebo**

**LANZAROTE**

*Bahía del Salado*

*Salinas del Río*

*El Risco*

---

a low crest and rise to a higher plain, where more *cosco* (see opposite) brightens up the inclines.

Reaching a SIGNPOSTED THREE-WAY JUNCTION (**❶**; **3h**) on a broad saddle in front of **Montaña del Mojón**, turn left for 'CALETA DEL SEBO'. You have a superb view over the white houses clustered along the water's edge to the dramatic Risco de Famara and the striking Playa del Risco curving round the foot of the cliffs on your return to **Caleta del Sebo** (**3h30min**).

### Short walk: Bahía del Salado

**Start out** as for WALK a, but keep rounding the bay. Turn inland on a walkway just past HOUSE 63 and go straight ahead on Calle El Portillo, crossing a few streets. Coming to a T-junction, turn left and immediately right. At the next 'T', turn left; then keep straight on past the HELICOPTER PAD (right) and the CEMETERY (left). From here head seaward to **Bahía del Salado** and the LAGOON (**❻**) … if the tide is in. Return along the seashore (**1h**).

## Walk 3: RISCO DE FAMARA

**Distance:** Access is best for motorists. Travelling by 🚗, allow 9km/5.6mi; 3h10min. By 🚌, the nearest stop is at Máguez, 4.6km away. Or get off the bus in Haría and pick up a taxi (see page 40; that's how I've described the walk): ask the driver to take you to the parking place for motorists but, at the end, walk to Máguez for a 🚌 (just under 14km/8.7mi; 4h10min).

**Grade:** ●┋ very strenuous — a steep, gravelly descent/re-ascent of 420m/1378ft down a cliff face,

with a possibility of vertigo for inexperienced walkers. *No shade en route: the return is sheer slog. Don't attempt in wet or windy weather. Only recommended for experienced and fit walkers.*

**Equipment:** walking boots, light jacket, sunhat, raingear, swimwear, suncream, picnic, plenty of water

**Refreshments:** in Haría or Máguez

**Transport:** 🚗 Travelling by car, park southwest of the Mirador del Río: descending from the *mirador* on the LZ202 alongside the Risco

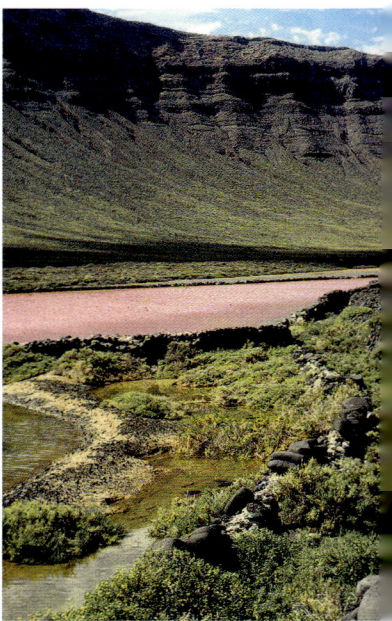

*The pink and orange ponds of the abandoned salt pans*

cliffs, watch for a derelict building on the right, a little over 2km from the *mirador*. Just past it (about 2.4km from the *mirador* — and just before the large Finca La Corona on the left — turn right on a narrow stone-paved track. Follow this track 100m to a small car park

(29° 11.789'N, 13° 29.52CW). Coming from the south, the track is on the left, just past the Finca La Corona. Or 🚐 to/from Máguez (Line 7; alight at the 'Sociedad' stop) and walk due north, with the church of

Santa Bárbara on your left, to the starting point (see map and add about 1h to reach waypoint ❶). Or 🚐 to Haría (Máguez bus, Line 7; alight at the 'Plaza' stop) and take a taxi (see below).

This is a truly spectacular walk. You descend into the landscape viewed from the Mirador del Río and zigzag steeply down the sheer Risco (cliff) de Famara. You discover that the captivating beach that sits imbedded in the lava tongue hundreds of metres below you is accessible after all! In the early morning and in the evening, this setting is no less than an oil painting.

*Travelling by bus to Haría,* alight at the Plaza stop and pick up a taxi. Ask the driver for 'Finca La Corona', luxury accommodation in six five-star villas on the narrow cliff-top LZ202 to the Mirador del Río. Just metres past the *finca*, start walking along the stone-laid track off left, immediately before a wall. A stunning panorama slowly unravels, as you near the cliff-tops.

You look straight out on to La Graciosa, bare of vegetation, desolate, and yet quite beautiful in the eyes of many beholders. The fishing village of Caleta del Sebo nestles around the exposed shoreline. Montaña Clara is the blade of rock that bursts up out of the sea behind La Graciosa and, further afield, to the right, lies the hilly island of Alegranza.

The track ends in a small CAR PARK (○), **where the walk proper starts**. Continue straight on, now descending a rocky, sometimes stepped, path — the **Camino de los Graciaseros,** an ancient path used by the inhabitants of Graciosa to climb to the market at Haría, where they could sell their fish. Standing on the very edge of the cliff, you look along a sheer wall of rock that plummets to a flat shelf below. Playa del Risco steals your attention with its golden sand and shallow turquoise-green water. Another sight distracts you: the strangely coloured pink, maroon and orange ponds of abandoned salt pans — the Salinas del Río.

The path swings down to the right of a magnificent VIEWPOINT by a POWER PYLON (❶). The very steep zigzag path now drops 200m/650ft, demanding keen attention, but no stretches of it are really vertiginous. An astonishing amount of vegetation clings to these cliffs, which harbour the richest plant life on Lanzarote. A number of very rare species, as well as nearly all the island's endemics are found in this northern massif. In and around these *riscos* you can find *Pulicaria canariensis, Asteriscus schultzii, Aichryson tortuosum, Kickxia, Reichardia,* two species of *Aeonium, Limoniums,* the rare *Echium decaisnei,* a yellow-flowering *Argyranthemum,* and many different grasses.

The desert-like Jable plain and the assortment of volcanic cones that constitute the Timanfaya National Park soon become visible over to the left. The path, easing out, soon reaches a faint track that cuts across the sea-flat at a junction. Turn right here (❷; **50min**). (The path to the left used to lead to one of my favourite walks — down along the cliffs to La Caleta — but the trail is badly broken now and too dangerous to be recommended.) Looking back up the way you came, you're bound to be impressed. Moreover, you know that at least here you can escape the press of tourists. Five minutes along, clamber across a dry, gouged-out stream bed. Five minutes later, the track passes through a stone wall. Some 100m *before* the wall, fork off left to the **Playa del Risco** (❸; **1h**). Nirvana! At last you can fling off your clothes (hoping that the telescope at the Mirador del Río isn't trained on you …) and plunge into the cool sea.

Now, whether you decide to swim first or explore the salt pans, your continuation is along this lovely stretch of beach. La Graciosa is just across the strait — almost within swimming distance. At the end of the beach, scramble over the stones and rejoin your track, following it to its end by an TRANSFORMER STATION that sends power over to La Graciosa via an undersea cable (❹; **1h25min**). The cliffs stand before you — a formidable barrier of rock. See if you can locate the *mirador* in the cliffs above: this will show you just how well camouflaged it is.

From here make your way over to the **Salinas del Río,** passing the remains of a DERELICT BUILDING which once housed the salt pan workers. Towards the end of the salt pans you come to the second 'sight' of the walk: a magnificent pink, milk-of-magnesia-coloured pond enclosed by crumbling stone walls. On a fine day you have a clear reflection of the Risco in it. The pools of the shallower pond in front of it sometimes glow a brilliant orange.

### Salt pans on the Canary Islands

Salt production was a crucial source of income in the Canaries before fishermen had the possibility of freezing their catches; they needed to keep tons of salt on their boats to preserve their fish before they could return to port. There was also a significant canning industry on the islands up until the mid-1900s.

All the islands had salt pans, but when modern methods of preservation were introduced, they had to adapt their economies rapidly; tourism is of course now the main source of income.

Today the major salt pans still in operation are the Salinas de Fuencaliente on La Palma (at the end of Walk 40) and the Salinas de Janubio on Lanzarote.

The disused Salinas del Río, shown above, are among the oldest in the Canaries, and they were viable until the 1970s. There are plans afoot now to restore many of the islands' salt pans — not least for the wildlife they attract — but with coronavirus losses coming on top of the world-wide financial crisis, progress will be slow.

---

Return by crossing a WALKWAY between the ponds, cutting across the salt pan. You come on to a track some 12 minutes back, where you turn left. When this track fades out a few minutes on, veer left uphill — quickly coming to a T-junction with another track. Turn right and remain on this track until you reach your outgoing descent path, then retrace your steps up the cliff to the CAR PARK (**3h10min**).

If you're making for a return bus at Máguez, *it is easiest to follow the roads highlighted in violet on the map.* Off-road alternatives exist (see map), but there is a short gap where a somewhat vertiginous old path rounds a private house in Las Rositas by hugging the edge of the cliff (keep the house on your left). When you come on to a track, follow it up over the crest, below a white house. Ignoring all branch-offs, descend to the main road and turn right. The BUS STOP in **Máguez** is opposite the CHURCH PLAZA (**4h10min**).

# Walk 4: ABOVE GUINATE'S VALLEY

**Distance:** 11.5km/7.1mi; 3h05min

**Grade:** ●❗ easy-moderate, with overall ups and downs of 250m/ 820ft. You must be sure-footed and have a head for heights at the cliff edge. Avoid windy days!

**Equipment:** comfortable walking shoes or boots, jacket, sunhat, raingear, suncream, picnic, water

**Refreshments:** bars and restaurants in Máguez and Haría

**Transport:** 🚐 to Guinate, sign-posted west off the LZ201. At the Y-fork some 400m along, go left, past the church, to park at the Centro Socio Cultural (29° 10.821'N, 13° 29.802'W). Travelling by 🚌, see Walk 3 on page 36 and take Line 7 to Máguez or to a taxi at Haría.

The high Guinate valley is one of the island's most attractive, and after a stiff hike from the valley floor up to the edge of the Famara cliffs, your reward is spectacular views to La Graciosa — views you won't be sharing with any crowds from Guinate's Tropical Park or *mirador*. The walk can be shortened to make a great leg-stretcher during a drive: go only to the cliff-edge viewpoint and return on the wide track, the Camino de Gayo. Try to visit in spring, when this area is an 'Easter basket' of yellow, white and violet wild flowers.

**The walk starts** from the CENTRO SOCIO CULTURAL (**O**) in **Guinate**: follow the track further along the **Guinate valley** between ridges left and right. The ridges show signs of terracing, but are no longer cultivated and have been taken over by prickly pear (*Optunia ficus-indica*), *vinagrera* (*Rumex lunaria*) and *verode* (*Kleinia neriifolia*). Some 450m/yds along, not far past a fenced-off farm on the right, note a FARM TRACK (**❶**) leading uphill right to some buildings just where the ridge peters out: if you're sure-footed, you could take this track and then follow the cliff-top path to the viewpoint where you are heading.

At the start the climb is gentle, passing beautifully farmed plots of potatoes, onions and vines in black volcanic soil; the track lined with *Argyranthemum maderense* (Famara marguerites) and *cerrarajón* (*Sonchus pinnatifidus*). But soon

you begin a noticeable ascent. Almost at the end of the valley, if you spot a CAIRN indicating a path climbing up to the right, *ignore it* and continue for another 100m, to a SECOND PATH (**❷**) up right — about 40m before the main track makes a fairly sharp U-bend to the left. This (better) path climbs steeply in less than five minutes to a *mirador* (**❸**; **35min**) with a great outlook over the Bay of Famara.

From this viewpoint return to the track and follow it round the bend to the left. This brings you up to the main track on the ridge, the **Camino de Gayo**. Turn right, to an info board about the **Fuentes de Gayo** (**❹**), two circular wells that were in use for centuries but are now dry as a bone. Some 800m (half a mile) further on, turn right at a notice board to a wonderful clifftop VIEWPOINT (**❺**) over the Risco de Famara to La Caleta and its sweep of beach.

*Right: the Guinate valley from the Camino de Gayo, focussing on the pretty farm with, behind it, La Graciosa island and its 'capital', Caleta del Sebo*

Return the same way or, if it's not windy and you're sure of foot, take the cliff-top path back to the Camino de Gayo. Turning right on the track, you come to a tarmac road and a circular white building with conical antennae behind it (a METEOROLOGICAL STATION; ❻; **1h35min**). A cinder track turns left uphill just past the meteo building — your route to the trig point on Los Helechos. Even if

you are omitting the climb to the summit, *do* carry on with the main walk for just a few minutes more — just to admire the neatly walled-off potato plot shown on page 39, with its own Lanzarote-green picket gate.

The main walk heads half-left before reaching the end of the plot, taking a grassy track/trail towards a plateau — yet another angle from which to enjoy 'the' perfect view of

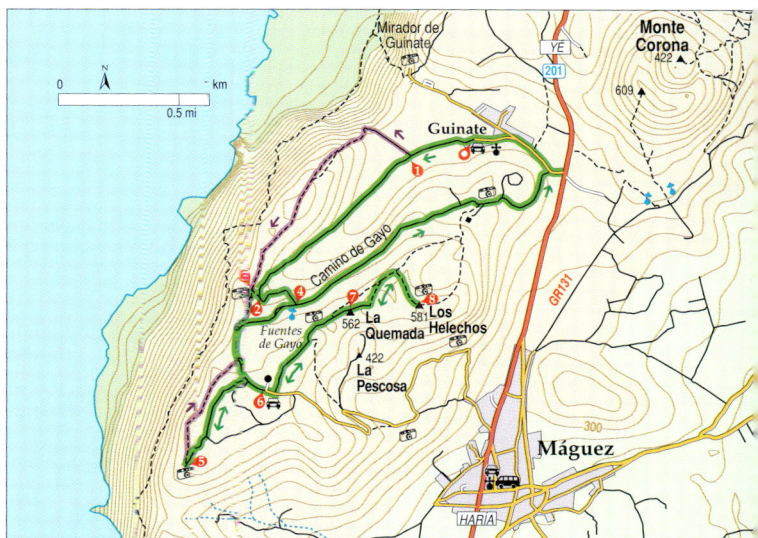

*From left to right: pimpernels* (Anagallis arvensis); *storks's bill* (Erodium malacoides); *mauve-flowering Canarian stock* (Matthiola bolleana) *and yellow* Reichardia tingitana; *a tangle of white and yellow cress* (Hirschfeldia incana). *A walker at the trig point on Los Helechos, looking into the cultivated double crater, out to La Graciosa and over to Monte Corona. Bottom — the 'star of the floral show':* bejeque de malpais (Aeonium lancerottense) *flourishing on La Quemada, flowers in spring and early summer.*

La Graciosa and the Risco cliffs. Continue uphill to a small white TRANSMITTER HUT on **La Quemada** (**❼**; 562m/1845ft; **1h50min**). Here's where you'll spot the endemic *Aeonium lancerottense*

## Lanzarote potatoes

A beautifully walled potato plot in black volcanic soil *(picón)* marks the start of your short hike to La Quemada (on the left in the photo) and the trig point on Los Helechos (on the right).

Once you've tried Canarian potatoes *(papas arrugadas* or 'wrinkled spuds'), you'll realise why they are an island speciality — despite not being very attractive to look at! The secret is that these small potatoes are cooked in salt water and then the water s left to evaporate, leaving a salty crust on the skins. This makes them tasty even when they are served on their own. But usually you will see them offered with a spicy red sauce made with chillis *(mojo picón)* or a refreshing green sauce made with either parsley or coriander *(mojo verde).*

The potatoes were originally cooked with sea water. To make something similar, use small or new potatoes and dissolve sea salt in the water until the potatoes no longer sink, but float!

with their beautiful pink blooms … if you're here in spring or early summer. From the hut make for the trig point seen ahead: keep to the left of the hut and aim for the saddle between the hill you are on and Los Helechos. Your way over the grass-covered hillside is obvious. As you admire the pristine farm you passed at the start of the walk, with its walled fruit trees, a

clear path comes underfoot and takes you to the TRIG POINT on **Los Helechos** (❽; 581m/1905ft; **2h**).

*(To return, the sure of foot could continue by circling the rim of this heavily terraced crater counter-clockwise if it's not too windy. On reaching a fork at its lowest point, head right and, a good five minutes later, keep straight ahead where a path goes left. Rejoining the Camino de Gayo, turn right with the main walk.)*

But the MAIN WALK retraces steps to the Camino de Gayo and now follows it to the right. Eventually you descend back into the Guinate valley, walking above the FARM passed at the start of the walk and admired from the climb to the trig point and soon enjoying a view to Playa del Risco, reaching out towards the port at Caleta del Sebo. The narrow strait of El Río is a turquoise mirror. When you reach the GUINATE ROAD just short of the LZ201, turn left and left again, back to the CENTRO SOCIO CULTURAL (**3h05min**).

## Walk 5: AROUND HARIA

**Distance:** 8.3km/5.1mi; 2h30min
**Grade:** ● easy, but some scrambling through brambles. An initial descent of just under 300m/1000ft, followed by an ascent/descent of 200m/650ft. ⚑ You must be sure-footed and have a head for heights near the cliff-edge in the second half of the walk, but this stretch can be avoided.
**Equipment:** walking shoes/boots, sunhat, light jacket, raingear, long trousers, suncream, picnic, water
**Refreshments:** bars or restaurants in Haría
**Transport:** 🚌 (Line 7) to/from the 'Plaza' bus stop (ⓐ) in Haría or 🚗 to/from Haría's large car park 200m northwest of the Plaza bus stop (ⓑ; 29° 8.838'N, 13° 29.934'W). Then taxi to the Restaurante Los Helechos. It is best to arrange this in advance (taxiharia.com, ☎620-315350). Other taxis, all English-speaking, are at ☎928-835368, ☎928-529806 or ☎629-331827. Ask to be met at the 'Plaza' bus stop on the east side of the church.

### Short walks
**1 Restaurante Los Helechos to Haría** (3.3km/2mi; 1h). ● Easy descent of just under 300m/1000ft, but slippery underfoot when wet. Equipment, access/return as main walk. Do the first half of the main walk only.
**2 Haría — Valle de los Castillejos — Valle del Rincón — Haría** (5km/3mi; 1h30min). ●⚑ Grade/equipment/transport as main walk. Do the second half of the main walk only. For a *very* short walk (just 45min), leave the Castillejos Valley via the track at ❺ and return on the far side of the valley.
**Alternative walk: From the Ermita de las Nieves to Haría** (adds 3km/2mi; 40min; ●⚑). From Haría, take the taxi to the *ermita* (ⓒ), and from there follow the lane (PR LZ 16) northeast past the 'golf balls' of **Peñas del Chache** to the LZ10. Then turn left downhill for 200m to the **Restaurante Los Helechos** (◉) and pick up the walk below.

---

This delightful countryside ramble takes you down a centuries-old trail into the palm valley of Haría, with wonderful views all the way. After a break, you leave the village to walk up the Valle de los Castillejos, along the edge of the Famara cliffs, and then down the Rincón Valley back into the village. The ramble ends at the lively square on the west side of the church — the Plaza León y Castillo.

Meet your pre-arranged taxi at the *'PLAZA' BUS STOP* in **Haría** (ⓐ) and ask for the Restaurante Los Helechos. Circling up the impressively walled hairpins by taxi, you may wonder how you're going to get back down to Haría on an 'easy' path! After enjoying the view from the *mirador* at the (unprepossessing) restaurant, **start the walk** (◉) by heading down the road in the direction you've just come (passing the KM17 sign),

with the **Barranco del Cuchillo** a deep gash on your right. As you approach a sharp bend, just below electricity wires, there is a break in the roadside barrier on the right with a *WALKERS' SIGNPOST* (❶). Step through — into history. Stone paving underfoot recalls the days when this was the pilgrims' route from the north to the Ermita de las Nieves. This is the PR LZ 16, which runs between Haría and the *ermita* (see the Alternative walk).

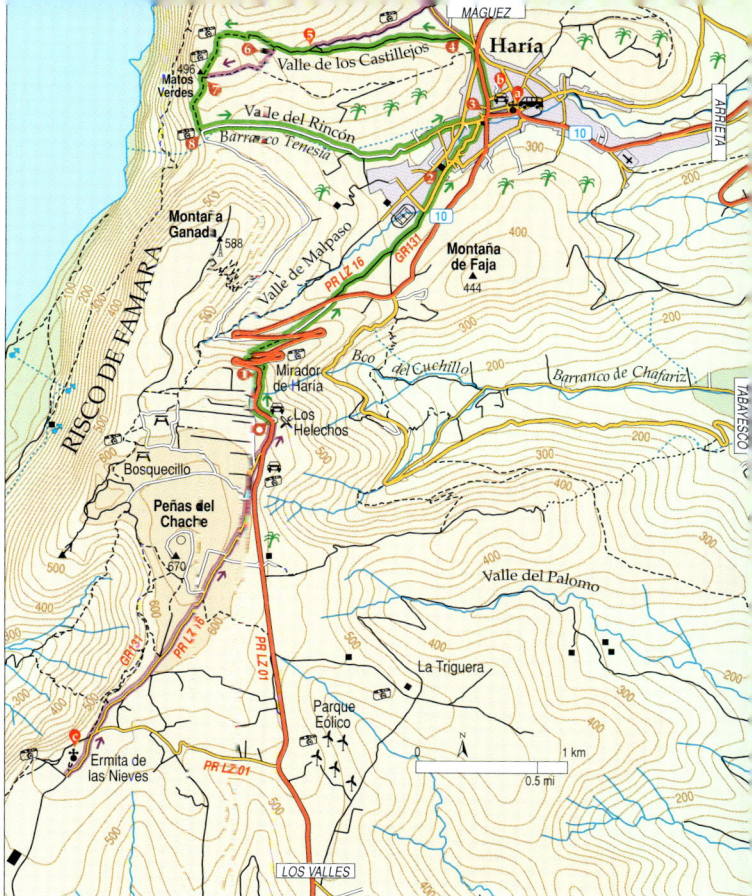

You head straight for the newly rebuilt (2021) **Mirador de Haría**, a white building on the **Filo del Cuchillo** ('knife's edge') but, before you reach this *mirador* with its glass-floored 'skywalks', the path veers off to the left. All the way down, on a very gentle gradient, you enjoy long-range views over Haría … while you step through a veritable botanic garden. You'll cross the road (*carefully*) three times. At the second crossing, in addition to a walkers' sign, there's another, '**Valle de Malpaso**'). After the third crossing (**30min**), the way becomes a cart track, and you can pluck some wild fennel to add to your herbs if

you're in self-catering accommodation. Monte Corona rises in the background, just to the left of the large school building. The plots of maize, potatoes, marrows and vines are festooned with huge fig trees.

On coming to a T-junction (**40min**) with a diagonally crossing track, head left towards the SCHOOL, soon passing an OLD FARM flanked by two palms and then some derelict cottages (the latter a rare sight on Lanzarote). Coming onto tarmac, keep straight ahead — ignore the road to the left. Now watch for the house on the left surrounded by palms and lava-stone walls: this was CÉSAR

41

MANRIQUE'S HOUSE (**2**) at the time of his death. At a Y-fork not far past it, bear right; then ignore any side-streets. When you reach a triangular 'square' of sorts, continue by keeping left against the no entry sign for vehicles.

You come to a T-junction, where the flags of the town hall are over to your right. Turn right at this junction and immediately left and left again, to the eucalyptus-shaded **Plaza León y Castillo** at the back (west side) of the church in **Haría** (**3**; **1h**). This is the place to take some refreshment before continuing … starting out … or ending the walk. If you *are* ending the walk, cross the square to the car park on the left or the CHURCH and your bus stop on the far side.

Moving on, with the square on your right and a supermarket on your left, follow the main street north uphill. Ignore a fork back left into the village in five minutes, but at a junction a minute later, go left: pass Calle Romero and head downhill on CALLE CASAS ATRÁS. After about 100m fork left up an EARTHEN TRACK (**4**) with grass down the middle. Monte Corona is ahead to the right, with the green spread of Máguez below it. This delightful track through cultivation and wild flowers takes you up the **Valle de los Castillejos**, where a dry *barranco* falls away gently on the right.

The bulk of Montaña Ganada with its TV transmitter looms ahead. To the left is a series of hillocks, with neatly-terraced 'aprons' of vineyards. Pass a house (**1h20min**) and ignore tracks off left into fields. Some 400m further on, a TRACK joins from the right (**5**). (For a very short walk, you could turn right and follow this track across the valley and back to the main road.)

By **1h30min** or less you're at a CINDERBLOCK WALLED ENCLOSURE (**6**). Continue uphill on the track.

In five minutes the track ends at a terraced plot. You've climbed up to the right (north) of a castellated ROCKY OUTCROP that rises just at the edge of the **Risco de Famara**.

You have a choice of routes from here. *To continue via the cliffs,* walk between the two palm trees about 20m away to your right. A faint path now becomes visible; follow it straight ahead towards the long, low stone wall that borders the edge of the cliff.

This route to the cliff-tops is steep and can be skiddy. And you may also find the cliff-top path too vertiginous, especially in the strong Lanzarote winds. *To take a safer route,* go back inland to the cinder-block enclosure and climb up the steep hill beside it. When you get to the top of the ridge, go through the gap in the wall and keep right to follow paths through more gaps in walls and join the path along the cliffs south of the Matos Verdes outcrop at **7**; see the map

When you reach the cliff-edge, you will be astounded by the stunning views. But the views are even better from the very top of the **Matos Verdes** outcrop on your left, so climb it, using the faint path (which some people may find vertiginous). From up here you're 'on top of the world': on the right is La Graciosa, Alegranza and Roque del Oeste. On the left, beyond the long golden beach of Famara, you can see the wastelands as far as La Santa and Sóo. On the horizon are the Montañas del Fuego, and behind you are Haría and Máguez.

From the top of the cliff follow the faint path downhill (it runs at a safe distance from the edge). The path takes you past the ALTERNATIVE ROUTE (**7**) rising from the cinderblock enclosure and down to the **Mirador Montaña Ganada**(**8**; **2h**) with drystone walls and a (motorable) track, where you turn left downhill

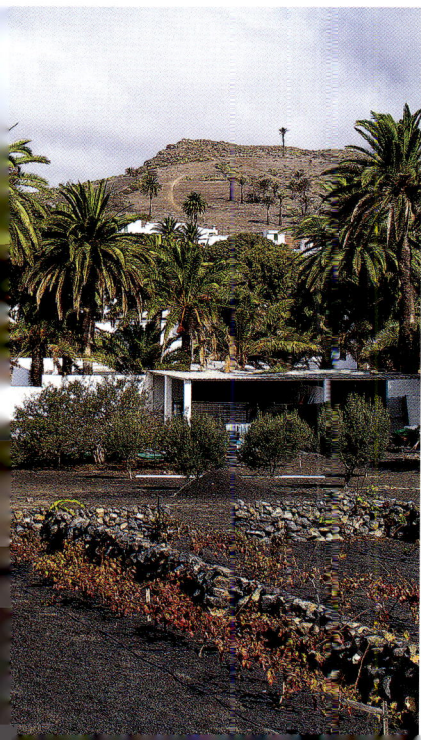

**Haría's valley of 1000 palms**
Haría's location, high in the north of Lanzarote, attracts cloud cover and condensation from the northeasterly trade winds that buffet the island. So it has always been green.

But late in the 16th century, during a pirate raid, both houses and palms were incinerated. Over the next couple of centuries, it became the custom for one palm tree to be planted when a baby girl was born — and two for each baby boy! Over the years this (politically incorrect) tradition has led to the plethora of palms in the valley.

Most of the palms in Haría — like the ones in this photo, are date palms. Unfortunately these dates are skimpy and quite tasteless — only suitable as cattle fodder.

### César Manrique
*Wherever you go on the island you will come across the legacy of César Manrique. So many major buildings and designs — from the Mirador del Río to Jameos del Agua, and from the Timanfaya 'devil' shown on pages 24-25 to many intriguing roundabout centrepieces — are his creations.*

*But apart from that, Manrique had a major influence on island planning regulations. It is thanks to him that there are no high-rise towers (save the Gran Hotel in Arrecife, built during his absence and too expensive to demolish on his return) and that the buildings are mostly 'colour-coordinated' in white and Lanzarote green.*

*You can see Manrique's simple grave (shown above) in the village cemetery off the LZ10 in the direction of Arrieta.*

through the **Valle del Rincón** — rather different in character from the Castillejos. There are no far-reaching views, fewer flowers, and less cultivation.

What catches the eye instead are the soft rosy-rusty hues emanating from the soil and the rock, set off by isolated splashes of cultivation. Notice, for instance, some 10 minutes down the track, a fruit tree on the right, completely enclosed by a circular drystone wall. On the hillsides opposite this tree, the stone walls not only help prevent erosion, but also capture water coming off the hillside and trap it in pools — at least in spring. Two minutes later a mini-reservoir on the left allows one lucky farmer to irrigate his smallholding: outside summer, pink carnations thrive among his marrows and onions. Around here the track is embroidered with ice plants like those on page 30.

Looking south, you should be able to spot your descent route in the first part of the walk. Pass the SCHOOL on the right and come into a noticeable grove of palms, with a ruin ahead. From here you continue on tarmac. A parade of palm trees takes you back into **Haría**. Soon a *barranco* is just on the right. Go straight over all junctions until you come to the town hall and return to the PLAZA LEON Y CASTILLO (❸). Cross the square to the CAR PARK on the left or go on to the CHURCH and your BUS STOP on its east side. (**2h30min**).

## Walk 6: CIRCUIT FROM UGA VIA MONTAÑA TINASORIA (AND MONTAÑA GUARDILAMA)

**Distance:** 7.3km/4.5mi; 2h10min
**Grade:** ● moderate; ups/downs of 300m/920ft, *excluding* the ascent of nearby Guardilama. A couple of short steep gravelly descents
**Equipment:** walking shoes or boots *(boots if ascending Guardilama)*, jacket, sunhat, suncream,

raingear, picnic, water
**Refreshments:** in Uga
**Transport:** 🚌 (Playa Blanca bus, Line 6); alight at the 'Iglesia de Uga' bus stop. Or 🚗 to/from Uga; travelling by car, park in the large car park east of the church (28° 56.920'N, 13° 44.594'W).

This entire walks takes place in La Geria, a perfect example of how man's need to tame nature for agricultural purposes results in the creation of a stunning landscape. The many thousands of half-moon drystone walls *(zocos)* of La Geria are dizzyingly beautiful.

**The walk starts** at the 'PUNTO SENDERISMO' in **Uga** (⊙), an attractive open space with a walkers INFORMATION BOARD. It's just 130m/yds east of the CAR PARK and 70m north of the BUS STOP called 'Iglesia de Uga' (Uga church). Leaving the info board off to your left, walk past Calle La Recontra and then turn left on the next street (60m further on; Calle los Arenales, but not signed when last checked). Two minutes (230m) along, leave the road and climb a farm track on the right, the first one you come to, with WALKERS' SIGNS (❶; GR131, PR LZ 40). The route overlooks the village, which nestles in a shallow depression of gardens, its back to a

*The tens of thousands of half-moon drystone walls* (zocos) *of La Geria*

### Viniculture in La Geria

Don't miss a visit to La Geria, a protected area covering some 52 sq km (20 sq mi) — it's a work of art. That's how César Manrique presented it in photographs at New York's Metropolitan Museum of Art.

The eruptions in the 1700s left land covered in granular volcanic ash about 3m (10ft) deep. To set the vines for which La Geria is famous, first all this ash must be hollowed out. Once the vines are planted in the soil beneath (only one to a hollow!), much of the ash *(picón)* is spread back over the soil because these porous volcanic granules not only protect the soil from drying out, but actually absorb moisture from the night air, which can then drip down into the soil.

Crescent-shaped lava stone walls *(zocos)* surround the precious plants, protecting them from breaking or drying out due to Lanzarote's quite strong winds.

vast expanse of crusty lava. Out of the lava rise the great fire mountains of Timanfaya, their inclines splashed with rust browns and reds. The cluster of hills to the south of the village climbs into the southern massif — Los Ajaches.

The track carries you up to the LZ30, where you turn left. Then, under 150m along, fork right on another track bristling with walkers' and mountain bikers' FINGERPOSTS. You're now entering the **Geria Valley**. Vines and fig trees fill the small hollows. The ash fields are ornamented by an assortment of stone walls. Your route will take you straight over the *cumbre,* the island's spine. Ignore all turn-offs.

Wandering through this blackened world is quite extraordinary. Over to the left, the lava fields grow into a vast lake ruptured by weather-worn cones, and above you stands a line of grass-capped hills that glow with greenery. The solitary white farmsteads stand out like sanctuaries in this inhospitable landscape.

Before long, walls take over the countryside. You're entering the vineyards, and the inclines are pock-marked with depressions collared by half-circles of stone walls *(zocos)*. This myriad of walls could be the ruins of a grand ancient city. You're in malmsey territory, where the well-known *malvasía* originates. These vines were introduced from Crete — where they were shown to thrive

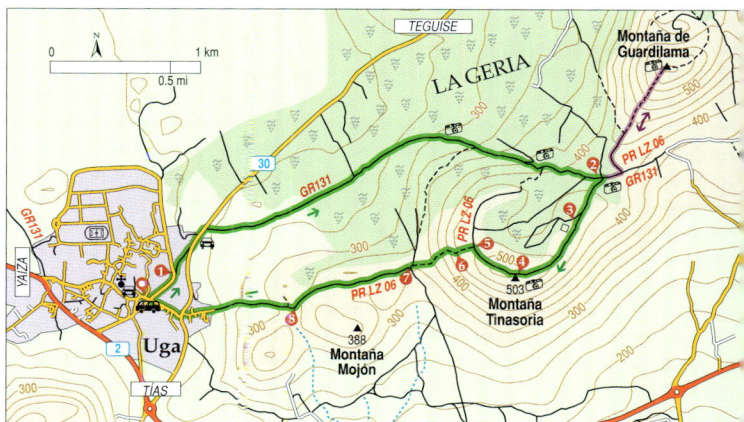

in a sunny, dry climate — and make up about 75 percent of Lanzarote's wine production.

Crossing the saddle of the *cumbre* the way eases out. You'll have a superb view back over La Geria and Timanfaya. Having ignored all offshoots from this main track, you come to the TOP OF THE PASS (**2**; **1h**). Turn right here* on a wide track through vineyards and head straight up the hill past a PARAGLIDERS LAUNCH SITE (**3**) and a large RUN. You'll spot what looks like an old stone wall some 10m to your right — in fact an old AQUEDUCT.

The track/path rises to a TRIG POINT and bench atop **Montaña Tinasoria** (503m; **4**; **1h20min**). A fantastic view unfolds over the southeast coast, with Lobos and Fuerteventura in the distance — while the crater below you is a maze of *zocos* filled with vines. Now, facing Uga and Yaiza, watch for a LINE OF LARGER ROCKS on the mountainside below and, 260m past the trig point, descend (**5**) pathless towards them. Your onward path (**6**), steep and narrow, but not difficult, descends

from the leftmost rock in this line. In just 10 minutes you reach a TRACK below (**7**; **1h45min**).

Go straight on, walking right through the middle of **Montaña Mojón** (**8**). Coming out of this crater, ignore a path off right to a 'baby' crater. Soon the track becomes tarred, then you cross the LZ30 and keep ahead into **Uga** (**2h10min**).

---

*If you would like to climb Montaña Guardilama first, it is just beyond this turn-off: head left up a track at the right of vines. This will add a full hour to your walk, and heighten the grade to fairly strenuous (●●). You will climb another 100m/330ft, and you must be sure-footed, with a head for heights for this ascent/descent, sometimes over loose stones (avoid it in hot weather, and on very windy days, when the Guardilama summit is potentially dangerous). When the track ends, continue zigzagging straight up to the summit — a tiring climb, as it's very steep and there are loose stones underfoot.

## Walk 7: RIDGE WALK TO THE ATALAYA DE FEMÉS

**Distance:** 14.2km/8.8mi; 5h20min
**Grade:** ● strenuous, with an over-all ascent/descent of 535m/1755ft. Mostly good, but sometimes steep tracks and paths underfoot. Can be cold and windy!
**Equipment:** comfortable walking shoes or boots, jacket, sunhat,

raingear, suncream, picnic, water
**Refreshments:** in Haría
**Transport:** 🚐 to/from the 'Supermercado Yaiza' bus stop (Playa Blanca bus, Line 6), or 🚗: park in the car park west of the church (28° 57.114'N, 13° 45.952'W)

This walk is all about the joy of ridge walking, with views right and left as you head (sometimes steeply) up to the Atalaya de Femés. Try not to notice the forest of transmitter masts that make this peak so easily identifiable for miles around; instead, enjoy the 360° panorama — you can almost count the colourful volcanoes on Timanfaya!

**The walk begins** at the PLAZA DE LOS REMEDIOS in **Yaiza** (●) — 200m/yds west of the 'Super-mercado' BUS STOP and just north of the CAR PARK. With the CHURCH on your left and the square on your right, walk south uphill past another (huge) plaza on your left. On your right are the lovely VOLCANIC GARDENS shown overleaf, laid out to commemorate the 250th anniversary of the 18th-century eruptions.

Turn left on a wide street beyond the plaza (about 100m *before* the walled-in CEMETERY, which can be seen ahead on the left-hand side of the road). Cutting across the valley floor, you look up into a tapering valley and see the

hamlet of La Degollada ensconced at the end of it. Your ongoing track is visible ahead. When the tarmac ends at an intersection, go straight ahead on this CINDER TRACK (❶). Ascending the valley wall, pass a faint fork off to the left. As you mount the crest, you pass to the right of a RUINED WINDMILL (❷; **35min**) — only the moth-eaten stump remains. A track coming up from Uga joins from the left; you continue to the right up this plump ridge, which will carry you all the way to the Atalaya de Femés.

As you climb, the island opens up, revealing a variety of scenery. Yaiza is in full view below, its brightness accentuated by the

*On the ridge, looking back from the Atalaya de Femés to Yaiza: on left is the Valle de Fenauso with La Degollada, on the right is the Valle de Femés.*

intense green garden plots and the dark sea of lava. A barrier of volcanoes, one running into the next, fills in the backdrop. About 1km along this wide track, 15m beyond the brow of the hill, take a right turn between *TWO BOULDERS TOPPED BY CAIRNS* (**3**; **1h05min**), going through a gap in the 'wall' formed by these huge lava boulders. Cross the field ahead on a clear path; it varies from year to

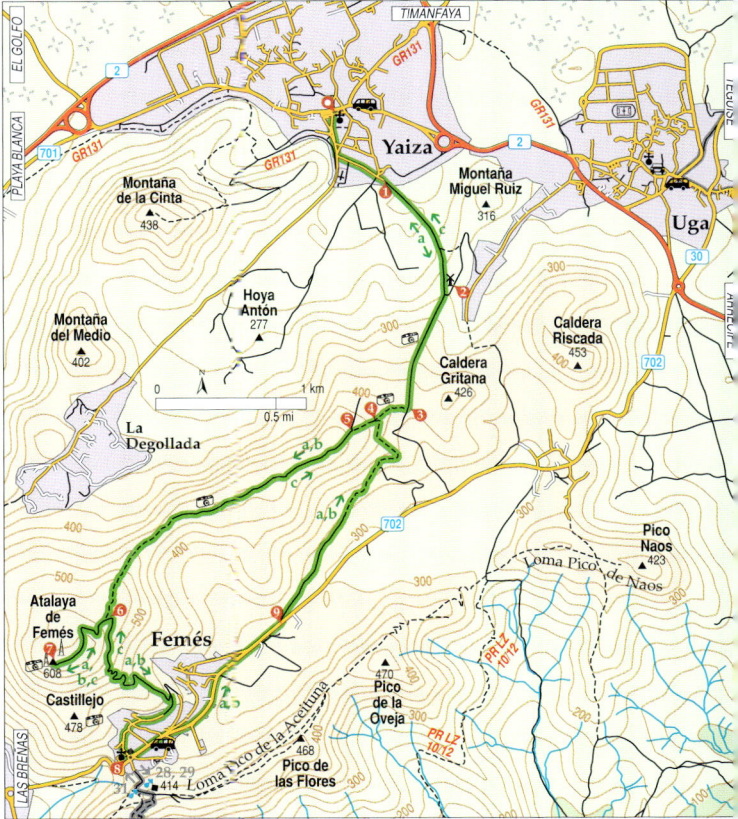

## Yaiza's Volcanic Gardens

Early in the walk you pass gardens commemorating the cataclysmic events of just under 300 years ago. As Yaiza's parish priest described it: 'the earth suddenly opened up and an enormous mountain rose from the bosom of the earth and from its apex shot flames which continued to burn for 19 days'. This eruption lasted intermittently for some six years (1730 to 1736), burying one-third of the island (including eleven villages and many more hamlets) under metres of lava … an eruption unsurpassed in recorded history.

year — just remember to keep uphill! Your view becomes more expansive and more rewarding — dipping down now onto Uga and stretching all the way up the dark, shadowy Geria Valley. Some 200m past the turn-off, at a FORK (**4**), keep right (your return path enters from the left here). Mounting another step in the ridge, you see over the sloping plains of the east to Puerto del Carmen and Arrecife.

When you meet a track at a T-JUNCTION (**5**; **1h15min**), follow it to the left along the ridge, still ascending, while overlooking both sides of the island. Timanfaya, the king of the volcanoes, dominates the national park to the north, with its distinct reddish-brown

slopes. The way fades to a path as it remounts the top of the crest, which in turn narrows into a sheer-sided 'neck'. Another striking sight follows: the shimmering off-white salt pans and khaki-green lagoon of the Salinas del Janubio.

When the path meets a track at a CAIRN (**6**; **2h05min**), head right, up to the SUMMIT of the **Atalaya de Femés** (**7**; 608m/ 1995ft; **2h30min**). A stupendous view unfolds. The remote (for this island!) little village of Femés lies straight below, huddled around the pass that descends to the Rubicón plain. Fuerteventura and Lobos fill in the backdrop. On the far side of the transmitter station, you look down onto Las Breñas, stretching along a raised shelf of cultivation.

Back at the cairned JUNCTION (**6**), follow the rather skiddy track down to the right. Some 20m past a chain barrier, turn right. When you meet asphalt at a Y-fork, go left. Then keep ahead on concrete. Ignore a road to the left, but turn left 30m further on. Follow the brick-paved road to the square at Femés (**8**; **3h10min**).

After a break, walk down the main LZ702 (past the village BUS STOP) for 1.4km, then turn left on a CART TRACK (**9**; **3h30min**). When this peters out, take the cairned path at the northern edge of black *picón* fields and then uphill towards a side-ridge — via a series of gullies. Sparse but helpful CAIRNS mark the route; if they are missing, just keep heading northeast uphill. Coming to a crossing track in front of another black field, turn left for one last uphill slog. The faint track/path bends right and meets your outward route at **4** (**4h25min**). Turn right and retrace your steps via the GAP IN THE 'WALL' (**3**) and MILL (**2**), back to **Yaiza** (**5h20min**).

## Walks on
# Fuerteventura & Lobos

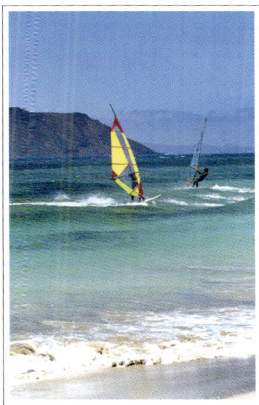

### Fuerteventura
AREA: 1660/km² (641sq mi)
LENGTH OF COAST: 304km (189mi)
HIGH POINT: Pico de la Zarza
   (807m/2648ft)
POPULATION: 126,227 (2020)
POPULATION DENSITY: 70/km²
   (182/sq mi)
CAPITAL: Puerto del Rosario
   (pop 28,357)
PROVINCE: Las Palmas

### Isla de Lobos
AREA: 4.6/km² (1.8sq mi)
LENGTH OF COAST: 13km (8mi)
HIGH POINT: La Caldera
   (127m/417ft)
POPULATION: 4 (2018)
PROVINCE: Las Palmas

Fuerteventura is different from all the other islands in the Canaries. Being the closest to Africa, there's a definite taste of the Sahara about it. The landscape is thirsty, barren and severe. Tourism, after having side-stepped Fuerteventura for many years, struck suddenly like a bolt of lightning, leaving the populace reeling from the blow.

In two things this island excels and outdoes all the others in the archipelago: it has the best beaches and the best climate. Beaches are what Fuerteventura is all about — mile upon mile

51

**FUERTEVENTURA**

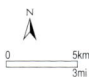

N

0            5km
3mi

**8**

Corralejo        El Puertito

**9**

DUNAS
DE
CORALEJO

El Cotillo        Lajares

Villaverde

La
Oliva

Tindaya

Tetir

Los Molinos        Tefía

**Puerto
del
Rosario**

Llanos de la
Concepción

Casillas
del Angel

Caleta
de
Fuste

Betancuria    **11**    Antigua

**10**    **14**

Ajuy        Vega de
Río Palmas

**13**    Tiscamanita

Pájara        Tuineje    MALPAIS    Pozo
Negro

Gran
Tarajal

La Pared        Giniginamar

Tarajalejo

La Lajita

Costa Calma

EL
JABLE

PENINSULA DE JANDÍA

Cofete    **12**

Punta de
Jandía        Morro
Jable

of untouched golden sand, great
billowing white sand dunes, foaming
surf, and quiet turquoise coves.

But there are walks to suit all appe-
tites as well — rambles across the old worn
hills, fairly easy mountain ascents, seaside
hikes and rocky *barrancos* in which to flounder.

Lobos — the tiny island of 'anthills' just offshore — is another
world again. It's a charmer.

Fuerteventura is the richest of the islands in Guanche relics
(sorry, Gran Canaria). Few people are aware of this. The island
is littered with Guanche settlements — all untouched. Unfortunately, they are also mostly unprotected and crumbling away.

## Walk 8: AROUND LOBOS

**Distance:** 10km/6.2mi; 2h45min
**Grade:** ● easy, but there is no
shade, and it can be hot, windy
and dusty. The ascent of Montaña
La Caldera is just over 100m/330ft.
**Equipment:** comfortable walking
shoes, fleece, sunhat, suncream,
picnic, plenty of water, swimwear
**Refreshments:** simple local in
Cases El Puertito; also Corralejo
**Transport:** 🚢 from Corralejo

to/from Lobos. There are three
boats sailing to Lobos from about
10.00 to 16.00: see www.naviera
nortour.com. The crossing takes
about 20 minutes; 'El Majorero' is
a glass-bottomed boat. Note that
the Visitors' Centre and adjacent
WC open immediately after the
the 10.00 boat arrives and usually
close promptly at 15.00. There are
no other facilities on the island.

Y‍ou can have Jandía and El Jable; I'll settle for Lobos any
day. A 20 minute — sometimes rough — boat crossing
with amiable seafarers takes you over to this strange little
island of sand and rocky mounds. Seen from Corralejo,
Lobos may not even arouse your curiosity. But once you've
seen the exquisite lagoon cradled by Casas El Puertito and
you've climbed the crater, then finished your day with a dip
in the turquoise-green waters off the shore, you'll remember
it as one of the most beautiful spots you've visited. Lobos
takes its name from the monk seals that once inhabited these
waters. The island is only 3km off the coast of Fuerteventura
and measures just 6.5 sq km.

You follow a track that circles the
island. A quad, which belongs to
the park rangers, is the only vehicle
you'll encounter. On Lobos all the
paths and tracks are very clearly
marked — *with signs warning you
not to leave the marked route: Lobos is
a bird sanctuary and protected area!*

Straight off the JETTY (○), **start
out** by heading right, past the
VISITORS' CENTRE, to make for the
tiny port of Casas El Puertito, a
jumble of buildings with the
island's only (simple) restaurant. A
neat wide path leads you there
through a landscape dominated by
mounds of lava and littered with
rock. These small mounds, called
*hornitos* ('little ovens'; see overleaf)
are caused by phreatic eruptions.
You'll see the beautiful *Limonium
papillatum*, with its paper-like
mauve and white flowers. And
fluorescent green *tabaiba* glows
amidst the sombre rock. You'll also

notice plenty of *cosco (Mesembryanthemum nodiflorum)*, the noticeably
bright red ice plant shown on page
34, and *Suaeda vera*. A reef of
rocky outcrops shelters the lagoon,
making it into a perfect natural
swimming pool. Through the
rock, the sand dunes of Corralejo
are visible in the background.
**Casas El Puertito** (❶; **7min**) is a
picture postcard setting. (*Tip:* if
you want to eat here after your
walk, order your meal now!)

Once past the little houses,
continue around the LAGOON.
Almost at once, swing back inland
and, at a T-junction, head right on
the coastal path to **Las Lagunitas**
(❷), the tidal pools where salt-
resistant plants thrive and the
habitat of several bird species.
*Arthrocnemum fruticosum* (a fern-
like plant) grows in the hollows.
Ice plants (see the panel on page
34), with transparent papillae

Punta Martiño
Faro de Martiño

Caleta
del Palo
a
La Caldera
127

GR 131

Playa de
la Concha
P
GR 131

LOBOS

Casas El
Puertito
Caleta de
la Rasca

CORRALEJO

resembling water droplets, also catch the attention. The track loops its way through these miniature 'mountains'. The rock is clad in orange and faded-green lichen. Overlooking all this is Montaña La Caldera (the crater), the most prominent feature in this nature park.

Shortly, you cross a sandy flat area. The track loops up the embankment; a small fork off to the left cuts the loop and rejoins the track at an INFORMATION BOARD. Lanzarote begins to grow across the horizon. Ignore the forks off to the right (**30min, 37min**). (The second fork leads past a patch of sisal — an aloe-like plant with exceptionally tall flower stems, sheltering in a hollow just a few minutes away.) Soon (**55min**), ignore paths to some ugly concrete buildings. Then join a surfaced track coming in from the left.

In a few minutes you're along-side the abandoned building and outhouses of the **Faro de Martiño** (❸; **1h10min**). If you don't plan to climb the crater, this will be your best viewpoint in the walk. You look out over the dark lava hills and the tiny valleys of golden sand that thread their way through them. To the right of the broken-away crater of Montaña La Caldera you'll glimpse Corralejo. Across the straits, just opposite, lie some of Lanzarote's magnificent beaches, from Playa Blanca to Punta Papagayo.

From the lighthouse follow the main track (the GR131) off to the right. Within 30 minutes from the lighthouse (at about **1h40min**), you will turn off to climb Montaña

### The *hornitos* of Lobos

This aerial view of the north of the island shows the lighthouse and, behind it, the islet's highest volcano, La Caldera.

But what is most noticeable is the 'lumpy' landscape all round: these are *hornitos* (a Spanish word meaning 'little ovens'); they are also called 'spatter cones'.

When volcanic tubes are formed in pahoehoe lava (see pages 26-27), sometimes the gas and steam produced causes the air pressure inside the tube to increase enough to cause phreatic eruptions — lava is forced up through an opening (called a 'skylight') in the cooling crust. Lava 'splutters' or 'spatters' out. The pressure ejects small bits of lava out of these openings over and over again, so that layer upon layer of 'spatters' builds up on top of the vent.

Most *hornitos* are just a few metres high, but they can be up to 15m/45ft high.

*Montaña La Caldera is home to a large seagull colony: take time to observe the fascinating social behaviour of these beautiful and elegant birds.*

La Caldera, by taking the *second* fork off to the right. (But first you might like to take a 30 minute return detour to Caleta del Palo (**a**), a beach inside Montaña La Caldera's crater. If so, take the *first* right turn and follow the track along a sandy depression. *Careful: in late spring and early summer breeding seagulls around here can be very aggressive!* You pass a water tank and continue on a path through a narrow 'valley' of rock, which leads down to this black-sand beach. Return the same way.)

The signposted **Montaña La Caldera** turn-off comes up four minutes after the detour route. Straight into this track, the route forks. Go right and follow the well-worn, partly cobbled and stepped path that ascends to the *RIM OF THE CRATER* (**4**; **2h10min**). A brilliant sight awaits you. You find yourself on a razor-sharp ridge, looking down sheer walls onto a beach, hidden inside this half-crater. Your vista encompasses

the profusion of *hornitos* that make up this island, the dunes of Corralejo, and Fuerteventura's hazy inland hills. To the north, you can trace Lanzarote's coastline as far as Puerto del Carmen. The crater is also home to a large seagull colony. The birds here are apparently used to visitors, as they are not aggressive.

Returning to the GR track, head right. Fifteen minutes after joining the track, watch for the turn-off to the main beach: it comes up two minutes past two concrete buildings that sit in a hollow on your left. This exquisite bay (**Playa de la Concha**; **5**; **2h30min**) is actually a shallow lagoon that curves back deeply into the coastline. Here's where you'll end up passing the rest of the day, no doubt. Keep an eye on the departure time of your boat! To return to the ferry, just continue along the track, keeping right at the fork, to return to the *JETTY* (**2h45min**).

## Walk 9: THE CRATER ROUTE

**Distance:** 12km/7.4mi; 2h55min
**Grade:** ● easy-moderate, with a steady 160m/525ft climb at the outset — or ● including the detour to Bayuyo (another 150m/490ft of ascent and 40min)
**Equipment:** comfortable walking shoes, light jacket, sunhat, raingear, suncream, picnic, plenty of water
**Refreshments:** café in Lajares; bars and restaurants in Corralejo

**Transport:** 🚐 to Lajares (Lines 7, 8); return on 🚐 from Corralejo (Lines 7, 8)

***Shorter walk: Calderón Hondo***
(8km/5mi; 2h15min). ● grade/equipment as above. 🚐 to/from Lajares: park by the stadium (28° 40.807'N, 13° 55.940'W); or 🚐 as above. Follow the main walk to **Calderón Hondo** and the *HERDERS' CORRALS* (❷); return the same way.

T his hike along the Bayuyo alignment is one of the most fascinating walks in the Canaries — and especially worthwhile if you've not been to Lanzarote or done Walk 38 on La Palma. Those of you interested in vulcanology will have a field day. And even if you couldn't give a hoot about volcanoes, it's *still* a brilliant walk — especially done early in the evening under the setting sun.

**Start out** from the BUS STOP (◯) in **Lajares** next to the FOOTBALL GROUND. Head north on the road at the right of this stadium (CALLE MAJANICHO). Follow this road for 10 minutes (1km). Then, just past the last house on the right, turn off right on the wide, green/white waymarked SL2 footpath signposted 'CALDERON HONDO'.

Your way is exquisitely cobbled and bordered by stones on both sides — a work of art. Surrounded by a lichen-covered *malpaís*, ignore a faint path to the left and head straight towards a dark reddish-brown volcanic mound, **Montaña Colorada**, which rises boldly in front of you. The path skirts the foot of this volcano to the right (white/green waymark), then ascends to an elevated plain. Magnificent stone walls stretch across the inclines below. The next volcanic mound to appear on the left is Calderón Hondo. Crossing a crest, you pass through a wall. To the right you look out over the sand dunes of Corralejo, separating

the dark lava flow and the blue sea.

On coming to a fork at the base of **Calderón Hondo** (**50min**), head uphill to the left. After five minutes ignore two paths forking off to the right very close together; continue steeply uphill to the left, to the VIEWPOINT (❶; **1h02min**). An impressive crater lies 70 metres below the perfectly circular rim shown overleaf. A surprising amount of vegetation grows on and out of the rock here. You have excellent sea views both left and right. Majanicho is the small seaside village seen to the left. The plains below are littered with corrals and dotted with buildings, many of which lie abandoned.

Now head back to the two forks you passed on your way to the *mirador:* they are now descending on your left. Take the second turning. Minutes along, you come to a traditional *HERDERS' STONE BUILDING* (❷). The small stone conical construction to the right was used for cooking. Nearby is a corral, also made of lava stone.

57

### The Bayuyo alignment

Calderón Hondo, shown above (with Montaña Colorada and Lajares behind it), is one of several craters that erupted about 50,000 years ago. Theses eruptions actually added over 100 sq km to the island's northern land mass — and created the island of Lobos as well. This walk takes in the 5km alignment on Fuerteventura itself, heading north via Colorada, Hondo, Rebanada, Encantada, Caldera, and Bayuyo. This last volcano, which gives its name to the alignment, comes from one of the pre-Hispanic tribes which inhabited the island in days past.

Return to the point where you turned off to the *mirador,* and now head left towards Corralejo. Crossing this elevated plain, you look into **Caldera de Rebanada**, the collapsed crater on your right. Five minutes later, a track cuts across in front of you. Follow it (it's the GR131) to the left

downhill towards the scattered dwellings of **Cotos Tamboriles**. Ignore a track forking left to this hamlet and continue straight on towards Corralejo. You can now safely ignore all turn-offs and just follow the track along the foot of the volcanoes *(but see the note opposite, beside the map).*

*Recommended detours:* Ten minutes after the Cotos Tamboriles junction, a short path to the left leads to the **Cueva Natural** ( **a** ): a hole in the lava caused by a volcanic gas bubble. Some 150m past the 'bubble path' a cairn-marked path heads right and climbs to the summit of **Bayuyo**. After 20 minutes you reach the top of the lower ridge, 10 minutes more take you to the TRIG POINT ( **b** ). Ignore the path down off to the right from here; go left along the ridge for about 200m to

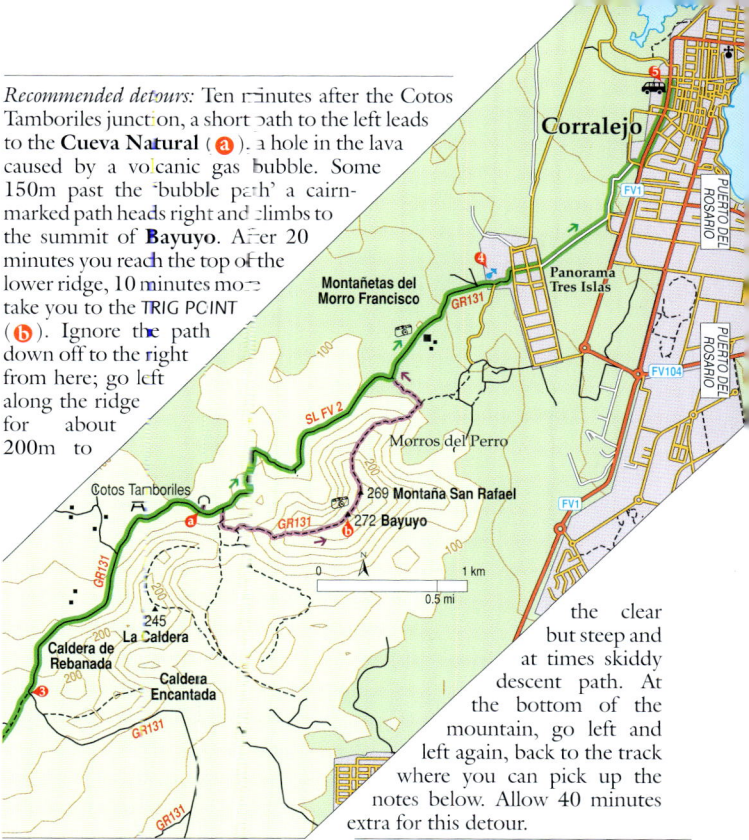

the clear but steep and at times skiddy descent path. At the bottom of the mountain, go left and left again, back to the track where you can pick up the notes below. Allow 40 minutes extra for this detour.

**La Caldera**, another prominent volcanic cone, overshadows you on the right. Heading into an undulating landscape of lava, the way now ascends, and you twist and wind through hillocks and depressions. Amidst the stone and rock there's a surprising amount of greenery about in spring — if the island's been blessed with the normal February rains.

Forty minutes along the track, you cross a crest and dip into the gaping crater of **Bayuyo** (**2h 05min**), a landmark for miles around Corralejo. This amphitheatre of mountain is about to encompass you when your way swings off left. You pass some abandoned sheds and stables and one or two illegal tips. Soon after, rounding a bend in the hillside, Corralejo comes into sight (but it's not as close as it looks!) … and a corner of Lobos.

Descending, and out of the lava, you pass a large white WATER TANK (**4**) on the left and come to a crossing road at a lone housing estate (**Panorama Tres Islas**) with few properties. Cross straight over to the far side of the estate, then follow a motor track through a grim wasteland. It approaches the main road, then moves away to the left before joining the main dual carriageway again (Avenida Juan Carlos I). Turn left and follow this for 10 minutes, to the BUS STATION (**5**; **2h55min**) in **Corralejo**, on the left.

## Walk 10: FIVE-STAR CIRCUIT FROM AJUY

**Distance:** 8.7km/5.4mi; 2h25min
**Grade:** ● easy, but on the return walk from Playa del Jurado don't venture too close to the edge of the cliffs — they could crumble away easily, *and be prepared to take extra time on the narrow steps to the caves.*
**Equipment:** shoes with good ankle support (or walking boots), fleece, sunhat, raingear, suncream, swimwear, picnic, water
**Refreshments:** ample in Ajuy

**Transport:** 🚌 to/from Ajuy. Park at the turning circle at the entrance to the village (28° 23.970'N, 14° 9.267'W), or down by the beach (28° 23.959'N, 14° 9.355'W). No bus access.
**Shorter walk: Barranco de la Madre del Agua** (5.3km/3.3mi; 1h25min). ● very easy. Follow the walk to the PALM GROVE shown below (**❷**), then return the same way.

This walk makes the most of the varied landscapes in this little pocket of Fuerteventura *and* delves into some recent history linking Ajuy's caves with World War II. The first part of the walk leads into one of the island's most salubrious corners, where you'll fine a tiny stream that flows all year round; in the second half you'll be awed by the striking coastal scenery and perhaps as intrigued as we were to read about the history of the two enormous caves below the *mirador.*

**Start out** at the ROUNDABOUT (**○**) in **Ajuy**: head down to the beach (or park there and begin there). Then, rather than following everyone else straight to the cliffs, curl right and follow the track up the **Barranco de Ajuy**. Eventually you will notice another TRACK crossing the *barranco* (**❶**; **30-35min**) — note this for your return, but keep straight on. Some 500m further on, you come to a side valley on your left, crammed with palms — the **Barranco de la Madre del Agua** (**❷**; **45min**). It's sheer bliss in the shade of trees here, listening to the trickle of water.

When you're ready to leave, retrace your steps for about seven minutes, to the TRACK (**❶**) crossed earlier. Follow this up to the right, past some RUINED HOUSES. *(But for the Shorter walk, keep straight ahead, retracing your outward route.)*

*At the mouth of the Barranco de la Madre del Agua — a tiny, permanently flowing stream and a profusion of palms*

Ignore a track off to the right. Shortly after, go through a rickety FENCE. Then ignore another track to the right.

Coming into the **Barranco de la Peña**, turn left. Tamarisk trees (see panel on page 75) huddle along the valley floor. Unfortunately, bottles are often scattered about, so watch out for broken glass. Well under an hour after leaving the palm oasis you are facing **Peña Horadada** (**3**), Fuerteventura's own 'Arc de

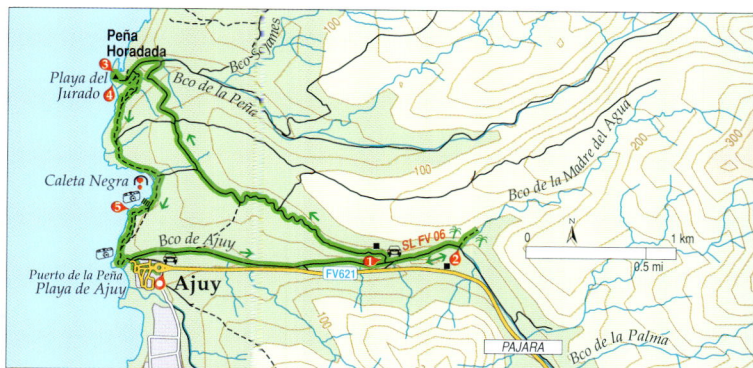

Triomphe' — at **Playa del Jurado** (❹; **1h35min**). Please remember that beaches here on the island's west coast are *very dangerous!*

From the beach you can either climb straight up to the cliffs or take the gentler inland path. The way along the cliffs is straight-forward, marked with sporadic cairns. You pass through a FENCE via a gate or gap and, as you approach **Caleta Negra** you can see a cliff-face viewpoint ahead.

Reaching this *mirador* (❺; **2h10min**), you will see that the paved steps down to it are protected by very sturdy railings — as are those down to the TWO ENORMOUS CAVES mentioned above. Be prepared to lose some time on the narrow steps — it's single file only!

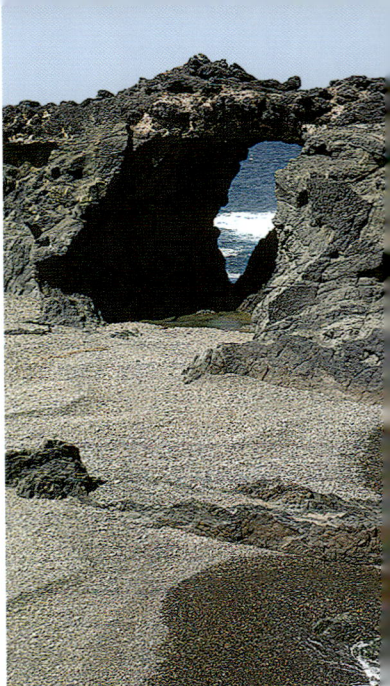

### The Cofete connection

At isolated Cofete, on the southern tip of the island, there's a large house surmounted by a turret. It was built by a certain Señor Winter who forbade anyone else to live in the area. The house is now inhabited by the grandson of one of the builders, who has become a bit of a celebrity — running tours of the property. He even has a facebook page. But it's a sad story, which you can read on casawinter.com.

News broke in 2017 that these huge caves may have harboured German U-boats during the Second World War — under the direction of Señor Winter. You can read about it by just keying in 'Ajuy sea caves' for news articles (including some from the BBC). There are also videos on YouTube, including tours of the house. Was the white-tiled 'kitchen' really an operating theatre performing plastic surgery on notorious Nazis before they fled to South America? Fascinating stuff.

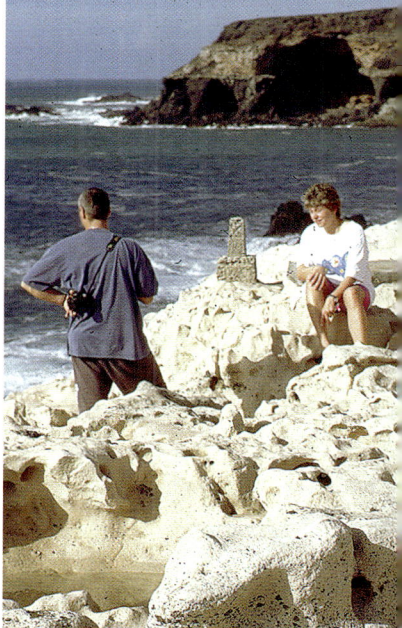

*Opposite: Fuerteventura's own 'Arc de Triomphe' at Playa del Jurado. Right: the fossilized dune landscape at Caleta Negra, near the mirador, is fascinating to look at, but quite tricky underfoot. Below: flights of narrow steps with sturdy railings lead down to a first sea-cave; it's certainly large enough to shelter a submarine (see panel below left). If the sea is not too rough, you can make your way into the adjacent cave.*

These caves form part of the Betancuria Rural Park and are one of the world's 150 main sites of geological interest: they are the oldest rock formations in the Canary Islands, created by the flow of lava which rose 100 million years ago from a depth of 3000 metres beneath the sea.

From the viewpoint it's little more than 10 minutes back to **Ajuy** and your car (**2h25min**).

## Walk 11: FROM ANTIGUA TO BETANCURIA

**Distance:** 5.5km/3.5mi; 1h50min
**Grade:** ● fairly strenuous, with
an ascent of 340m/1120ft, often
on a stony path; well waymarked
(SL FV 29 and partly GR131)
**Equipment:** walking boots,
sunhat, light jacket, suncream,
picnic, plenty of water; raingear in
winter
**Refreshments:** restaurants and
bars in Antigua and Betancuria

**Transport:** 🚌 to Antigua (Line
1); return on 🚌 from Betancuria
(Line 2). If travelling by car, you
could park in Antigua and take the
16.30 🚌 from Betancuria part
way to Puerto del Rosario and
change to a Line 01 bus back to
Antigua (ask the driver where to
set you down) — but it would be
easier to call a taxi (📞 928 878094).

T his is the pilgrim's walk. Every year on the third Friday
in September hundreds of pilgrims make their way
across these hills to pay homage to the Virgen de la Peña in
Vega de Río Palmas. But the contrast you'll see in vegetation
is reason enough to do this hike. In winter there's a rare
lushness on the hilltops rarely seen on this island.

**The walk begins** at the CHURCH
in **Antigua** (○). With the belfry
behind you and the leafy church
plaza on your left, head along the
street to the first junction. Turn
right here (GR131 fingerpost for
the 'DEGOLLADA DEL MARRUBIO'
and 'BETANCURIA'). Go through
another junction and soon cross
the valley floor. Palms edge the
road on the right. You come to an
ELECTRICITY TRANSFORMER/BUS
STOP (❶; **10min**) on the right; the
well-restored Durazno windmill is
about 100m behind it. At the
Y-FORK here, go left on the lower
road, straight towards the barrier
of hills cutting across in front of
you. You can see your ongoing
route from this point — a wide
path ascending a lateral crest not
far ahead, slightly to the right.
    Around 10 minutes later ignore
a road to the left. Some 90m/yds
further on, when the road forks
right, continue straight ahead on a
track (FINGERPOST). Most of the
garden plots on the left lie fallow.
Just below a WATERHOUSE (❷), the
way forks. Head right up the wide
SL FV 29 path, the ascent now

noticeable. A lush little cultivated
valley unravels to your left and,
looking back down over the
scattering of Antigua, you have a
sweeping view. Low volcanic
humps and razor-backed ridges
stretch across the horizon.
    A SIGN designating the area
'parque rural' comes up at just over
**30min** en route. You zigzag your
way uphill towards the crest.
Nearer the top, the spiny *aulaga*
bushes give way to bright green
*tabaiba*. The path fades briefly, but
traces of stone walls come to the
rescue. In winter low cloud may
brush the ridges. The terrain gets
rockier, and the greens of the
*verode, tabaiba* and asphodelus
bring life to these otherwise insipid
slopes. Then the grass becomes
noticeable; the landscape softens.
Quite a treat! Soon goats and
sheep will keep you company.
    Crossing the **Degollada del
Marrubio** (or Degollada de la
Villa; ❸; **1h20min**), brace
yourself for a blasting on windy
days! A brilliant sight awaits you
now, as the vegetation changes
completely. The inclines are dotted

## The pilgrimage festival in honour of Nuestra Señora de la Peña

The patron saint of Fuerteventura is the focus of a pilgrimage every year on the third weekend in September. Although many people now travel by car, some make the journey on foot. They start out from their homes on the Friday (a bank holiday) and gather at Antigua to begin the mountain crossing.

It's a cheerful pilgrimage, as you can see! The groups 'parade' with decorated carts, guitars, and music — and with gifts for the Virgin, which they either carry or load on donkeys or camels. On arrival at the church in Vega de Río Palmas where the statue resides, the joyous atmosphere is enhanced by stalls with food and drink, the singing of traditional songs, dancing and midnight fireworks. All the gifts intended for the Virgin are donated to charity after the vigil and church services.

The tiny statue of the Virgin came to the island by sea in the early 15th century, brought by Jean de Béthencourt, who captured Fuerteventura for the French and after whom Betancuria is named. It's the oldest image of the Virgin in the Canaries. It was damaged several times, particularly in the late 16th century during a Berber raid. After being repaired, it was reputedly hidden in a cave in the Barranco de Mal Paso …

… where it was discovered in the 17th century by two Franciscan monks from the monastery in Betancuria. It was first housed in the chapel in the river bed where it was found (shown on pages 74-75), but this was difficult to reach when the river was flowing, and the dampness was harming the statue. Its new nearby resting place was inaugurated in 1716.

65

with wind-battered pines, and grass carpets the ground. Straight below lies Betancuria, ensconced in these hills. Keeping straight over the crest, you descend on a very wide path. Thick leathery-leafed aloes border the path and nearby

fields. Baying dogs welcome you into **Betancuria** 25 minutes below the pass, and you turn right on reaching the FV30. The bus stops about 200m beyond the Valtarajal Restaurant, just before the BRIDGE (**4**; **1h50min**).

*Betancuria, with the 17th-century cathedral church of Santa María*

# Walk 12: PICO DE LA ZARZA

**Distance:** 15.6km/9.7mi; 5h
**Grade:** ● strenuous, with an
overall ascent of 820m/2650ft —
nearly all on a track, except for the
last 25min, where you follow a
path to the summit. It can be very
hot — or very cold and windy. Not
recommended on very windy days
— nor on cloudy days, since the
climb is only worth it for the view
and, if you were lost in mist, the
climb could be dangerous as well.
But everyone fit should try this
hike, beginners included. Yellow/
white waymarked PR FV 54
**Equipment:** walking boots or
stout shoes with ankle support,
warm jacket, raingear, sunhat,

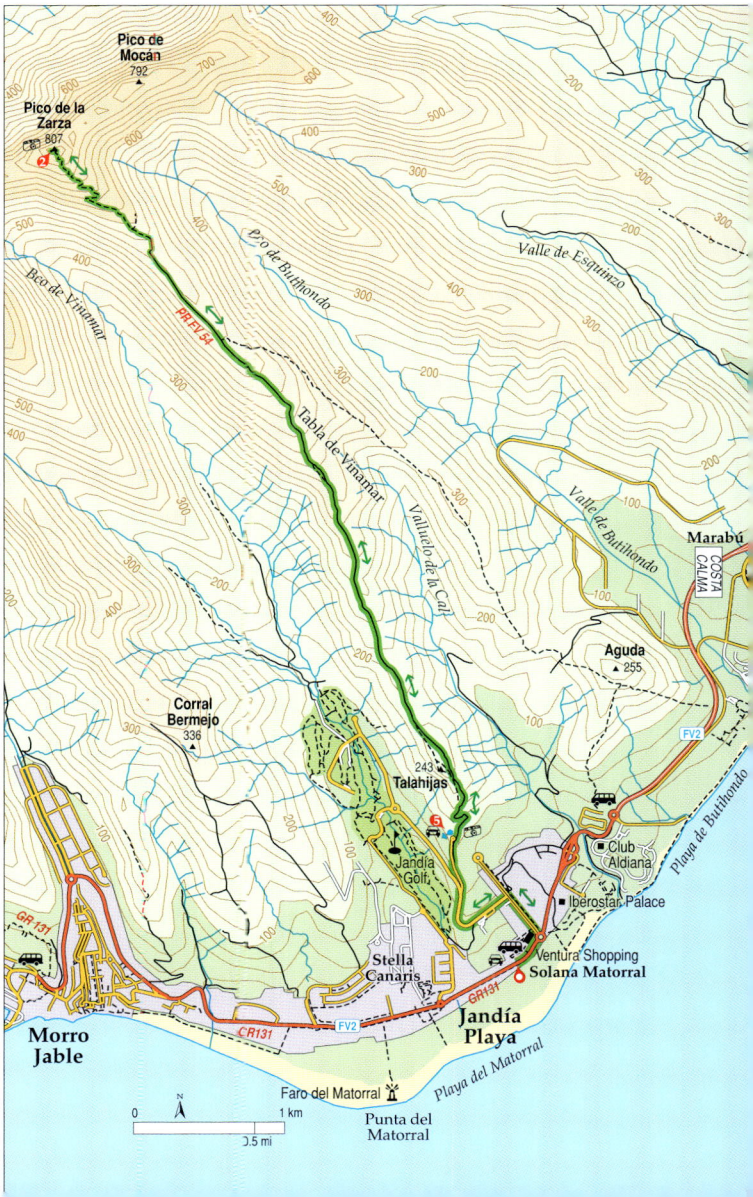

suncream, picnic, plenty of water
**Refreshments:** plenty of
possibilties in Jandía Playa
**Transport:** 🚌 to/from the Ventura
Shopping Centre at Jandía Playa,
where there is a large car park

(28° 3.172'N, 14° 19.424'W) — or you
could park by the water tank
10min uphill (28° 3.555'N,
14° 19.699'W). Or 🚐 (Lines 01,
04, 05, 09, 10) to/from the Centro
Comercial Ventura

**P**ico de la Zarza is Fuerteventura's highest peak and worth
climbing for two reasons: the grand panorama that
tumbles away below you and the wealth of botanical
specimens to be seen en route. The best time to scale this
mountain is in spring, when the summit is resplendent with
yellow-flowering *Asteriscus* (as in the photo above). But be
warned: it can be very windy! On a calm day, it's one of the
most exhilarating spots on the island.

*From the summit of Pico de la Zarza, you look out towards the tip of the Jandía Peninsula. There's a surprising amount of greenery up here, including the furry-leafed yellow* Asteriscus, *an island endemic.*

When the road forks, keep right and right again on a track a minute later, to pass to the right of this WATER TANK (❶). Nearby is a WALKERS' INFORMATION BOARD for the trail. Follow the track uphill; it quickly becomes rough and winds its way up the rock- and stone-strewn slopes. You pass to the right of twin-peaked **Talahijas**; its lower summit can be quickly reached, but for the ascent of Zarza a stiff climb lies ahead. Meanwhile, you already have a superb view back over the long white Playa del Matorral with its turquoise-green shoreline. The Barranco de Vinamar, as bleak as the rest of the countryside, cuts straight back into the massif.

Climbing higher, you catch sight of corrals hidden in the depths of the ravine. On heading round to the eastern side of the ridge, you overlook another harsh valley (**Valluelo de la Cal**, with a stone quarry and rubbish tip), where more ridges hint at a succession of ravines in the distance. You have an excellent view that stretches to the hills at the centre of the island. Pico de la Zarza is the unimpressive peak that rises a thumbnail above the rest of the massif at the very end of this ridge.

Reaching the cloud zone, you find that the top of the crest is very herbaceous. It's quite a wild garden! (Keep well clear of any goats you may encounter up here; they are very easily frightened and

**The walk starts** at the BUS STOP (⊙) in front of the CENTRO COMERCIAL VENTURA. Follow the FV2 a short way east, to the ROUNDABOUT with the tall modern sculpture. Turn left here and walk up the dual carriageway beside the Occidental Jandía Playa Hotel. After 300m/yds, turn left on CALLE SANCHO PANZA (there may be a sign here for 'Jandía Golf'). As this road bends round to the right and edges the **Barranco de Vinamar**, aim for a huge white WATER TANK you can see up ahead.

will dart off in all directions if startled; in particular, avoid any with kids.)

Climbing higher, you head alongside a bouldery crest, flooded with *tabaiba* bushes, *verode* and asphodels. Look, too, down on the *barranco* walls below, where you'll spot some enormous *candelabra*. When the track reaches about 500m/1640ft (**2h**) it deteriorates. The track stops dead on the crest of the ridge (**2h35min**), leaving you to continue to the top on a good path. *Lamarzkia aurea* (it resembles the bottle-brush plant) flourishes up here, and soon the slopes are ablaze with golden yellow *Asteriscus*. About 200m

### Cardón de Jandía
The Jandía Nature Park takes up the northern part of the Jandía Peninsula — a wide arc of mountains falling precipitously to the north coast. It culminates at the highest point on the whole island — Pico de la Zarza.

The Park harbours a wealth of flora, many of them endemic to the Canaries or to Fuerteventura. In addition to the plants mentioned in these walking notes, you will certainly spot *cardón de Jandía* (*Euphorbia handiensis;* shown above). Not only is it endemic to Fuerteventura, but it only appears in the Nature Park! It's the symbol of the island.

from the summit, the environmental authorities have erected a high barbed-wire fence, to protect the very special flora from goats and sheep. Go through the gate, *making sure to close it behind you.*

Eventually, windswept and exhausted, you're on the roof of the island, atop **Pico de la Zarza** (❷; **3h**). And what a view! To the left you look across the lofty crags that rupture this impenetrable wall of rock. The jutting southwestern coastline unfolds as this barrier of mountains dies down into sand-patched hills and finally a sea-plain. Don't venture too near to the edge of the peak; it plummets hundreds of feet straight down.

A mysterious mansion with a turret sits back off the flat, in the shadows of the cliffs — the Cortijo de Cofete (or 'Villa Winter': read about its history in the panel on page 62). More in keeping with the landscape is Cofete, the hamlet over to the left. To your right stand the high rolling sandhills of the Pared isthmus that joins these mountains to the northern half of the island. On hazeless days, it's possible to see well down the eastern coastline to Lanzarote.

Botanists will want to tarry here on the summit for quite some time to discover more of the island's floral treasures, some of them illustrated on pages 18-19: *Echium handiense, Bupleurum handiense, Sideritis massoniana, Argyranthemum winteri,* and the more common *Ranunculus cortusifolius, Andryala cheiranthifolia* and *Minuartia platyphylla.* The summit also houses a tiny meteorological hut and two large antennae.

Home is all downhill — sheer bliss — two hour's descent away. You'll be back at the VENTURA SHOPPING CENTRE in about **5h**.

**Distance:** 9.2km/5.7mi; 3h40min
**Grade:** ● fairly strenuous, with an ascent/descent of 515m/1690ft (almost all in one go). All paths are clear, well-waymarked and signed (green/white SL FV 31) except for the detour to the Gran Montaña summit which is almost pathless.
**Equipment:** walking boots,

walking pole(s), sunhat, light jacket, suncream, picnic, plenty of water; raingear in winter
**Refreshments:** bars and restaurants in Tiscamanita
**Transport:** 🚌 to/from Tiscamanita (Line 1). Or 🚗 to Tiscamanita; park near the bus stop (28° 21.085'N, 14° 2.143'W) .

If you have the energy for the climb, this is a beautiful walk with far-reaching views in all directions. The walk I suggest here is the first part of an old trail between Tiscamanita and Vega de Río Palmas which has recently been restored by the island government — the SL FV 31. I've made it an out-and-back for transport convenience … and so that you can take in Tiscamanita's Windmill Interpretation Centre when you finish the hike.

**Start out** on the main road in **Tiscamanita**: watch for the sign 'CENTRO DE INTERPRETACIÓN DE LOS MOLINOS' and turn west on CALLE JUAN PEÑATE (●). Ten metres along is a hikers' INFORMATION BOARD on the left. Continue into the village, ignoring all side-streets and tracks; stay on JUAN PEÑATE. After passing an ALOE VERA FARM on the right (derelict when last seen), the way becomes a signposted dirt track, and you climb past some traditional wind-pumps and *gavias* (see overleaf) over to the left. An INFORMATION BOARD explains the different types of agriculture in this area

When you reach a SHELTER with two picnic tables and a SIGNPOST (❶; **35min**) climb the stone-lined path at the left of the shelter, accompanied by ravens and goats. You pass fields of *tuneras* (*Opuntia* cacti used in the past for cochineal production) and *pitas* (agaves yielding sisal and rope). There are also *cuernúas* (*Caralluma burchardii*, a small and endangered plant endemic to the eastern Canaries), *acebuche majorero* (*Olea*

**Windmill Interpretation Centre**
*One of the things you'll discover at the Centro de Interpretación de los Molinos is the difference between 'female' and 'male' mills: the slender female construction on the left is a molina: a wooden contraption that rotates and is built onto the rooftop of a house. The house normally has a room on either side of the mill. More robust is the male molino: it's conical and is moved by pushing the long arms, thus rotating the cap with the windmill blades. This building is not inhabited. Both mills were used for grinding gofio (which you can buy at the centre).*

71

*europea ssp guarchicha,* an olive tree species), *tabaibas* and *verode*.

The higher you climb along the **Majada de Mujeres** (a protected area, where shepherds kept their flocks overnight), the better the view. Eventually, you can see to Montaña Cardón in the south, the Jandía Massif, and the Chilea mountain range behind Pájara. To the north are views over Antigua and the central mountains.

You reach an elongated SADDLE above the Majada de Mujeres (**2**; **1h10min**). Continue to another saddle, **Morro Jorjado** (**3**; **1h40min**) which harbours, as the name suggests, colonies of *jorjado* (*Asteriscus sericeus*). From here head up steeply left on a barely visible but signposted path. You pass a ruined OLD SHELTER (**4**) and after 15 minutes you're on the summit of **Gran Montaña** (**5**; **1h55min**).

### Gavias

*Gavias* are seen throughout Fuerteventura. In this traditional Canarian system of irrigation, land is levelled, then surrounded by metre-high walls of soil (or soil and stone) called *trastones*. Run-off water is sent via canals or pipes into the *gavia*, where it is slowly absorbed. Every *gavia* has an overflow opposite the side where the water comes in: superfluous water is sent on to the next gavia or emptied into a *barranco*.

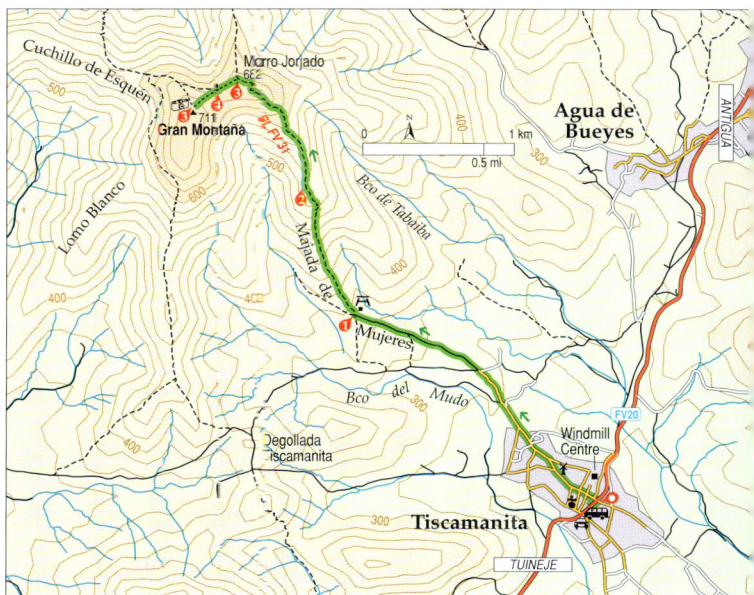

*Left:* gavias *below Montaña Cardón; below: the aloe vera farm at the start of the walk: although recently abandoned, I nevertheless found it very attractive.*

Now it takes another 15 minutes to slide back down to **Morro Jorjado** and retrace your steps to **Tiscamanita** (**3h40min**).

## Aloe vera in the Canary Islands

The cultivation of aloe vera is becoming a major Canarian industry, especially in Fuerteventura and Lanzarote. The plant flourishes in the dry climate and thrives on the rich minerals in volcanic soil.

Probably endemic to the Arabian peninsula, the plant has been known since ancient times to have curative properties; Egyptian pharaohs were buried with it; Columbus took it on his voyage to America. Its fleshy leaves, harvested and cut by hand, produce a gel used in medicines and cosmetics. Or a gooey juice can be extracted and easily mixed into smoothies. Some of Fuerteventura's production is organic, but there are also fraudulent products which have not even come from the Canaries.

## Walk 14: BARRANCO DE LAS PEÑITAS

**Distance:** 4.4km/2.7mi; 1h40min
**Grade:** ●❓. quite easy, well
signposted and waymarked (SL
FV 06/27), but the path to the
chapel could prove unnerving for
those prone to vertigo. *Be very
careful if it's wet!*
**Equipment:** comfortable shoes or
walking boots, fleece, sunhat,
suncream, raingear, picnic, water
**Refreshments:** in Vega de Río
Palmas, at Don Antonio by the
church or the Casa de la Naturaleza
**Transport:** 🚌 to/from Vega de
Río Palmas. From the church (goal
of the pilgrimage described on
page 65) drive south on the FV30
and turn right after just under
400m on the narrow road to the
reservoir (signposted to Vega de
Río Palmas); park by a bridge at
the signposted entrance to the
path/track into the stream bed
(28° 23.617N, 14° 5.266'W). Or 🚙

to/from Vega de Río Palmas
(Line 2); alight at the 'Casa de la
Naturaleza' bus shelter ( **ⓐ** ) and
walk downhill 150m to the bridge
where the signposted walk begins.
**Short walk: Nuestra Señora de la
Peña** (2.4km/1.5mi; 30min; ●❓).
Grade/equipment as above. *Not
signposted.* Transport by 🚌: take
the FV605 from Pájara towards La
Pared and turn right after 1.5km
on the FV621. Turn right again
after 3km on a road signposted to
Buen Paso (FV627). After 1.2km
the road is chained off: either park
here ( **ⓑ** ; 28° 23.165N, 14° 6.682'W)
and walk along the track into the
**Barranco de Mal Paso**, or drive to
where you can see the chapel in its
narrow gorge. Cross the *barranco*
bed at this point and follow a
walled-in water pipe to a RUIN,
from where a pretty path leads to
**Nuestra Señora de la Peña** ( **❷** ).

This stroll is short and sweet; it takes you down one of the island's most picturesque valleys, the Barranco de las Peñitas. Palm trees dot the valley, and a small reservoir rests in the floor. From the reservoir wall you look through a corridor of rock out onto more palms and salubrious garden plots far below. In winter you may find dark green pools embedded in the floor of the *barranco*. Hidden in the sheer walls lies the delightful little Ermita de Nuestra Señora de la Peña — just the kind of place where one might feel inclined to offer up a prayer.

**Start the walk** in **Vega de Río Palmas** at the ERIDGE over the **Barranco de las Peñitas (●)**: take the gravel track that strikes off right just before the stream bed and drops down into this dry *barranco* (SL FV 06/27). A healthy sprinkling of tall palms graces the valley floor and indeed, the entire valley. For Fuerteventura, this is the height of arboreal luxury! Abrupt craggy ridges dominate the landscape. Follow the stream bed

### Tamarisk trees

The endemic *Tamarix canariensis* (Spanish: *tarajal*) colonises all the islands in the Canaries except El Hierro. It is especially prevalent in the eastern Canaries, with Fuerteventura even having a village named Gran Tarajal.

The trees or shrubs, up to about 4m/12ft high, have showy, aromatic sprays of tiny pale pink florets in summer. Tamarisks are adapted to moist soils and tolerate a moderate salt content, which is why they are often found near the coasts (even on Gran Canaria's dunes of Maspalomas, by the lagoon).

They also commonly grow in copses in river deltas, *barranco* beds and slopes on Fuerteventura — making them look like green rivers, as above by the reservoir in the Barranco de las Peñitas.

until, a little over **10min** off the road, the ways climbs up right out of the *barranco* on a wide old washed-out track. When the track forks, go left to skirt the reservoir. This track quickly becomes a narrow trail. A sign indicates that this area is a bird sanctuary.

The valley floor quickly fills with tamarisk and then forks. The left-hand fork swings back up into the hills; the right-hand fork cradles the reservoir, before folding up into a narrow ravine that drops down to join the Barranco de Mal Paso. You're surrounded by hills; pointed Gran Montaña (708m/ 2320ft; Walk 13) dominates the valley. The now-narrow trail winds amidst large boulders. Soon the **Presa de las Peñitas** is just below you — murky green in winter and spring, probably bone dry in summer. Green garden plots set amidst palm trees terrace the slopes on your left now. The *barranco* is freckled with verode — the brightest plant on the slopes. Less than 10 minutes along, you're on the *RESERVOIR WALL* (❶; **30min**). The bare escarpment stares down on you, as the ravine closes up into a deep V, before emptying out onto an oasis of palms and gardens and continuing its seaward journey.

Beyond the reservoir wall you follow a stone-paved path built into the sides of the *barranco*. Parts have crumbled away, requiring steady footwork … and the lizards darting about are distracting. The pools may be just puddles by the time you visit, but they *can* be very deep. A couple of minutes down the path, you spot the tiny white chapel of **Nuestra Señora de la Peña** (❷), perched on a rocky out-crop above the stream bed. A short stretch of path leads to it. This path clings to the face of the rock and is quite unnerving, but it's fairly short — only about 25m.

Inside the chapel you'll find bits of clothing, plastic flowers, and a visitors' book that makes for interesting reading. On a scorching hot day, the chapel provides the perfect retreat for a picnic. Beyond the *ermita* the trail hangs out over the side of the *barranco*. This stretch of path might also prove unnerving for those without a head for heights. It's an impressive piece of path-building, that's for sure. A few minutes along, near the end of the gorge, there's a fine viewpoint by a *RUIN* (❸; **50min**) — a good place to turn back.

Returning, follow the same route, remaining on the path just above the reservoir until you re-enter the stream bed. You should be back at the *BRIDGE* in **Vega de Río Palmas** in **1h40min**. The *BUS SHELTER* is just 150m up the road, in front of the *CASA DE LA NATURALEZA*.

## Walks on
# Gran Canaria

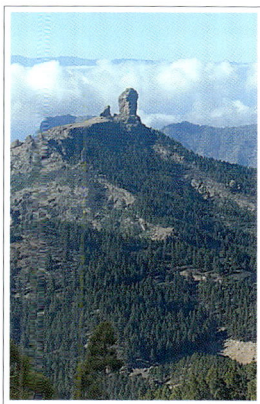

**Gran Canaria**

AREA: 1560/km² (602sq mi)
LENGTH OF COAST: 256km (159mi)
HIGH POINT: Morro de la Agujereada (1956m/6417ft),
 by the viewpoint on Pico de las Nieves (1949m/6393ft)
POPULATION: 870,595 (2020)
POPULATION DENSITY: 546/km² (1413/sq mi)
CAPITAL: Las Palmas (pop 379,925)
PROVINCE: Las Palmas

A wealth of diverse landscapes and a wonderland of curious flora await the explorer on Gran Canaria. So special are these ecosystems that almost half the island has been designated a nature protection or preservation area. It's hard to believe that such a small island has so much to offer. And yet it has often been referred to as a 'continent in miniature'.

From the *cumbre*, the island's great saddle, ravines are born and fan out seaward like spokes on a wheel, gouging enormous valleys in their wake. For me these magnificent *barrancos* are one reason why Gran Canaria is so special. Dams and reservoirs are another: these small reflections of

# GRAN CANARIA

calm water are Gran Canaria's lifeline. Every valley cradles at least one.

The harsh and often inhospitable character of the countryside is softened by a wealth of flora. The slopes of the *cumbre* are like a wild garden in spring, ablaze with bright yellow *retama (Teline)* and flecked with mauve *Cheiranthus*, pale blue *Echium*, and the white to carmine florets of *Senecio*. Palm-studded valleys and giant *Euphorbias*, like *cardón* (candelabra spurge), on the barren sea-slopes, hint of nearby Africa. Spacious Canary pine woods cloak the highest summits … surviving several recent conflagrations.

Gran Canaria, like Fuerteventura, is inundated with sites and relics of the past — the Guanche epoch. Little is known about these deeply religious and moral people. It is believed that they arrived on the islands about 4000 years ago. Vestiges of their civilisation can be found in ancient settlements — intriguing troglodyte villages carved high into often-inaccessible crags.

## Walk 15: ROQUE NUBLO

**Distance/time:** 4.8km/3mi; 2h
**Grade:** ● Quite easy; overall climb of 250m/820ft. Not suitable in wet weather. All trail S70
**Equipment:** comfortable walking shoes or boots, sunhat, long-sleeved shirt, long trousers, warm fleece, warm jacket, gloves, raingear, picnic, water

**Refreshments:** mobile kiosk at La Goleta; otherwise bar at Ayacata
**Transport:** 🚌 to/from the La Goleta parking area off the GC600, north of Ayacata (27° 57.937'N, 15° 36.088'W). Nearest 🚐 18 bus stop is 1.3km away at Ayacata (see map): follow the steep S70 trail up 300m/1000ft to La Goleta, allowing 1h.

**M**ysterious Roque Nublo ('Cloud Rock'), a monolith of rock balancing on a table-top mountain, is Gran Canaria's proud landmark. Whether seen from far away or nearby under its spell, it's easy to understand why this eye-catching rock was sacred to the Guanches. The panorama from this ancient sanctuary captures all the veins in the landscape — the sharp-edged ridges segmenting the valleys below.

**Start out** at the **Goleta** viewpoint and parking area (**○**): take the S70 trail signposted to Roque Nublo, just on the north side of the road. The surrounding terrain is a mass of round rocky abutments pierced by occasional fingers of rock. In the spring, yellow-flowering *retama* and *tabaiba* brighten the slopes. Roque Nublo becomes ever more impressive as you near it. Barely 15 minutes up the path, level with **El Fraile** ('The Monk', another rock monolith resembling a monk in prayer), ignore a turn-off to the right (**❶**); you will return that way.

On reaching a high pass, the **Degollada de las Palomas** (**❷**; **25min**), a small pine-studded basin appears below, swallowed up by these enormous abutments. (On the return, you will descend to the left here, down into this basin.) Enjoy the superb view over to El Teide on Tenerife, then clamber up the rocky ridge on your right, where more astounding views unfold, straight down onto Ayacata.

Now ascend the two gigantic platforms of rock, which lead you up to the once-sacred **Roque Nublo** (**❸**; **35min**), a magnificent sight against a backdrop of deep blue sky. Beside it is yet another massive rock, looking just like its name — the crouching 'Frog' (**La Rana**). You look straight down into the Barranco de Tejeda, seaward bound, in its attempt to cut the island in two. To its left lies the cleft of the Barranco del Corilla, narrower and more severe. Tejeda, a sprawl of white

*Be prepared for company on your visit to Roque Nublo — it's the most popular walk on the island.*

houses, lies on the gentler inclines below on your right.

Soak up the view, then return to the junction (❷) less than 10 minutes back. Descend to the right, into the basin below. At a junction 10 minutes downhill (**Hoyetas del Nublo**; ❹; **55min**), turn right. When the path forks again some 10 minutes later at the **Degollada Blanca** (❺; **1h05min**), keep straight ahead, back to your outward path at ❶. Descend back to **La Goleta**, 30 minutes away. (The Presa de los Hornos, a good five minutes up the road from the car park, is worth a short stroll; this is *included* in the 2h allowed for this walk.)

### Roque Nublo

For about 1500 years, up until the Spanish conquest in 1496, the original inhabitants of the Gran Canaria — probably Berbers from Africa — had a well-developed civilisation. They colonised the island's higher elevations, where they raised cereal crops (which could be stored in the many caves which can be seen in these areas, for instance on the GC607).

To survive, these people had to know when to plant, and their agricultural success was based on their knowledge of the seasons. It is believed that they made precise observations of the sun, moon and stars from sacred places called *almogarenes* — one of which was Roque Nublo.

The main *almogarén* was on Roque Bentayga — positioned in such a way as to be perfectly aligned with Roque Nublo, whereby the aboriginal astronomers could use the setting equinoctial sun to calculate the equinoxes with great precision — even to within one day, according to some scholars.

*View from the Mirador de Becerra across the Caldera de Tejeda, with Roque Bentayga at the right and Roque Nublo to the left*

## Walk 16: CRUZ DE TEJEDA • LA CULATA • TEJEDA

**See also photo on page 74**
**Distance/time:** 10km/6.2mi; 3h20min
**Grade:** ● fairly easy ascent of 200m/650ft overall; long descent of 600m/1970ft. But you must be sure-footed and have a head for heights. Not suitable in bad weather, and note that it can be very cold and windy. S50, S82, S80
**Equipment:** walking boots, sunhat, fleece, windproof, long trousers, gloves, thick socks, raingear, picnic, water
**Refreshments:** available at Cruz de Tejeda, La Culata and Tejeda
**Transport:** 🚌18 from Maspalomas at 09.30 to Tejeda, then 🚌305 to Cruz de Tejeda; journey time 2h20min. Or 🚌303 from Las Palmas to San Mateo, then change to 🚌305; journey time about 2h. Return on the same bus lines from Tejeda. Or 🚗 to Tejeda, then 🚌305 to Cruz de Tejeda to start the walk

Short and sweet, this walk gives you spectacular views from the roof of the island. Descending to La Culata, a charming country village where time seems to have stood still, you enter a beautiful valley gushing with water.

**Start the walk** at **Cruz de Tejeda** (○): take the cobbled S50 trail to the right of the BAR-ASADOR YOLANDA (opposite the stone cross). Heading though *codeso*, *retama* and chestnut trees along the grassy *cumbre*, after a few minutes ascend to the left at a fork. (The route to the right is the S85 to Tejeda, the fastest, lowest and easiest trail to the village, but at time of writing signposts had not yet been replaced after forest fires several years ago.) Already a striking panorama unfolds over the Barranco de Tejeda and its tributaries, to the distant greenhouses of San Nicolás. Tenerife rises above the clouds. Tejeda, on the slopes below, comes out of hiding. The two monumental rock landmarks to the south are Nublo and Bentayga.

Soon the path skirts a WALLED-OFF ESTATE on the left (**15min**). Keeping straight on, join a track and follow it until it turns sharp left. Here, take the path to the right. Now your view encompasses the northern hills, speckled with white houses; sheep graze the surrounding pastures. Dropping down to join the GC150, turn right. Then take steps on the right, to follow the trail above and to the right of the road, eventually passing a house.

After some 800m you reach the **Mirador de Becerra** (❶; **40min**) and enjoy the stunning view shown opposite. La Culata, the small clusters of houses set along the wall of the Tejeda Valley below, is your next destination. Your path leaves from the right-hand side of the road just past the *mirador*. Keep right at a fork five minutes down at the **Degollada de la Cumbre** (❷). Keep left at the next fork, where the S85 rises up on the right from Tejeda. You pass a SPRING at the **Barranco del Molino** (❸; **1h**) — a superb picnic spot, with its chestnut trees and small streams bouncing down the hillside.

Joining a LANE (❹; **1h20min**), you have a superb view of Roque Bentayga, Montaña Altavista and El Teide — all in a row. After two minutes (150m/yds), turn right down a narrow road. Under 200m further on, turn left down shallow

81

## The Caldera de Tejeda

From the viewpoints at the Mirador de Becerra (shown on page 80) or Cruz de Timagada, you can take in various angles of the huge Caldera de Tejeda — measuring 28km x 18km.

Formed about 14 million years ago, it is one of the world's true examples of a collapsed crater (as opposed, for example, to the Las Cañadas crater on Tenerife; see page 116).

A caldera — as opposed to a crater — is formed by the collapse of a volcano into itself. If not all magma is released in an eruption, heavy particles drop to the floor of the magmatic chamber and support the chamber roof above. But when a new eruption takes place, it needs to be much more violent to get through this roof. The earth's crust quickly bursts under this tremendous pressure and collapses into the empty chamber. It is thought that the Caldera de Tejeda was created in under two hours! Over millenia, the caldera rim keeps collapsing inwards: only about half of Tejeda's caldera rim still exists.

steps onto a cobbled path. After another 150m, when the path meets a concrete track at a house, turn left; turn right 25m/ yds further on and go under a wire frame with climbing plants. Then turn immediately left downhill on a concrete path with green handrails, looking into gardens, courtyards and animal pens. Step down to the centre of **La Culata** (**5**; **1h35min**). To the right is a PARKING AREA/BUS STOP.

Leaving the village, descend steps (S82) from the parking area down to the valley floor, where you cross a FOOTBRIDGE. Meeting a track at a T-junction, follow it to the left uphill for 10m, then turn right up a driveway. Go straight on past the house. Ignore a path to the right and cross a tributary. A steady ascent follows. The slopes are wooded with *escobón*, *tabaiba* and almond trees.

Eventually you come to the TURN-OFF RIGHT (**6**; **2h15min**) to Tejeda. Roque Nublo stands directly above you here. (Before going down into Tejeda, I suggest that you might like to go *left* here. A 10-minute detour would take you to **Cruz de Timagada** (**a**), with its two crosses and spring and on to the crest of the ridge, another fine VIEWPOINT across the Caldera de Tejeda (**b**).

Return to **6**; about 25 minutes (1km) down the Tejeda path, you pass above some gardens, go straight over an intersection, and join a farm track. After just a few

metres, this track bends sharp left: take the (faintly vertiginous) path to the right here, rounding the hillside. Descend to a track in the floor of the *barranco* (**3h**) and turn left, joining the TEJEDA ROAD (**7**; GC60). Turn right for 15 minutes, to the BUS STOP by the PETROL STATION in **Tejeda** (**8**; **3h20min**).

*Tejeda, with Roque Nublo in the background*

**Distance/time:** 9.7km/6mi; 3h30min

**Grade:** ●❢ moderate; overall ups/downs of 350m/1150ft. You must be sure-footed and have a head for heights: much of the path on the crater rim is vertiginous *(dangerous in wet and/or windy weather)*, as is the path to the Guanche caves; the descent into the crater is steep and slippery and the shadeless ascent of 200m/650ft back up very tiring

**Equipment:** walking boots, sunhat, long trousers, long-sleeved shirt, fleece, windproof, water, picnic

**Refreshments:** bar/bodega by the bus shelter; at the golf course hotel

**Transport:** 🚌 311 from Las Palmas to/from Bandama; journey time 30min. Take 🚌 30 or 50 from Maspalomas to Las Palmas if necessary. Or 🚗: park in Bandama, near the bus shelter (28° 2.158′N, 15° 27.616′W)

**Short walks:** The main walk can be divided into three parts, each a good short walk: **THE PEAK** and its *mirador* (● moderate, 180m/600ft ascent/descent; 1h), **THE CRATER RIM** (●❢ easy but vertiginous, 1h-15min), **THE CRATER FLOOR** (● fairly strenuous, 230m/750ft descent/ascent; 1h30min). Equipment, access as main walk.

---

U p to the peak, round the rim, and then down into the crater. You'll have seen Bandama from every possible angle when you've done this walk. Guanche caves, set spectacularly in the sheer walls of this perfectly-formed crater, make an intriguing detour.

when last seen it was overgrown with spiky agaves. Motorists may prefer to drive to the top.

All the way round, you're looking straight down into the crater, rising above dark shallow valleys that nurture some of the island's few vineyards. (At the end of the walk you might like to visit the Bodega San Juan de Mocanal, nearby on the GC802. This large old property, with a wine museum, is set in a park.) At the top of **Pico de Bandama** (❶; 35min), you'll find a bar and coachloads of tourists. Wonderful views encircle you here. Ridges stream down off the *cumbre*. Las Palmas, always at its best when seen from a distance, is a sprawl of white stretching all the way to the Isleta. And the crater lies below, 200m/650ft deep, 1000m/3300ft in diameter.

Next we explore the rim of the crater: walk about 1.2km back down the road to the junction

**Start the walk** in **Bandama**, at the JUNCTION of the GC802 and the GC822 (❍; 20m/yds uphill from the bus shelter). Follow the road signposted '*PICO DE BANDAMA*'. There used to be a path to the summit (shown on our map), but

where the path turns sharp left off the road (S25; **❷**; **50min**). After five minutes' descent, you will reach the EDGE OF THE CRATER (**❸**) and mount the crest by forking right. A path appears running along the rim. This spectacular ramble round the perimeter, quite vertiginous, offers fine views off the shoulder of the crater over villages sheltering amongst the surrounding hills.

Within an hour of circling the crater (just below a hotel and golf

*The plots at the Casas del Fondo in the Caldera de Bandama are still farmed.*

course), the path rises up log-stablised steps to a corner of the green. Keeping along the edge of the green, head across to the HOTEL; walk through the car park and take the access road out. At a fork, go right on the chained-off, LOWER TRACK (**4**), to pass above the tennis courts. Just after rejoining the golf course road, you meet the Atalaya road (GC802). Follow it to the right downhill, back to the BUS STOP and bar (**5**; **2h**).

To visit the floor of the crater, go right on a driveway (signpost: 'CALDERA DE BANDAMA'), into the tight cluster of houses. Just beyond a gate, you pass a *mirador* over-looking the caldera. *(There may be a sign on the gate, stating that it is only open between 08.00 and 17.00; if so, bear this in mind for your return!)* High stone walls flank your cobbled path; it quickly falls away into the crater, where the walls are covered in a wild tangle of prickly

### The Caldera de Bandama

*Once upon a time there were twin volcanic cones side by side. But 4-5000 years ago one of them collapsed, earning itself the name 'caldera'. But the Caldera de Bandama is not a true caldera or collapsed crater as described on page 82.*

*It is called a 'maar'. The reason for its collapse was that the magma came into contact with the groundwater table — heating it to boiling and causing shallow explosive eruptions. So although looking straight down into the 200m/650ft-deep crater is impressive, it is nowhere near as deep as a true caldera; the Caldera de Tejeda is over 1500m/ 5000ft deep in places.*

*The twin that didn't collapse is the cone of Pico de Bandama...*

pear, lavender and *vinagrera*.

Approaching the first bend, where the (now-earthen) path turns sharp right, take a path ascending slightly to the *left*. This narrow gravelly path crosses a steep slope; inexperienced walkers and those who have no head for heights may find it unnerving. Some eight minutes across the wall of the crater, you come to the MAIN GUANCHE CAVES (**6**; **2h15min**), set high in the escarpment.

From here return to the main path. Just after joining it, you come to another *mirador* built onto a rocky outcrop. Don't lean on the railings here! About 10 minutes below the *mirador*, as you approach the floor of the crater (just past an enormous boulder on the right; **7**; **2h35min**), turn right to circle the crater. At a fork encountered immediately, keep left (right goes to a couple of caves and later rejoins this path). Round the lower crater walls amidst a scattering of olive trees. After five minutes, the path from the caves rejoins from the right. The crater shelters varied vegetation — palms, eucalyptus, *retama*, *taginaste*, olive trees, and higher up, *cardón*.

Soon you reach an *era* (**8**), a circular threshing floor. Remain on the path to the right here, heading towards the very picturesque ruined farm buildings and garden plots in the crater floor, **Casas del Fondo** (**9**; **2h55min**). Walk below the gardens, ignoring the path off right that skirts the house. Keep an eye out for an old wine press behind the farm sheds. Two enormous eucalyptus trees offer shade here; there's also a water tap.

From here continue to the main path; huff and puff your way back up to the JUNCTION, then turn left, back to the BUS STOP (**3h30min**).

## Walk 18: GRAND CIRCUIT FROM SAN BARTOLOME VIA CRUZ GRANDE

**Distance/time:** 14km/8.7mi; 4h15min

**Grade:** ● moderate; fairly steep ascent of 450m/1475ft, gradual descent. *Highly recommended* for fit beginners, but not in wet weather. S50 to Cruz Grande; S60 then S58 to the Degollada de la Manzanilla; S57 back to San Bartolomé

**Equipment:** walking boots, sunhat, long trousers, long-sleeved shirt, warm fleece, windproof, picnic, plenty of water

**Refreshments:** in San Bartolomé

**Transport:** 🚌 to/from San Bartolomé; park near the bus stop (27° 55.537'N, 15° 34.438'W). Or 🚌 18 from Maspalomas to/from San Bartolomé (journey time 50min). From Las Palmas take 🚌 11 to Agüimes (journey 45min), then change to 🚌 34 to San Bartolomé (journey 50min); use the same buses to return, or else take 🚌 18 to Faro de Maspalomas, then 🚌 30 or 50 back to Las Palmas.

I f clouds threaten bad weather in the north, head south to walk. Although devastating fires have left their traces in this area (as elsewhere), there is still much of beauty to accompany you along this *camino real* (see history of these 'royal highways' on page 92) — it's one of the island's top walks.

**The walk starts** at the BUS STOP/ CAR PARK (🔴) in **San Bartolomé**. Follow the GC60 towards TEJEDA, and after 150m turn left on the GC603 signposted to a MIRADOR.

Climb steeply for 300m/yds to a junction by a SCHOOL on your right. Turn right here on CALLE JUGLAR FABIAN TORRES, running just to the left of the school (you

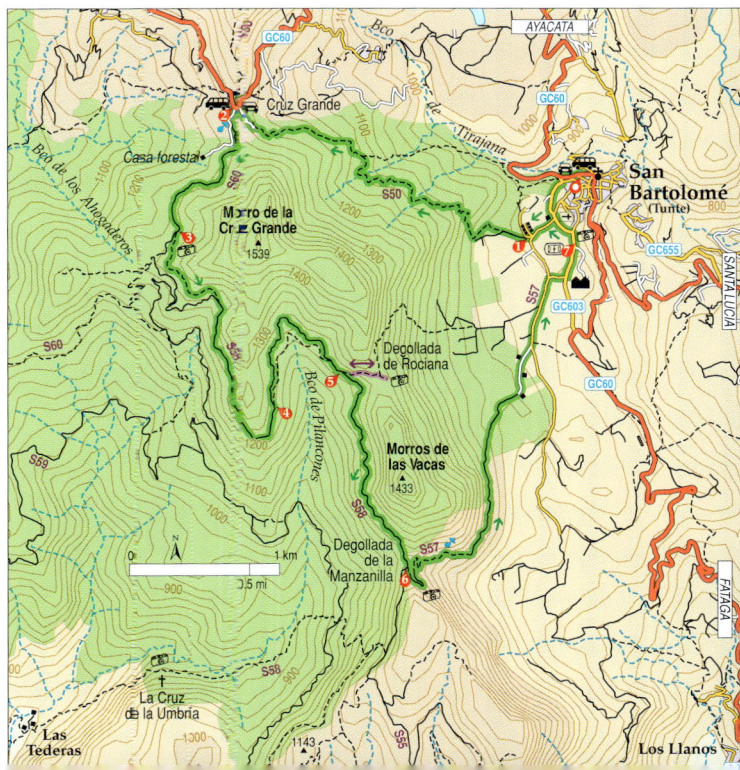

will return on the road to the left). After 200m, just past a street on the right, turn right on a track signposted 'CAMINO REAL, CRUZ GRANDE, CUMBRE' (❶; **20min**); there may also be a sign for the S50 at this turn-off.

After couple of minutes (150m), when the track bends left, continue straight ahead on the *camino real*, in a landscape full of *Cistus*, *tabaiba*, *retama*, aloes, *taginaste*, *Salvia blanca* and *escobón*. A fine cobbled trail comes underfoot,

*View over the route descending from the Degollada de la Manzanilla to San Bartolomé, with the Barranco de Fataga in the distance*

climbing to the upper reaches of the **Barranco de Tirajana**. When you join a track (**1h20min**), turn left uphill to **Cruz Grande** (❷), a signposted pass on the GC60 with wide views back east over the Barranco de Tirajana and west to the Pilancones pine woods which we're about to enter.

Follow this road to the left and, after 40m (just through the pass), turn left on a forestry track (trail S60, initially concreted). Ignore a track off to the right and then, by a large water tank, a road off right to a *casa forestal*. Your view reaches out over the wooded valley of the Barranco de los Ahogaderos. And behind you the *cumbre* rears up, an imposing mass of rock. Some 20-25 minutes from the road (1.2km), at a FORK (❸), take the path up to the left — leaving the S60 for a time — for better views out over the enormous **Barranco de la Data**.

The path shortly descends to the track again (now trail S58), which you follow south. After the track has bent back to head due north, you will pass another path on the right (❹), this time below the track. Path and track both round the **Barranco de Pilancones**. Eventually the path rejoins the track; just afterwards, watch for a wide path ascending to the left, by a small CAIRN (❺; **2h45min**). Here you could make an optional 12-minute return detour to the Degollada de Rociana, a fine viewpoint over the extensive Barranco de Tirajana and San Bartolomé.

When you reach a junction at the **Degollada de la Manzanilla** (❻; **3h10min**), take the first track to the left, trail S57 for San Barto-lomé. This pass affords a fine view over the upper Fataga Valley Descending, the way narrows into

a path and soon rubs against the hillside, where high craggy fingers of rock pierce the ridge above. Widening into a track again, your route eventually goes straight through an INTERSECTION (**3h50min**). Beyond some piggeries, you join a road coming from the right and follow it to the left, ignoring a wide track off to the left. Some 200m further on, fork right to a road (ANTONIO SANTANA). Turn left, passing the STADIUM (❼) on your left and a MIRADOR to your right. Turn left at the next junction. After 160m you're back at the SCHOOL, from where you can retrace steps to the BUS STOP/CAR PARK (**4h15min**).

### Cruz Grande and the Camino de Santiago

Cruz Grande, criss-crossed by trails, was for centuries the link between north and south on the Ruta de la Plata, the ancient transhumance route along which cattle farmers drove their livestock to greener pastures in the south after winter rains; it was also the main link for commercial travellers, workmen, shepherds…

But did you know that Gran Canaria has its own Camino de Santiago? After the Conquest in the 15th century, Spain built a church dedicated to St James (the country's patron saint) in Gáldar. Legend tells us that Spanish sailors were saved from shipwreck in the 16th century by an image of the saint which eventually found its way to San Bartolomé's church. A pilgrimage between the two churches developed, using the old transhumance route. But today's trail begins at the light-house in Maspalomas — in honour of the sailors who almost came to grief on the south coast.

## 19 FROM CRUZ GRANDE TO AYACATA

**Distance/time:** 9km/5.6mi; 3h35min
**Grade:** ● fairly strenuous, with an ascent of 500m/1600ft and descent of 420m/1375ft. Only suitable in fine weather; it can be quite cold. S50 to the GC600, then road-walking for 2.2km and S70 on the descent to Ayacata
**Equipment:** walking boots, sunhat, warm long trousers, long-sleeved shirt, warm fleece, warm jacket, gloves, raingear, picnic, ample water

**Refreshments:** sometimes a mobile snack van at La Goleta, bar/restaurant opposite the bus stop at Ayacata
**Transport:** 🚍18 from Maspalomas to Cruz Grande (journey time 1h15min, including a 10-minute stop at San Bartolomé). Or 🚗: park at Cruz Grande (27° 55.782'N, 15° 35.872'W). Return on 🚍18 from Ayacata — back to base, to Cruz Grande for your car, or to San Mateo to connect with 🚍303 to Las Palmas

This hike begins on the magnificent old *camino real* that crosses the *cumbre* from south to north. You climb the beautifully surfaced trail to the high plateau — where Pico de las Nieves is off to the right. But you head left for today, through light pines, down to the GC600 above the small Presa de los Hornos. After half an hour's walking on or beside the lightly trafficked road, you come to La Goleta and the take-off point for Roque Nublo (Walk 15), from where you descend to Ayacata. Thanks to the width of this well-built 'kings' highway', the walk is suitable for everyone.

**Start the walk** at the BUS STOP at **Cruz Grande** (○). Walk back through the pass towards San Bartolomé for 50m/yds, then ascend a concrete drive with various signposts, including 'RUTA DE LA PLATA/CAMINO DE SANTIAGO' and 'LLANOS DE LA PEZ' (the S50). Pass to the right of a house and climb straight uphill; there are no turn-offs to worry about. You have a choice of views — the vast San

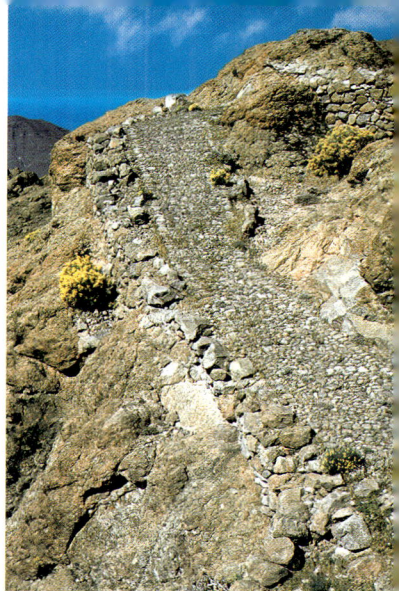

*Right and opposite: this old stone-laid camino across the cumbre is the island's masterpiece.*

Bartolomé basin to the east and, higher up, the shallow Ahogaderos Valley in the west. Tall agaves salute you on your way.

A *WHITE CONCRETE MARKER* (**25min**) is the first of many you will encounter. Sheer rock walls soon tower above you, and the path can be seen twisting its way up the bulging mountainside ahead. Your view now stretches over the Ahogaderos Valley to the Presa de Chira. A rock protruding from the mountain wall serves as a good *LOOKOUT POINT* (**40min**). Daisies splash bright white along

## The *caminos reales* ('kings' highways' or 'royal roads')

The *caminos reales* are the paths and donkey trails developed by the earliest inhabitants of the island and then extended, widened and cobbled after the Spanish Conquest (thus the epithet 'King's'). They were used by everyone who needed to cross the island or travel from village to village — from farmers to cattlemen, traders, pilgrims.

The 1990s was a ideal time to attract walkers to the island (and so compete with Tenerife!). The EU was lavishing money on its new member states in the south, and a program was set up to clean and mark the old footpaths: 410 million pesetas was allocated for the work.

In 1994 the local government announced that the first phase of recuperation (which they called the 'spinal column') was complete. It consisted of 43km in the centre of the island between Los Berrazales and San Bartolomé, with three 'offshoots': Cruz de Tejeda, the Degollada de la Cumbre, Llanos de la Pez–Roque Nublo.

The second phase (150km), well underway, included the stretch Cruz de Tejeda–Teror and San Bartolomé to Ayagaures. The third, final phase, would cover no less than 200km — less crucial circuits linking villages.

The project coordinator at the time of the announcement hoped that the local communities would get involved in keeping the trails maintained and that the trails would not be used by trial bikes because 'they will dislodge all the stones which we've laid with such effort'…

*View across the* cumbre *to Roque Nublo, with El Teide on Tenerife in the distance*

can be glimpsed through the pines, over the edge of the *cumbre*. Ignore a faint path to the right (**1h30min**).

At the pass of **Degollada de los Hornos** (❷; **1h50min**), continue down the S50 path for 15 minutes, to the GC600 (❸). Turn left for just over 2km along this little-trafficked road, eventually passing a fine viewpoint over the **Presa de los Hornos**. Then you come to **La Goleta** (❹; **2h40min**), the parking area for Roque Nublo, where you may be able to get sustenance if the mobile snack van is there.

Follow the Roque Nublo path for a few metres/yards, then fork left for 'AYACATA' (S70) and descend to the road. Turn right and, two minutes (230m) down the road, take the S70 path left through a *GAP* (❺) in the roadside guard rail.

Five minutes later, rejoin the road and turn left. After 80m, your path continues to the right: keep to the main path. After descending for 10 minutes past a bounty of almond almond blossom (in January/February), you pass between a couple of dwellings and join a private lane. On reaching the road again (for the last time), turn right for 20m, then go right to rejoin the path. Coming to a lane, turn right for 12m, then turn right on a walkway down to **Ayacata** (❻; **3h35min**). The bus stops opposite Casa Melo, where you can get refreshments.

your way. The path underfoot, shown on the previous pages, is a work of art, the island's master-piece. Soon it winds its way up into the bulging mass of rock. A tiny green *presa* (reservoir) appears, built into the rocky face of the escarpment below (**Charco Hondo**; ❶; **55min**). With a sweeping panorama, this makes the ideal rest stop ... unless it's dry as a bone.

After a zig and a zag above this contemplative spot the cobbled trail ends. At first you will see nothing but bedrock, but look more closely — a worn path, marked by CAIRNS, soon becomes obvious. It gradually bends over to the right and, 50m uphill, passes between two rocks and follows a dry stream bed on the left, which it eventually crosses. San Bartolomé

## Walk 20: FROM CRUZ DE TEJEDA TO ARTENARA

**Distance/time:** 7.5km/4.7mi; 2h45min

**Grade:** ●: easy descent of 550m/ 1800ft, after a steep initial ascent of 250m/820ft. But you must be sure-footed and have a head for heights. Avoid all cliff-edge paths in mist; *they are potentially dangerous in damp weather.* S90, S01

**Equipment:** walking boots, sunhat, long trousers, long-sleeved shirt, warm fleece, warm jacket, gloves, raingear, water, picnic

**Refreshments:** available at both ends of the walk; nothing en route

**Transport:** 🚌18 from Maspalomas at 09.30 to Tejeda, then 🚌305 to Cruz de Tejeda; journey time 2h20min. Or 🚌303 from Las Palmas to San Mateo, then change to 🚌305; journey time 2h. Return on 🚌220 from Artenara to Teror, then 🚌216 to Las Palmas (or 🚌220 direct to Las Palmas on Sat/Sun). 🚌30 or 🚌50 to Maspalomas if needed; journey about 1h30min

**Alternative circuit: CUEVAS DEL CABALLERO** (7.5km/4.7mi; 2h50min). ●: Access/grade/ equipment as main walk. Follow

*The walk passes this cave chapel carved out of the rock as it comes into Artenara.*

the main walk to the CAVES (**6**); then, to make a circuit, return along the clifftop path. Those who are less sure of foot can simply retrace steps.

From the rim of the enormous craggy basin at Cruz de Tejeda the world is yours: sharp ridges, bold peaks, and views in every direction — alas, much fire-ravaged. Cliff-top caves (sealed off by iron railings) set high on the brink of the Tejeda Valley offer an interesting detour. Artenara, your destination, is an artists' dream. Its little white houses poke their faces out of the richly-hued wall of the *barranco*.

**Start the walk** at **Cruz de Tejeda** (**○**). Follow the GC150 due north (the road to the right of the *parador,* as you face it). After 200m/yds there are car parks on both sides of the road. Take the trail off the far side of the left-hand car park, the route of both the S01 to Gáldar and the S90 to Agaete. After a few minutes, circle to the

left of a WATER TANK. Then ignore a path to the left.

A steep ascent now follows. You'll be captivated by the far-reaching views. Two rocks stand out in this rugged terrain: Roque Nublo (Walk 15) in the distance, to the left, and Roque Bentayga on the opposite ridge. Tejeda spreads across two ridges rising from the

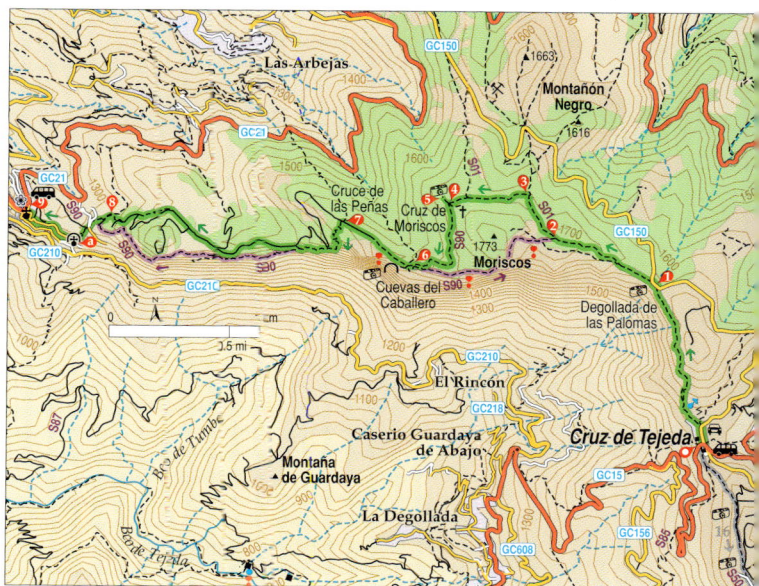

valley below. The path descends to the Pinos de Gáldar road, where the **Degollada de las Palomas** (**1**; **45min**) just to the left gives you another chance to absorb this wild panorama.

Continue along the path behind the shelter at this *mirador*. Soon the path widens into a track. Then, 750m further on, you come to a FORK (**2**). The S90 trail, signed to Artenara and Agaete, goes left here, hugging the edge of the cliffs. (This stretch, followed in reverse for the Alternative circuit, and other paths further west shown on the map, are more dramatic than the route suggested: use them on clear days, *if you are sure-footed and have a head for heights.*) The main walk turns *right* here (S01).

On meeting another FORESTRY TRACK (**3**; **1h**), turn left. After 7-8 minutes (450m), on the north side of **Moriscos**, the S01 turns off right; keep left here. A couple of minutes later, you arrive at a junction, the **Cruz de Moriscos** (**4**). There's a good VIEWPOINT (**5**) on the hillock 100m to your right: on a clear day El Teide on Tenerife seems to rise straight up out of the sea.

Return to the junction and take the first right. to continue along the main track. After 10 minutes, you pass huge boulders balancing on the lip of the ridge. The **Cuevas del Caballero** (**6**; **1h25min**; 'Gentleman's Caves', an ancient cave hamlet) are on the far side of these rocks, facing Tejeda. Take the slippery, vertiginous (*potentially dangerous*) path between the rocks. What a view to wake up to — straight out over the Barranco de Tejeda and, to the right, the flat-topped Vega de Acusa.

Again back on the main route, a signposted short-cut path to the left (from the **Cruce de las Peñas**; **7**) cuts some loops off the track. Ignore the track down right after some 600m (**1h55min**), followed

### Artenara

As you descend into Artenara, the highest village on the island, quaint little dwellings peep out of the face of the mountainside. Cacti, *valo* and *taginaste*, threaded with geraniums, have transformed the severe rock-face into an enchanting garden.

Cut across the plaza in front of the church (its red stone is from Tamadaba) and turn left past the Mirador Esquina. Walk along to the Mirador Unamuno, where the great Basque writer and philosopher, exiled to Gran Canaria during the First World War, looks out to the *cumbre* — which he described as a 'petrified storm'.

Some 80m further along this road is the Ethnographic Museum — a re-creation of cave houses dating from before the Conquest, but lived in until quite recently.

by a turn-off left 230m further on. But a couple of minutes later, take a short-cut to the right. Rejoining the main track, leave it after a minute or two: descend a stone-laid path on the right. Then, at a fork (**8**), keep left downhill for Artenara (right goes to Fontanales). Cross a narrow road (**2h25min**), and climb the wide path on the left. As you mount the ridge, Artenara comes out of hiding ... bit by bit.

After a few minutes' descent, you come out onto a neat paved area, rich in volcanic reds and purples. The Tejeda Valley lies before you. Visit the TINY CHAPEL (**a**) shown on page 94: carved into the rock, it lies a little way along to your left. Then follow the walkway and road some 500m into **Artenara**. The BUS leaves from the GC21, just below the plaza (**9**; **2h45min**).

## Walk 21: CIRCUIT OF LAKE CHIRA ... AND THE HIDDEN VALLEY

**Distance/time:** 5.6km/3.5mi; 2h; a detour to the 'hidden valley' adds 4.7km/3mi; 150m ascent; 1h45min
**Grade:** ● quite easy for the main circuit; ascent of about 100m/330ft
**Equipment:** comfortable walking shoes, sunhat, long trousers, long-sleeved shirt, picnic, ample water

**Refreshments:** bar/café at Cercados de Araña
**Transport:** 🚗 to Cercados de Araña: take the first right turn on entering the village, passing the 'Consultorio' on your right. Park after 280m, by house N° 26 (27° 54.917'N, 15° 37.683'W).

You round the Presa de Chira, one of Gran Canaria's impressive reservoirs, and then visit the charming rustic village of Cercados de Araña, near the tail of the lake. Before returning to the start, you can make a detour to one of the island's little-known gems, climbing to an overgrown ravine, hemmed in by two enormous loaves of rock, with small cave-dwellings peeping out from a tangle of vegetation.

Start the walk from the parking area (○): walk left (south) to the lightly trafficked GC604 and follow it to the right (southwest), to the head of the lake. Just before the Albergue de Chira, turn right

(S60) to cross the DAM (❶; **35min**).

At the end of the dam wall, pick up the path beside a *canal* (❷). This contours into another valley and crosses a RETAINING WALL (❸) below a tiny dam. Then the cairned path rises towards a plateau with a couple of pylons, where you meet a track (❹; **1h**). Turn right here but, after about 600m, switch left to a path. This crosses the track and comes to a

junction in front of a PRICKLY PEAR ENCLOSURE (**Cruce de Caminos**; ❺; **1h20min**).

To continue on the main circuit, turn right here, following the motorable track/rough road,

### Gran Canaria's *presas*

Each of the Canary Islands has its own way of collecting and preserving water — for instance the many underground *galerías* on Tenerife (see page 119).

But Gran Canaria's system of dams and reservoirs, the *presas* or *embalses*, adds so much beauty to the landscape! Every valley cradles at least one. In fact this tiny island has the highest number of reservoirs per capita of anywhere in the world, 69 in all.

Chira was built in 1941-4, but heightened in 1964-5. Although very large, Chira is designed to spill over into the neighbouring Presa de Soria, the largest dam in all the Canaries, with a capacity of 32 million cubic metres.

*Photo: view north over the Presa de Chira*

keeping right at any junctions. You will cross three bridges before coming back to your car at **Cercados de Araña** (**2h**).

But to detour to the 'hidden valley', continue straight ahead on a minor track past well-tended fields, ignoring a track off left just past the fields. Keep winding gently uphill. Behind you, the upper walls of the Soria Valley appear in the south.

Ahead, locate a house with fenced garden set in a first rock 'loaf'. Between you and it is a depression cradling the small **Presa de Bernadino**. After passing to the left of this reservoir, ignore a track off left and keep ahead, to pick up a path that rises to the house and runs below both the HOUSE AND ITS GARDEN FENCE (**❻**). Rounding a bend, you find a *canal* cut into the hillside. Follow it to the right; a path will soon appear. Enjoy the panorama back over the Chira reservoir and Cercados de Araña.

The path runs by the foot of the rock loaf. After a few minutes, you come to a stream bed, your ongoing route. Turn up left, just in front of another FENCED-OFF GARDEN. Be prepared to spend a few minutes finding the 'path' up the stream bed — sometimes you'll just be on bedrock. You find yourself in a tiny hidden ravine; a tangle of prickly pear, aloes, almond and fig trees fills the ravine floor.

Your general direction is up the valley floor, but little paths turn off here and there which are great fun to explore! You'll find fascinating cave-dwellings in every corner. It takes about takes about **10 minutes** to pass through this jungle of vegetation, then you ascend a path through a strip of terracing at the left and come to a dwelling that even has a SWIMMING POOL (**❼**; **2h20min**)! End your detour here, and walk back to the PRICKLY PEAR ENCLOSURE at **Cruce de Caminos** (**❺**; **3h05min**), to continue on the main walk.

# Walks on
# Tenerife

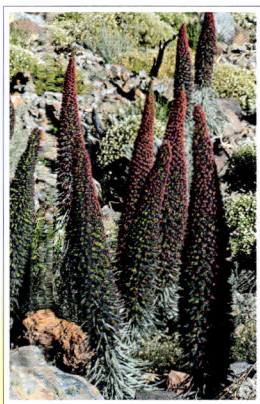

**Tenerife**
Area: 2034/km² (785sq mi)
Length of coast: 342km (213mi)
High point: El Teide (3715m/12,188ft)
Population: 966,354 (2020)
Population density: 445/km² (1152/sq mi)
Capital: Santa Cruz (pop 207,312)
Province: Santa Cruz de Tenerife

To absorb Tenerife's beauty takes time. Her moods are captured at sunrise and sunset, best captured in the country-side: no season is without its bloom and pot-pourri of colour.

Tenerife's bleak south is a mystery of dry terraced slopes, sliced through by deep ravines. The lush and green northern escarpment yields up pine-forested hillsides rolling off the central massif, soon burgeoning with produce as it steps its way down to an indigo sea. Las Cañadas, a world apart, is the focal point of every visit, where strange hues and tor-mented rock forms are dominated by the majesty of El Teide.

This island caters wonderfully for walkers, with well-marked trails criss-crossing an incredible kaleidoscope of

# TENERIFE

**28** El Pijaral

Taganana

Igueste

ANAGA

Taborno

San Andrés

Bajamar

Las Mercedes

Tegueste

Tejina

La Laguna

Santa Cruz

La Esperanza

Candelaria

Puerto de la Cruz

**24** Arafo

Aguamansa

Güímar

La Orotava

**26**

OROTAVA

Fasnía

CAÑADAS

Icod de los Vinos

El Teide

Guajara

Poris de Abona

Garachico

**25**

Arico

El Tanque

Pico Viejo

Paisaje Lunar

**23**

Buenavista

Los Silos

TENO

El Palmar

Granadilla

Teno Alto

**27**

Santiago del Teide

Masca

Vilaflor

Charco del Pino

Punta de Teno

Guía de Isora

San Miguel

Barranco del Infierno

Los Gigantes

**22**

San Juan

Adeje

Costa Adeje

Playa de las Américas

Los Cristianos

landscapes: the
Anaga (Walk 28) — specta-
cular coastal scenery and laurel
forests; Las Cañadas (Walk 25)
— the unforgettable moonscape;
Teno (Walk 27) — a world of tilting plateaus and deep
chasms; the Orotava Valley (Walk 26) embraced by pines;
and the sun-baked south (Walk 23). The fact that I saw so
few other walkers prompted me to write the first edition of
this book in the 1980s. Since then, of course, the island has
become one of Europe's best-loved walking destinations.

## *Walk 22*: BARRANCO DEL INFIERNO

**Important note:** Because of its fragile ecosystem and the danger of rockfall, this *barranco* is now within a Protected Natural Area; access is limited to 300 people per day. You must book in advance, choosing your time slot (last entry at 11.30; walk closes at 15.30); and there is an entrance fee of 9 € for adults (children half price). Full information and booking at www.barrancodelinfierno.es. *Note that lace-up shoes and helmet (you will be given one) are mandatory.*
**Distance:** 6.5km/4mi; under 3h
**Grade:** ● moderate climb/descent of 300m/1000ft requiring agility. The *barranco* may be closed after heavy rain or rockfall.
**Refreshments:** ample bars, cafés and restaurants in Adeje

**Equipment:** walking boots, fleece, sunhat, windproof, picnic, water
**Access:** 🚌 to Adeje. If you're early enough, you can park near the start of the walk at the top of Calle Los Molinos by the Restaurante Othelo (28° 7.575'N, 16° 43.427'W). To get there, turn left by the church at the top end of Calle Grande and follow the brown sign for the *barranco* (see violet line on the map). Otherwise use the car park at the foot of Calle Los Molinos. Or 🚌 447, 473 from Los Cristianos to/from Adeje (journey time 30min). Alight at the 'City Center' bus stop and walk uphill through Plaza Venezuela to the roundabout, then up Calle Grande to the church; follow the same route as motorists (above).

For years the Barranco del Infierno ('Hell's Ravine') has been the most walked gorge in the Canaries, with the resulting damage to flora and fauna. Visitor numbers are now strictly limited to protect the ecosystem. It is expensive, but with only 300 people allowed in on any day, the walk is more pleasant than in the crowded past. This *barranco* boasts one of the few permanent streams on Tenerife. High sheer walls close in on you as you make your way up the defile of jagged rock. Wild blackberry drapes itself over the trees and bushes, and ivy 'tunnels' convey you up to the three-tiered falls, the highest on the island. Adeje, at the foot of the ragged crags that confine Hell's deep chasm, is an immaculate village, with an appealing combination of old and new.

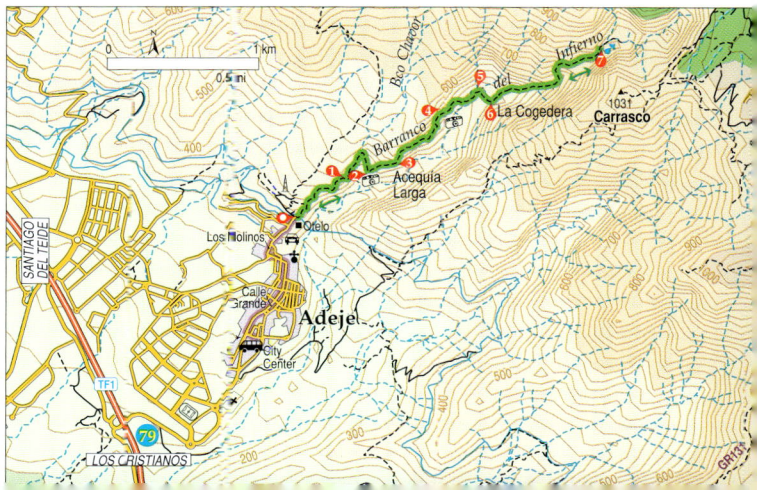

**The walk begins** from the top of *CALLE LOS MOLINOS* (⓿) in the upper, older part of Adeje. After gaining access (you will be given a map — and a helmet *which you must wear, even if it is hot*), descend into the *barranco*. From the outset you're looking down into a dry ravine: further up the *barranco*, the water has been diverted for irrigation in watercourses and pipes. Clumps of prickly pear, *valo, cardón* and *tabaiba* coat the steep slopes, white daisies grow alongside the path, and no doubt you'll see some tame Barbary partridge. Beyond some fine views down over Adeje, you come to the **Bailadero de las Brujas** at *INFO BOARD 3* ('Witches' Dancing Floor' — a legendary name for many mountain settings throughout the Canaries; ❶).

On rising gently to **El Gran Mirador** (❷; **15min**), at the very edge of the *barranco* walls, you enjoy another fine view down the *barranco* and over Adeje. Fifteen minutes later, past an info board about the **Acequía Larga** (❸), there is another fine viewpoint at

the **Mirador de la Cueva del Marqués** (**4**). Soon after, you descend to the BED OF THE STREAM at INFO BOARD 9 (**5**; **45min**).

Now the *barranco* comes alive with willows and a tangle of bramble, shrubs and ferns. Pools become frequent (*pity we're asked not to take a dip in them!*) and, if you're early, you will see and hear many birds. From here on the walk steepens and requires more agility, but this is the most beautiful and most dramatic part of the hike. The rocky path criss-crosses the stream between the perpendicular walls of the gorge. Beyond **La Cogedera** (**6**) and the start of the *canal*, you pass an old gnarled chestnut at BOARD 11. It's not far now to see the lovely three-tiered WATERFALL (**7**; **1h20min**) splashing down some 80m/250ft into a small pool. The *barranco* walls tower 1000m/3300ft above you here, virtually blocking out the sky.

Allow 1h20min to return to Calle de los Molinos for your car (**2h40min**) — or 10 minutes more to the bus stop (**2h50min**).

### Barranco del Infierno

For years we all hiked in this *barranco*, oblivious to the potential danger of rockfall. But in 2009 a walker was killed, leading to the walk being closed for almost six years. No sooner had it reopened in 2015 than there was another death. This time the *barranco* was closed for only four months, until it was made as safe as possible.

Now there are rangers in the *barranco*, and you must wear a helmet and stout shoes. Beyond La Cogedera (a good place for a break), when the path narrows, you are advised not to stop in your tracks, but to keep moving at a steady pace to the falls.

The *barranco* is not only a natural wonderland, but because of the permanent flow of water, it is known to have been inhabited by the Guanches in antiquity; their caves, cave paintings, tools and even a mummy almost 1700 years old have been found here. You can see the artefacts found in the *barranco* in Santa Cruz's Museum of Nature and Archaeology.

## Walk 23: FOUR WALKS TO THE PAISAJE LUNAR

### Walk a: PR TF 72 — the most popular circuit to Paisaje Lunar

**Distance/time:** 7.5km/4.7mi; 2h50min

**Grade:** ● moderate ascent/descent of 300m/1000ft; good, waymarked PR/GR paths

**Equipment:** walking boots, walking pole(s), sunhat, fleece, gloves, windproof, raingear, picnic, plenty of water

**Refreshments:** none; take a picnic!

**Access:** 🚌 to/from an info board for the PR TF 72 (28° 10.260'N, 16° 37.195'W); it's 3.5km along the Pista Madre del Agua, a motorable eastbound track from KM66 on the TF21

### Walk b: Circuit from Vilaflor

**Distance/time:** 13km/8mi; 5h

**Grade:** ● fairly strenuous ascent/descent of 670m/2200ft; good, waymarked PR/GR paths

**Refreshments:** available in Vilaflor

**Equipment:** as Walk a

**Access:** 🚌 to/from Vilaflor (car park just north of the church: 28° 9.624'N, 16° 38.219'W). Or 🚐 482 from Los Cristianos to/from Vilaflor Centro; journey time 35min

### Walk c: Parador — Paisaje Lunar — Vilaflor via Walk a

**Distance/time:** 16.5km/10.2mi; 5h05min

**Grade:** ● strenuous and long, with an ascent of 265m/870ft and descent of 1120m/3645ft; good, waymarked PR/GR paths

**Refreshments:** at the Parador de las Cañadas and in Vilaflor

**Equipment:** as Walk a

**Access:** 🚐 342 from Los Cristianos to the Parador de las Cañadas; journey time 1h15min. Return on 🚐 482 from Vilaflor; journey time to Los Cristianos 35min

## Walk d: Parador — Paisaje Lunar — Vilaflor via Campamento Madre del Agua

**Distance/time:** 19km/12mi; 6h
**Grade:** ●: strenuous and very long; ascents of 365m/1200ft and descents of 1170m/3850ft. Mostly good GR/PR paths but recom-

mended for experienced walkers: the descent into Paisaje Lunar is very steep and slippery, the way-marking hard to follow at times
**Refreshments:** at the Parador de las Cañadas and in Vilaflor
**Equipment:** as Walk a
**Access/return:** as Walk c

T he classic hike to the Paisaje Lunar (the tiny gem of a 'Moon Landscape') is a must for all walkers visiting Tenerife. Its setting is a forest of old Canarian pines. The real Canarian pine is the *roble* among peasants, and the pines of Vilaflor are renowned for their grandeur. Whether you're a beginner walker or a strong hiker, this walk is a must: just choose the version that suits you best.

**Start Walk a** at the *WALKERS' INFO BOARD* (**a**) 3.5km along the **Pista Madre del Agua**. Climb the *RED/ WHITE/YELLOW*-waymarked trail to a fork (**1**; **3min**). Both forks are signed to Paisaje Lunar; head left here (you'll return from the right).

The lovely stone-lined trail passes some terraces on the left, crosses a track, then passes a ruin on the left (**Casa Marrubial**; **35min**).

Having crossed a *barranco,* head right at the next two forks, always keeping to the same waymarks. But leave the GR131 at **1h10min** (**2**): it heads left at a fingerpost *(Walks c and d join here).* Continue right, downhill, towards 'PAISAJE LUNAR', still on the yellow/ white-waymarked PR TF 72. You pass a *FIRST VIEWPOINT*, from where there is a much-photoed side-on view of **Los Escurriales** — the **Paisaje Lunar**. A second viewpoint, the **Mirador de Los Escurriales** (**3**; **1h35min**), with full-on view, is rather more difficult to photograph. Soft creams, beiges, yellows, browns and greys saturate these smooth conical sandstone moulds rising like turrets on both sides of the **Barranco de las Aguas**.

From here continue ahead (right) towards 'VILAFLOR' on the easily seen trail, mostly in descent. You eventually come to a junction where you join the PR TF 83 (**4**; **2h15min**). Head right towards

*The tuff pilars of the Paisaje Lunar — damsel-capped fairies' chimneys*

'VILAFLOR', still on the PR TF 72. The trail runs above the **Pista Madre del Agua**, for a while with a high wall on the left. You cross two tracks rising from the *Pista*,

pass a ruin (**Casa de los Llanitos**), then join the *Pista* itself and follow it round a curve before forking right on the trail once more. You pass the path where you turned left

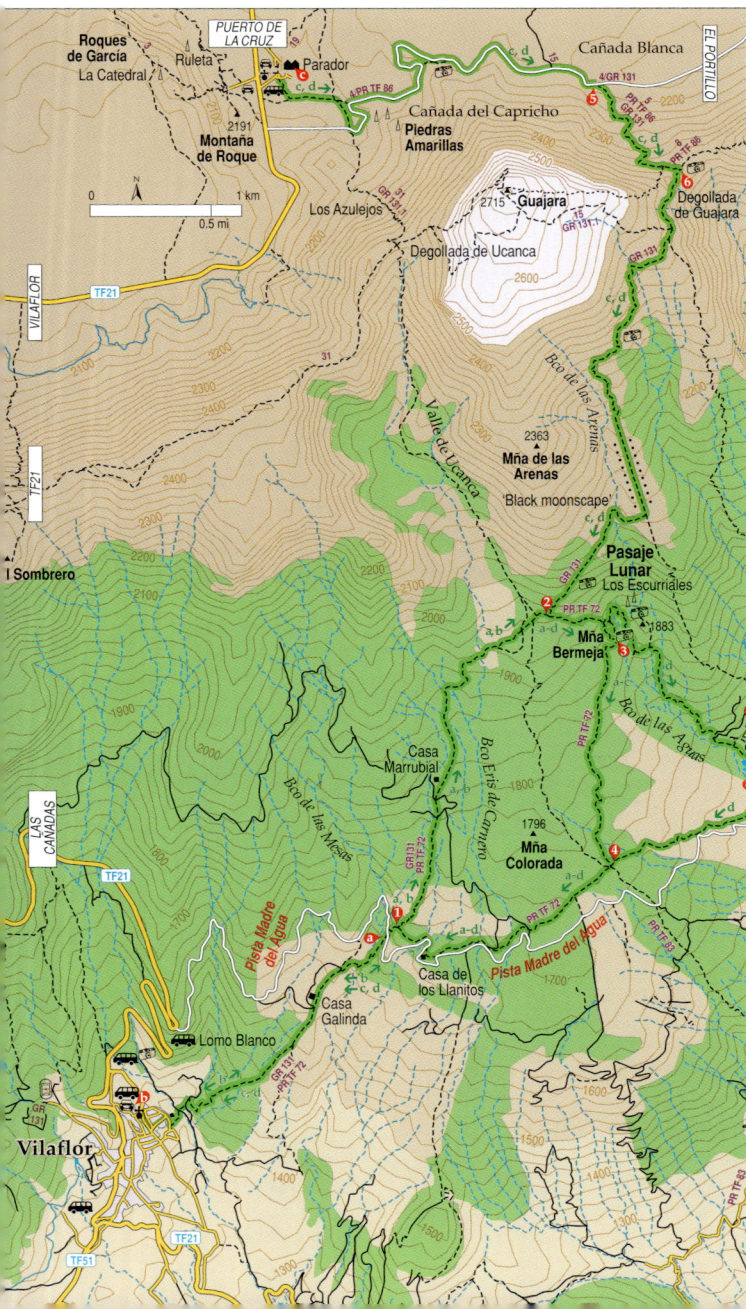

early in the walk (**1**) and rejoin the **Pista Madre del Agua** at the *WALKERS' INFO BOARD* (**1**; **2h50min**).

**Start Walk b in Vilaflor** (**b**). From the car park/bus stop by the church walk downhill at the left of the *PLAZA*, taking the third turning left (*CALLE EL CANARIO*; *RED/WHITE/YELLOW* waymarks). After 150m turn right at the T-junction; then, 75m downhill, just in front of two large round water tanks, turn left on the signposted stone-laid trail (PR TF 72, GR 131). It drops into a *barranco*, passes another large round *WATER TANK* and joins a track. Follow this left for 50m, then go sharp right on a walled-in cobbled trail. You rise steeply through pines to a very photogenic farm set amongst terraces, with an almond grove on the right (**Casa Galindo**; **55min**). Pass to the right of the farm and fork half-right through a gap in a wall about five minutes later. Descend into another *barranco*, then rise to the **Pista Madre del Agua** at the point where Walk a starts and ends

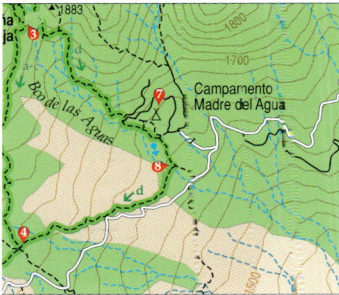

(**a**; **1h10min**). Now follow **Walk a**, adding 1h10min to all time checks, and when you return to this point, retrace your steps to **Vilaflor** (**b**; **5h**).

**Start Walk c at the Parador de las Cañadas** (**c**). Follow *NATIONAL PARK TRAIL 4* from the turning circle just south of the building. In

under 10 minutes the trail takes you to a motorable track, which you follow to the left (still Trail 4). A fascinating formation of pink and yellow rocks rises in front of you. The pastel colours give this fine natural sculpture its name — **Piedras Amarillas** ('Yellow Stones'). Behind them, you cross a small gravel plain, the **Cañada del Capricho**. Where the track makes a sharp turn to the left, you can save 500m by taking a short-cut to the right, quickly rejoining the track. Guajara — the bastion of the encircling walls — is seen at its best here, rising 500m/1640ft from the crater floor.

Your ascent begins five minutes beyond a turn-off to the left (National Park Trail 15). Here you join *PARK TRAIL 5*, the GR131 and the PR TF 86 (**5**; **50min**) to begin the ascent. Turn right uphill; cairns mark the way. You reach the edge of the crater at a pass with magnificent views, the **Degollada de Guajara** (**6**; 2373m/7785ft; **1h30min**). Gran Canaria seems surprisingly close from this vantage point. The PR TF 86 heads off to the left here, while you turn right on the GR131 and *PARK TRAIL 15*. After a brief ascent, the GR131 forks (by a *METAL POLE* and a *NATIONAL PARK INFO BOARD*; **1h40min**). The right fork is the main ascent route to Guajara; keep left for Paisaje Lunar. Barely a minute down, the path forks again: keep right with the GR131. Over to your right (still in the distance) is **Montaña de las Arenas**, with its charred sides and maroon summit. Below you, pines full of character dot the landscape.

The path turns down a low side-ridge. You pass a particularly large *PINE TREE* (**2h15min**) — a cool resting place. Minutes below it, you're trudging straight down across the gravelly black sand.

Rocks flank your route all the way downhill.

Just before the end of the sandhill and the first pines, the trail forks. Ignore the path straight ahead down the hill; go right. Scramble down a steep, gravelly bank — probably on all fours. You cross the **Barranco de las Arenas** (where you could make a short detour back up the riverbed to a black 'moon landscape').

From the floor of this ravine you ascend a gravelly ridge at the edge of another, lower ravine — the **Barranco de las Aguas**, home of the Paisaje Lunar. From this path you enjoy a first view down into

### Fairies' chimneys

The tuff pillars of the Paisaje Lunar were created millions of years ago by volcanic eruptions spewing out both ash and solid materials. The ash hardened into tuff, a light-coloured porous rock. Erosion caused by water and wind wore away the tuff, giving rise to the pillars we see today. Geologists call them 'fairies' chimneys'.

But they would disappear were it not for their 'caps' — the dark hard basalt that can be seen in the surrounding terrain and 'capping' some of the chimneys in the photo on pages 104-105. The basalt, known as 'damsel caps', is protecting these tuff pillars from being worn away completely.

While fairies' chimneys exist in many countries, the textbook example is Cappadocia in Turkey. One cannot help but wonder if Antoni Gaudí, whose work was so inspired by nature, ever thought of damsel-capped fairies' chimneys when creating the Sagrada Familia cathedral.

the 'moon landscape'. When you come to a crossing trail, turn left downhill on the WHITE/YELLOW-waymarked PR TF 72, joining Walks a and b at ❷ (**2h50min**).

Use the notes for **Walk a** from the **1h10min**-point, adding 1h40min to all times. You come to the **Mirador de los Escurriales** (❸) in **3h15min**. Now keep following Walk a until it ends at the parking place on the **Pista Madre del Agua** (ⓐ). Then, referring to the map, keep to the RED/WHITE/ YELLOW waymarks down to **Vilaflor** (ⓑ; **5h05min**).

**Start Walk d** at the **Parador de las Cañadas** (ⓒ). Follow **Walk c** to the SECOND VIEWPOINT (❸; **3h15min**). Here you *leave* the PR trail and head back the way you came. You come to a junction where the Paisaje Lunar is signed down to the right. Descending carefully, you're soon walking along the very edge of the **Paisaje Lunar**. At another path junction, head right, alongside the **Barranco de las Aguas**. Crossing a crest, you encounter a WATER PIPE, and minutes later you rejoin the left fork, heading right.

When you meet a track, follow it to the right: a minute downhill, a picturesque CAMPSITE comes into view through the pines. Cut down through the camp, keeping straight downhill, and in a couple of minutes you'll reach the front entrance to **Campamento Madre del Agua** (❼; **3h45min**). There's a water tap just above the office, to the right of the gate.

Just over 200m below the entrance, turn right on a TRAIL (❽) running above the **Pista Madre del Agua**. Follow this to the junction of the PR TF 72 and PR TF 83 (❹). Keep ahead on the PR TF 72, referring to the map and the PR TF 72 waymarks, to descend to **Vilaflor** (ⓑ; **6h**).

## Walk 24: THE CANDELARIA TRAIL: LA CALDERA • LA CRUCITA • ARAFO

**Distance:** 12.5km/7.8mi; 5h
**Grade:** ● very strenuous, with a steep climb (800m/2600ft) and steep *gravelly* descent (1500m/4950ft)
**Equipment:** walking boots, walking poles. sunhat, warm fleece, rain-/windproof, long trousers, whistle, picnic, water
**Refreshments:** snack bar at La Caldera; restaurants in Arafo
**Transport:** 🚌345 from Puerto to La Caldera; journey time 50min. Return on 🚌121 from Arafo to Santa Cruz; journey time 50min; *change to* 🚌102 to Puerto; journey time 1h *or* 🚌111 to resorts in the south

**Short walk: Chimoche circuit from La Caldera:** 5.5km/ 3.5mi; 1h45min. ● Easy-moderate climb/descent of 300m/1000ft; equipment as above, but stout shoes will suffice. Follow the main walk to the *MAJOR JUNCTION* met at 45min

(❷). Keep right here. Just uphill from the junction, below the large pine, bear right on a path (the main walk heads to the left of the pine). When the path ends (55min), follow the forestry track straight ahead downhill for a couple of minutes, to **Choza Chimoche** (❹). Descend the track behind the shelter: facing the *choza*, the continuation to La Caldera is the second (descending) track to the right. (The first track to the right climbs to Choza Bermeja on the TF21.) You swing behind the shelter, dipping into a small flat area — a very picturesque spot for a picnic. After descending for a little over 10 minutes, the track passes **Galería Chimoche** (ⓑ). A few minutes later, at **Pasada de las Bestias**, keep left downhill on track at the *T-JUNCTION*, to come back to **La Caldera** and the *BUS STOP* (**1h45min**).

---

This hike follows an old pilgrims' way known as the Candelaria Trail. It originally began at La Orotava. It climbs the steep escarpment of the central massif and then twists endlessly down to the sea at Candelaria. Today, the land between Arafo and Candelaria is so built up that the few pilgrims who still make the journey leave the trail at our destination, Arafo. The Virgin of Candelaria is Tenerife's patron saint, whose Assumption is celebrated each year on August 14-15th. This long, but gratifying walk offers superb panoramas, encompassing corners of immense beauty.

**The walk starts** at La Caldera (❶). Leaving the bus, take the road to the left. Walk past the *BAR* (closed Wed) on the PR TF 35/ GR131 and then fork left on the **Pista de Mamio**, a forestry track signposted to '*LOS ORGANOS*'; it runs through heather and pines. Not far along, you cross a bridge straddling the end of a narrow ravine. About **10min** along,

various *SIGNS* appear; follow the main track around to the left, past **Choza Pedro Gil**. Leave the GR131 here by taking the wide earthen path off right, signposted '*CAMINO A CANDELARIA*'. The *THREE LITTLE CROSSES* you pass give this path another of its names: Camino de las Crucitas.

Fifteen minutes further uphill, at a small flat area (**Lomo de los**

**Brezos**; ❶; **25min**) you cross a track and follow the path slightly to the left, up the hillside. The way divides here and there, braiding itself up the slope. The side-on view of Los Organos and the eastern escarpment is quite impressive. It's hard to believe that the route winds up into those walls!

You come to a MAJOR JUNCTION (❷; **45min**), where a left turn is signposted for Los Organos; keep right here to make for La Crucita. Under 40m up, at another FORK, the main path veers off round the right-hand side of the ridge to Chimoche. You do *not!* At this point you are just below a large pine: continue up the ridge, to the left of the pine. *(The path to the right is the Short walk route.)* For the first few minutes of the climb, you are in a sunken path. A couple of minutes up, ignore a path branching off to the left. The route will eventually take you up and over the *cumbre*.

As the climb steepens, more of the valley becomes visible through the sparse pine growth. Some 25 minutes from the last turn-off, on a bend, you look over into a strip of bare *barranco* that emanates a soft mixture of pinks, mauves, browns and greys. Seconds up,

your path briefly runs alongside the DYKE (❸) shown opposite. The vegetation undergoes a change here: small bushes of Canarian edelweiss (*Sideritis*) turn white as their velvety leaves catch the sun, and scraggy chimney broom (*escobón*) and *retama* take control of the slope. The path is so colourful that it's easy to forget the wider landscapes on view.

All the way up, the vast view stretches across the upper inclines of the Orotava Valley, where more and more land is being given over to buildings. At **1h35min** you find yourselves sheltered between a low DYKE (❹) and a few pines. A faded arrow indicates the best place to cross this natural rock wall. From here, you can see the path heading across the escarpment. Another patch of writing on rocks, and a WHITE ARROW pointing left, are your next landmarks. The path climbs steeply through rocks and over stones in a multi-coloured volcanic landscape. A good look-out point lies midway between the dyke and the TF24 above.

When you reach the TF24 at an altitude of 1980m/6500ft, get out your anchor! From here on it's down, down, as you descend

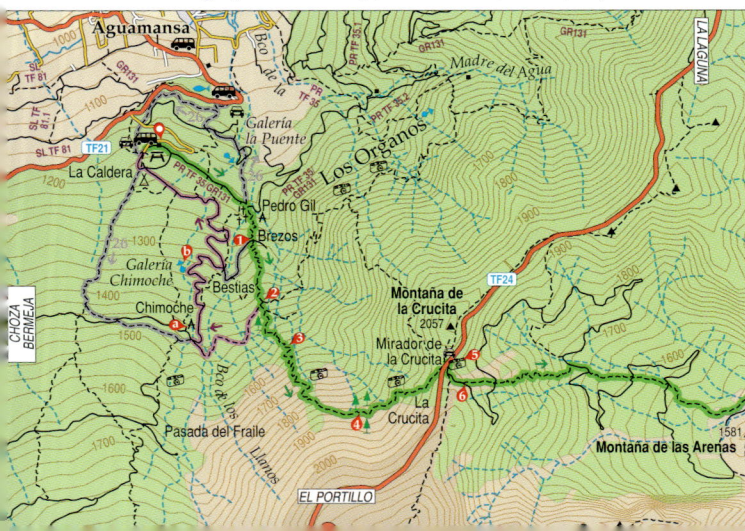

the southern escarpment. Cross the road and, 30 m along to the left, at the **Mirador de La Crucita** (❺; **2h20min**), turn right on a forestry track. The isolated valley you are about to enter lies far below. The

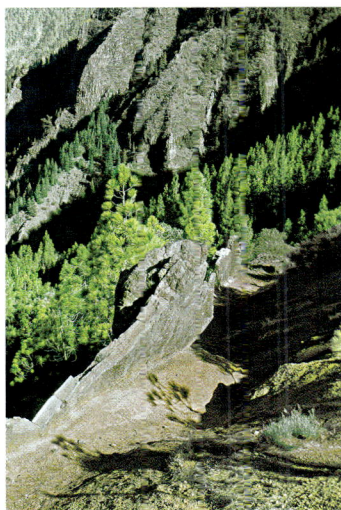

entrance to the valley is blocked by an enormous naked black mound, Las Arenas. You have the stupendous view shown just below: dark, pine-sprinkled slopes drop down to a coastal plain tessellated in faded browns and greens. The sea stretches out into the distance.

Ignore National Park Trail 17 up to the right but, three minutes (250m) down the track, your PATH strikes off to the left (❻) and slithers its way down the stark slope. The descent will be at a snail's pace: there's loose gravel under foot, and the slope looks almost vertical. Within minutes, you cross the track. Turn left: your continuation is 10m downhill, on the right.

Soon you head back into pines, under which *codéso* and broom shelter. The path forks just above the point where you the track once again. If you fork right, along the crest of the ridge, the stretch is vertiginous, but railings help part of the way. (An alternative is to fork left to the track, then turn right.) Where the main (crest) path rejoins the track by a CAIRN, continue downhill for 20m, then take the path on the left, on a bend. It squiggles through the trees, past lovely picnic spots on relatively flat land and, at the edge of the wood, with spectacular views. Where the path is faint, keep the shallow ravine on the left

*Top: Montaña de las Arenas from the main road at La Crucita, with the endemic white-flowering Teide broom* (retama del Teide; Spartocytisus supranubius) *in the foreground; left: an hour into the walk the path runs alongside this dyke.*

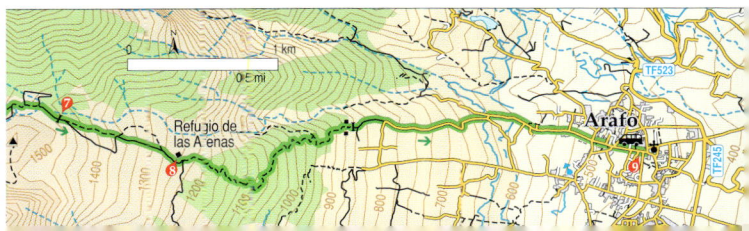

*View to El Teide and over the mist-shrouded Orotava Valley from La Crucita*

within sight, and you're sure to be okay. Sporadic small dots of red paint help you along.

Recross the track once more, and again find the path slightly below and to the left. At the next track crossing, find the ongoing path a few metres downhill to the left. A minute downhill finds you in a shallow *barranco:* descend this

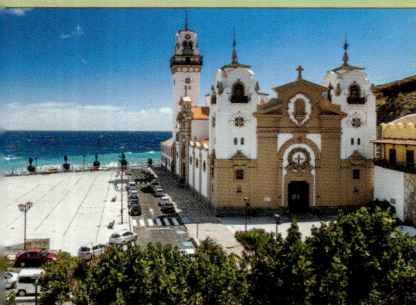

### The pilgrimage basilica of Nuestra Señora de la Candelaria

The basilica in Candelaria is the most important place of worship in all the Canaries. Its history is fascinating. Legend tells us that in the late 14th century Guanche herdsmen found a wooden image with fair colouring on the beach after a storm. In one hand she held a child, in the other a candle.

After some miradulous cures, the Guanches — including their southern chieftain — attributed the image with miraculous powers.

They sheltered the statuette in a dome-shaped cave very near to where the huge cathedral stands today. Even the last king of the Guanches, Bencomo, led one of the first pilgrimages from the north of the island to worship. (Carbon dating proves that this cave was a place of worship for thousands of years previously.)

When in the 15th century the Spanish invaders eventually conquered the Tenerife (after being repulsed by the Guanches for almost 100 years), the missionaries who came after them installed the image in a chapel beside the cave. Later the Virgin Mary was delared by the Pope to be patroness of all the Canaries in 1559.

The original image was saved when the chapel burned down, but lost again in a flood. A new image was consecrated in 1830.

It is thought that the merging of Guanche and Christian cultures makes Candelaria very special.

for a couple of minutes, then swing out of the ravine and around the hillside.

Smooth black sand soon comes underfoot. The outline of a rounded volcanic hill completely disrupts the landscape as it appears through the trees. You come face-to-face with this bulging black monster, **Montaña de las Arenas**, at **3h15min**. It obliterates everything. The track is not far below; shortly, you rejoin it. Follow it downhill for about a minute; then, on the next bend, cut off right across the sand. On meeting the track again. leave it after two minutes — just past a METAL GATE (**7**): take the path that veers straight ahead off the track, and keep alongside the ravine. (The track heads slightly away from the ravine, to the right, at this point.) Gran Canaria is on the horizon. Arafo, your destination, is far below, and the immediate land-scape reveals an intriguing beauty: chestnut trees are the sole survivors in these black sands. Bent and crippled, these 'triffid' creatures have never managed to raise their backs. It's a unique sight.

Some seven minutes later, when you next meet the track (on a bend), follow it downhill. In ten minutes you reach the simple stone

**Refugio de las Arenas** that the pilgrims visit (**8**). To continue, head to the bend in the track just below the refuge and take the small path down to the left (CAIRN), briefly encountering scrub and bushes.

Scrubland is eventually replaced by a Canary pine forest, and you pass some proud old specimens. The way (always marked with CAIRNS) splinters and rejoins. In just over 600m/0.4mi the path swings left across the hillside and, a few minutes later, heads right, soon crossing an old (probably dry) *canal*. Five minutes below the *canal*, you come to the edge of the forest. Again you wind your way through scrub.

Meeting a narrow lane just beyond two WATERHOUSES and a chain barrier (Camino Mora del Estanque; **4h25min**), follow it straight ahead for just under 1km. Here you turn left for a mere 20m to another lane (Camino la Canal Alta), where you go right. The lane, now called Calle Eduardo Curbelo Fariña, heads straight to the main square in **Arafo** (**9**; Plaza José Antonio; **5h**). The BUS STOP is just to your left, with plenty of seating; the church is straight ahead.

# Walk 25: MONTAÑA DE GUAJARA

**Distance:** 9.7km/6mi; 4h30min
**Grade:** ● moderate-strenuous climb and descent of 650m/2130ft. The ascent is quite easy, and the newly engineered descent path is clear and without exposure. Still, the walk is not recommended in unsettled weather. National Park Trails Nos. 4, 5, 15 and 31.
**Equipment:** walking boots, sunhat, fleece, windproof, long trousers, gloves, thick socks, picnic, water
**Refreshments:** at the Parador

**Transport:** 🚐348 from Puerto (journey time 2h) or 🚐342 from the south (journey time about 1h30min) to/from the Parador de las Cañadas; or 🚗: park at the Parador (28° 13.422'N, 16° 37.674'W)
***Shorter walk: Parador — Degollada de Guajara — Parador***: 8km/5mi; 2h40min. ● easy-moderate climb and descent of under 250m/820ft; access and equipment as above. Follow the main walk to ❺ (1h30min); return the same way.

Guajara is Tenerife's third highest mountain, standing at 2717m/8910ft. This is an easy, straightforward climb, offering superb views down into the crater of Las Cañadas. As you ascend Guajara's back, the southern coastal plain unravels in a haze below. After taking a break at the summit, protected from the wind by stone walls, you can look forward to an exhilarating descent via the Degollada de Ucanca on a recently engineered path.

**Start out** at the **Parador de las Cañadas** (⊙). Follow NATIONAL PARK TRAIL 4 from the turning circle just south of the building. Your destination is the prominent mountain protruding from the crater wall southeast of the Parador. In under 10 minutes the trail takes you to a motorable track. Straight across is National Park Trail No. 31 (❶; your return route) but, for now, turn left to continue east along Trail No. 4.

A fascinating formation of pink and yellow rocks rises just in front of you. The pastel colours give this fine natural sculpture its name — **Piedras Amarillas** ('Yellow Stones'; ❷). Behind them, you cross a small *cañada* (gravel plain), the **Cañada del Capricho**. Where the track makes a sharp turn to the left, fork right on a short-cut path, quickly rejoining the track and

saving 500m. Here Guajara — the bastion of the encircling walls — is seen at its best, rising 500m/1650ft from the crater floor. Splashes of yellow lichen, like paint daubs, decorate the higher rock faces. In spring, *taginaste rojo* — some as tall as 3m/10ft — add bold strokes of red to this canvas.

Not far beyond the trail off left to Montaña de Majuá and the cable car (❸; Trail No. 31) you begin your ascent. Your turn-off right to the Degollada de Guajara is marked with FINGERPOSTS and BOARDS for Park Trail 5, the GR131 and the PR TF 86 (❹; **50min**). The clear, cairn-marked path takes you to the edge of the crater at the **Degollada de Guajara** (2373m/7785ft; ❺; **1h30min**), where the PR TF 86 and National Park Trail No. 8 head left. The views are magnificent. The tones are the most dramatic aspect of this landscape, as they flow into and across each other. *(The Shorter walk turns back here).*

Follow NATIONAL PARK TRAIL NO 15 (and the GR131) southwest off the pass; it swings back to the left almost immediately. Gran Canaria seems surprisingly close from this vantage point. After a brief ascent, by a METAL POLE and a NATIONAL PARK INFO BOARD (❻; **1h40min**), keep right on Trail No. 15 for Guajara. (The path to the left is the GR131 to Vilaflor with a connecting path to the famous 'moon landscape' visited in Walk 23.) An eroded watercourse briefly becomes your path. Metal poles help to keep you on route. The way eases out as it swings across the *retama-* and *codéso*-patched slope.

*View to the crater from Trail 15 on the descent to the Degollada de Ucanca*

You eventually come to a fork with fingerposts showing an out-and-back path to the summit, as well as your onward path to the Parador. Turn right here. El Teide slowly reappears until it is seen in its full magnificence when you reach the Guajara *SUMMIT* (**7**; **2h 30min**), marked by a trig point. There's also a rock enclosure here — a good picnic shelter on a windy winter's day, but it gets crowded. The panorama from Guajara's summit can only be

matched by that from El Teide.

From the summit the descent is via the Degollada de Ucanca: return to the signposted fork and now follow the path southwest. Whereas the descent of the Guajara escarpment used to be only suitable for sure-footed hikers with a head for heights, this recently rebuilt path is clear and well waymarked, with no exposed points. The left side of the crater is now in full view — its walls very impressive. The Llano de Ucanca is the expansive lake of gravel that lies on the edge of a dark lava flow. Tall red *taginaste* flourish amidst the rock.

The path continues through stumpy pines, heading downhill on the left side of a ridge. Just after crossing a small flat area and ascending a little, you reach the **Degollada de Ucanca** (**8**; **3h30min**). Ignore the path climbing to the left here.

Once over the pass, the cairned path (now *PARK TRAIL NO 31*) briefly descends to the left before swinging back to the right to make tight zigzags down the hillside. The colours in the immediate landscape are a stunning mixture of green, yellow, pink, mauve and white, while over to your right are the Piedras Amarillas. Coming onto a dazzling patch of white and yellow hillside, the path veers right and soon takes you to the road, from where you follow the path opposite, back to the **Parador de las Cañadas** (**4h30min**).

## Walk 26: CIRCUIT FROM AGUAMANSA

**Distance:** 7km/4.3mi; 2h30min
**Grade:** ● easy-moderate climb/
descent of 400m/1300ft, *but note
that the descent from Lomo de los
Brezos is steep and slippery.*
**Equipment:** stout shoes or
walking boots, sunhat, fleece, rain-
/windproof, picnic, water
**Refreshments:** bar/restaurant at
La Caldera; several in Aguamansa
**Transport:** 🚌345 from Puerto
(journey time 45min) to the
Aguamansa trout farm; from the
south first take 🚌343 to Puerto

(journey time 1h20min). Or 🚗
to/from the trout farm (main
entrance; 28° 21.653'N, 16° 29.782'W)

***Short walk: Aguamansa — La
Caldera — Aguamansa:*** 3km/
2mi; 1h. ● easy. Follow the main
walk to the CRATER (**1**), circle it,
and return the same way.
***Alternative start:*** Just after the
25min-point at **1**, take the first
turn-off right, the steep, signposted **Camino de los Guanches**
up to **Choza Chimoche** (**5**), then
return via the main walk.

Although it's often misty here, no trip to Tenerife is
complete without a visit to the Orotava Valley. This
walk — and Short walk 24 — make good introductions to
the valley's patches of forest, ravines, high and naked escarp-
ments, shady moss-green paths … and above all, the island's
water collection *galerías*.

**The walk begins** 30m/yds uphill
from the main entrance to the
AGUAMANSA TROUT FARM (●). on
the other side of the road, follow
the wide earthen path that heads
up into the pines and heather by
the bus shelter (there is a TRAIL
BOARD here for the PR TF 35). A
few minutes uphill, turn right on a
narrower trail. You cross the access
road to La Caldera in 15 minutes,
then climb a bit more steeply to
the recreation area itself. On
reaching the tarred road that circles
**La Caldera** (**1**; **25min**), bear
right; through the trees, you will
see the crater (*la caldera*) below
you on the left. There's a pleasant
bar/restaurant (closed Wed) and a
large parking area and bus stop.
    Continue by circling the crater
on the road. Ignore a first turn-off
right. *(But turn right here on the
Camino de los Guanches if you are
following the 'Alternative start'
above.)* Turn right on the next track
(signed 'ZONA DE ACAMPADA').
*(But for the Short walk remain on the*

*tarred road.)* Follow this track
through slender pines and past the
CAMPSITE (**2**).
    About 45 minutes uphill, a
wide earthen trail strikes off to the
left at **Pasada de las Bestias** (**3**;
the sign may be missing). You will
return on that trail after visiting
Choza Chimoche but, for now, be
sure to *turn sharp right on the main
track.* A small gorge lies below.
    Beyond an enormous gravel
deposit, you pass **Galería
Chimoche** (**4**), a very important
water source — as explained
overleaf. Behind the two buildings,
hidden in the rocky-faced embankment, is the *galería* ('water gallery'
or tunnel). **Choza Chimoche** (**5**;
**1h40min**) sits in a sheltered
hollow further up the track.
Continue up the track at the left of
the shelter for a few minutes, to an
even lovelier picnic spot by the
mouth of the **Barranco de Los
Llanos**.
    From this ravine retrace your
steps for 20 minutes. past the *choza*

**117**

*Three little crosses give the trail one of its names: Camino de las Crucitas*

and *galería,* and head back to more garden-like surroundings. Turn off right at the **Pasada de las Bestias** T-junction (**3**) below Galería Chimoche. The track to the left is the route you climbed from La Caldera; you now head right on a wide earthen trail which skirts the ravine below. Five minutes from the turn-off you come to a small flat area called **Lomo de los Brezos** (**6**; **2h10min**). (The track ends just around the bend.)

From Lomo de los Brezos descend to the left on a path, the **Camino de Candelaria** (see Walk 24) is also called the 'Camino de las Crucitas' — for the three little wooden crosses standing on the left near the bottom of the path (**7**). You soon cross a forestry track at **Choza Pedro Gil** (**8**) — going straight ahead down a path shaded by tall heather, leafy trees, and the occasional pine. The trees are bearded with moss and lichen.

Having crossed the track 120 **Galería La Puente** (**9**), your path rejoins the same track, which you follow to the left. A few minutes along (some 220m), you pass a track forking off to the right. Just 40m beyond it, you'll see your return path, also on the right. Two minutes downhill this path collides with a magnificent old pine that must be about 5m/15ft in circumference at the base of its trunk. Ignoring all the narrow side-paths, in five minutes you reach the main TF21 road and *BUS STOP* where you started out, by the main entrance to the *TROUT FARM* (**2h30min**).

*Water gallery at Las Hayas, near the El Lagar picnic area*

---

## Water collection on Tenerife — Canary pines and *galerías*

The majestic Canary pine plays a very important ecological role. The prevailing northeasterly trade winds carry clouds to the northern slopes and create an atmosphere which causes condensation. The drippings from this moisture were measured over the period of a year and yielded an incredible 2000 litres per square metre! This may not mean much to you — until we tell you that a reasonable rainfall for a year yields about 500 litres per square metre. This is the reason for the continuous planting of trees in bare or denuded areas of the forest: to feed the underground reservoirs, the *galerías*. From these *galerías* (tunnels), water is piped to all parts of the island. Tenerife relies very heavily on these water sources, because there are no natural wells and few streams with a permanent flow of water. 'Railway tracks' are are commonly seen near *galerías*, where a great deal of soil has been excavated — one of the water tunnels in the area where the photo above was taken is over three kilometres long!

## Walk 27: FROM EL PALMAR TO THE TENO

**Distance:** 8.5km/5.3mi; 3h35min (under 3km/1.9mi; 40min to Punta de Teno)

**Grade:** ●❗ strenuous, with a total climb of 400m/1300ft and (sometimes skiddy) descent of 800m/2600ft. Possibility of vertigo on two short-cut paths. PR TF 57, then PR TF 51

**Equipment:** walking boots, sunhat, fleece, rain-/windproof, picnic, plenty of water, swimwear

**Refreshments:** Buenavista, by the 'Las Canales' bus stop, Teno Alto

**Transport:** 🚌363 from Puerto to/from Buenavista; journey time 1h20min; *or* 🚌460 from the south to Icod, then *change to* 🚌363. At Buenavista *change to* 🚌366 to El Palmar; journey time 15min; alight at the 'Las Canales' bus stop, 90m south of the road to Teno Alto. Or taxi for this short trip (5km). From Teno Bajo (or Punta de Teno) 🚌369 to Buenavista

**Alternative walk: Buenavista coastal path:** 8km/5mi; 2h.
● Easy, with a climb of just 130m/425ft at the end; equipment as above, but stout shoes will suffice.

Transport to Buenavista as above. Or 🚗: several places to park are shown on the map if you want to shorten this ramble. Referring to the map, start from Plaza San Sebastián (**ⓐ**) west of the BUS STATION. With the **San Sebastián** chapel on your right, cross the main road and follow the street directly opposite. Walk to the left of the main CHURCH, turn left at a T-junction, turn right after another 100m and finally fork left 100m short of the CEMETERY entrance. Coming down to a seaside CHAPEL (**ⓑ**) at the **Mirador Barqueros**, follow the lovely coastal path north of the GOLF COURSE to **Playa de las Arenas** (**ⓒ**). From the end of the beach, cross the bridge and continue to **Playa del Fraile** (**ⓓ**), where the path ends. Retrace steps past the Mirador Barqueros and after 200m/yds, at a fingerpost, turn right up an old trail signed 'CENTRO HISTORICO' and 'ERMITA DE LA VISITACION'. Beyond the pretty *ermita* (**ⓔ**), walk on to the TF445 and turn left, back to Plaza San Sebastián.

The high, hidden, segmented valleys of the Teno are a must for walkers with stamina. This isolated severe landscape has a stark beauty; solitude and peace immediately come to mind. The hardships that these few inhabitants face leave one admiring, perhaps even envying, their fortitude.

**The walk begins** in **El Palmar**, just by the road to Teno Alto: take the PR TF 57 (**○**) trail running alongside a low concrete-block wall on the left, where the sign reads 'TENO ALTO'. Head up between sagging stone walls. You will follow this well marked, lush green trail all the way to Teno Alto. In the first 20 minutes you cross both a track and the Teno road. Closer to the pass, the path is very steep and slippery. Your view commands the entire valley.

You reach a PASS on the **Cumbres de Baracán** (**❶: 40min**) and enter the hidden valleys of Teno — a completely different world, bleak and rugged. You're at about 800m/2600ft here; the highest point of this great mass is Montaña Baracán at 1003m/3290ft, not far away on the left. (For a better all-round view pop up to the road above.)

The now-shady path continues straight on over the pass, below the road. In a couple of minutes you meet the road again, on a bend: cross over the track branching off the road, to pick up the continuation of the path. A FINGERPOST for the PR TF 57 reassures you. As you round the hillside, a short stretch of path may prove vertiginous for some.

Around 15 minutes later, bear right along the crest and begin to

**Cardón (Euphorbia canariensis)**
Punta de Teno is one of the best places in the Canaries to see huge colonies of Canary Island spurge.

The 4- to 6-sided branches can be thick as your arm and grow to 250cm (10ft) high. Their shape gives a clue to their other name: caldelabra spurge — and what a candelabra; they can be up to 360cm (12ft) or more in width. It flowers in mid- to late spring, but the reddish-green florets are modest and hardly noticeable.

Beware! The milky sap is an irritant and could burn your skin. The Guanches used to put the sap in the sea to drug fish, which they could then catch in their hands…
122

descend into a valley (**1h10min**). After climbing a neatly-paved section of path on the far side of the valley, you round a bend and soon find yourselves on a concrete track above a small farm building. Follow this track for seven minutes (about 440m), then take the wide cobbled path off to the right (just where the track swings left). You meet the Teno Alto road again several minutes uphill and cross it, passing a SHRINE dedicated to San Jerónimo on your right. Soon your curiosity is satisfied: you rejoin the road and head left into **Teno Alto** (❷; **1h40min**).

To make for Teno Bajo, keep straight ahead across the junction/ plaza, on the PR TF 51 signposted 'PUNTA DE TENO'). You cross a slight crest and descend into another valley. Within 10 minutes you reach another crest and a JUNCTION, where there is a house with shutters on the right. Fork right, straight over the crest and then downhill, ignoring a track off to the right after just 70m. The

*Opposite: the lighthouse at Punta de Teno; right: Barranco de las Cuevas*

road now reverts to motorable track. Barely 10 minutes down, you round a bend and come to a junction. Your way is downhill, to the right, signposted *'LA CUEVA'* (**3**). A few minutes later you meet a road. Just beyond it, follow a faint path down to the left, on the edge of the **Barranco de las Cuevas**. The path becomes clearer further along. For the first stretch, stay to the left of the road, following the edge of the *barranco* downhill. A 5cm/2in diameter WATER PIPE is beside you.

On reaching the road again, above a few buildings, follow it to your NEXT TURN-OFF (**4**): this comes up some 20m below a house on a bend, just before the road veers right. Here you pick up the path again, descending to the left (some people may find this stretch vertiginous). Keep following the WATER PIPE. You head down the hillside, at times quite close to the edge of the ravine. A tired rock wall is on your right, and you pass several abandoned stone buildings. Some metres/yards *before* the last of the dwellings in the valley, fork left, quickly reaching the bed of the *barranco.* Here you join another TRACK (**5**; **2h35min**) and follow it to the left.

As you leave the ravine, go right at a fork and, soon after, go through a GATE (please leave it as you find it). Along this part of the track, more of the coastal tongue comes into view, where dark lava shades meet the royal-blue sea. Fifteen minutes beyond the last houses, the track comes to a dead end, high above the plain. A wall of rock here, **Roque Chiñaco** (**6**), serves as a good windbreak. This is an excellent viewpoint and lunch spot: to the right, the jagged ravine cuts back into the mountainside; to the left is the subdued coastline's only landmark: the lighthouse, sitting on a promontory of black lava. Flickering below you are greenhouses for tomatoes. On clear days La Gomera is visible — its mountains rise very clearly out of the sea, and the two humps of La Palma stand out over to the right.

Your path continues behind the windbreak to a viewpoint, then veers left. Zigzag down the sheer escarpment. Loose rocks and gravel make it very slow going, so enjoy the superb descent *in pauses, not while on the move!* Your only landmark on this stretch is a small covered WATER TANK (**7**), about 25 minutes downhill. The path ends at the left of some large sheds at **Teno Bajo** (**8**; **3h35min**). Opposite is an enormous farm … and a windfarm. There's a BUS STOP here as well — or you could stroll on to the lighthouse and pick up the (hourly) bus there.

123

## Walk 28: THE 'ENCHANTED FOREST'

*NB:* A permit is needed to walk in the protected Pijaral reserve, and numbers are limited to 45 people a day. But the application on the government website is only in Spanish (centralreservas.tenerife.es/actividad/1), despite the fact that the website has English pages. So either email them in advance *in English:* medionatural@tenerife.es, or telephone 00 34 901 501 901/922 633 576. They will want to know your name, address, email address, what day you wish to visit, time of day you plan arrive/leave, and the number in your group (limited to five people). If you are on the island, you might call in at the Visitors' Centre at Cruz del Carmen for help with the permit.

**Distance:** 6.8km/4.2mi; 2h20min

**Grade:** ● moderate, with an ascent/descent of 300m/1000ft; the trails can be slippery when wet

**Equipment:** walking boots, fleece, walking poles, rain-/windproof, whistle, picnic, water

**Refreshments:** none en route — take a picnic! Nearest restaurant at the Albergue de Anaga

**Transport:** 🚗 to KM4.8 on the TF123 (28° 33.374'N, 16° 10.790'W), where you will spot some parked cars or 🚌 247 to KM4.8 on the TF123 — this is a *request stop:* ask for '**La Ensillada**' (a former picnic site, no longer signposted)

This walk, through the remains of the original laurel forest that covered the Mediterranean basin and Macronesian archipelago until decimated by advancing glaciers, is one of the most beautiful on the island, running through one of UNESCO's Biosphere Reserves. While trees darken and roof your way along this spine of the Anaga range, there are some fine viewpoints as well. Botanists especially will be in their element with so many Canarian endemics to admire.

The walk starts at La Ensillada (⊙), a one-time picnic site off the TF123, 200m west of the KM5 road marker. Turn into the wide path blocked to traffic by bollards. The walk will take you through the 'enchanted forest' — a name aptly describing the fairy-tale atmosphere that will surround you — especially in the mist and fog to which the spine of this peninsula is prone.

About 20 minutes along this path, a turn-off left (**1**) leads to the **Chinobre** *mirador,* a rocky nodule three minutes uphill (910m/2984ft). Unfortunately, this volcanic chimney is *closed to walkers at present, even those with a permit.* Reason: it is now the *only* site on the island where the rare endemic Anaga violet (*Viola anagae*) can be found. Chinobre is

### The Pijaral

Located in one of the oldest geological zones on the island, dating back to the Tertiary Era, the Pijaral is crucial in preserving the underground aquifer. Its northeasterly aspect faces the trade winds, leading to high humidity, mist, fog and horizontal rain. It condenses all this moisture, and the dense greenery also protects the soil.

It's a corner of the island of great ecological value. In the 'enchanted forest' you'll find not only laurels, but other specimens of fauna and flora endemic to Macronesia — from pigeons and snails to lily of the valley trees, small hollys, stinklaurels, tree heath, ericas, native mahogany, bush oleander, mosses, fungi, lichens... and the fern for which the area is named — the *pijara* (*Woodwardia radicans*).

This fern, which can grow up to 3m (15ft) long, is also a memorable feature on Walk 36 at Los Tilos on La Palma (shown on pages 4-5).

*Roque de Anambro is simply spectacular.*

fork to the right (**2**); you will be returning that way. Your onward path rises and falls gently past trees dripping with moss and ferns waist- or shoulder-high.

A further 30 minutes brings you face-to-face with a spectacular rock towering above the trees. Another volcanic chimney, this one is called **Roque de Anambro** (**3**; **50min**), and it makes another good viewpoint over the hidden northern valleys. It was a sacred site for the Guanches, and legend has it that Beneharo, one of the nine Guanche chieftains, jumped into the void from this rock rather than be captured by the Spanish conquerors. He fell onto an *acebiño*, and his drops of blood are why the berries of that tree are blood red. (The *acebiño* is a small holly, *Ilex canariensis,* and the symbol of La Gomera.)

The **Cabezo del Tejo** (**4**; **1h**) is yet another magnificent lookout, with many views similar to those from Chinobre, especially along the coast to Taganana and as far west as Almáciga.

You meet a track here at the viewpoint. Now follow this track back to the TF123 (**1h55min**). It's very awkward going on this muddy track when conditions are wet; you may be glad of walking poles.* Turn right on the road and right again almost at once (**5**), on a rising path which takes you back to **2** in under 15 minutes (**2h15min**). Turn left, back to **La Ensillada** (**2h20min**).

one of the best viewpoints on the island, equalled only by Teide and Guajara. Presumably, if they succeed in propagating the violet elsewhere in the Anaga, they will reopen the path to the viewpoint.

A minute downhill, ignore a

*If you're not dependent on a car, you could follow the steeply descending path at the end of the viewpoint to a junction, and there turn right (PR TF 6/7). Keep left at the fork about 15 minutes down. In under 40 minutes you'll be in **Chamorga** (restaurants; 947).

# Walks on
# La Gomera

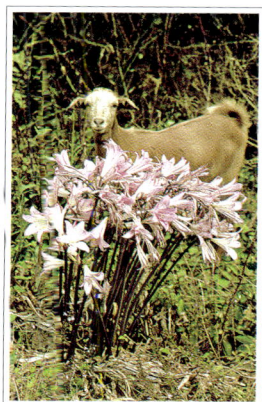

**La Gomera**
AREA: 370 km² (143sq mi)
LENGTH OF COAST: 100km (62mi)
HIGH POINT: Garajonay (1487m/4879ft)
POPULATION: 22,426 (2020)
POPULATION DENSITY: 58/km² (151/sq mi)
CAPITAL: San Sebastián (pop 9093)
PROVINCE: Santa Cruz de Tenerife

The little dome-shaped island of La Gomera sits some 32 kilometres/20 miles southwest of Los Cristianos on Tenerife — just 50 minutes away by high-speed ferry … and that's the only way to get there from northern Europe. There are no direct flights because the few beaches and the limited touristic infrastructure on the island don't warrant an international airport. The good ferry schedules have allowed Sunflower's team of walk-checkers to hop back and forth for a few days at a time … but we recommend at least a week.

La Gomera is Noel's favourite Canary Island. It's a place where people go to appreciate the simple things in life — peace and quiet, space to breathe and splendid rural scenery.

## LA GOMERA

In all three of these it excels, and, on top of this, the island has remained largely unspoilt.

La Gomera is a walkers' paradise. Admittedly there are a lot of ups and downs, but we've tried to include a few easier versions with some of the moderate hikes — so you can get the 'feel' of the landscape without hiking for miles. Perhaps, unawares, you will find yourself drawn deeper and deeper into this countryside of moss-coated laurel forests and palm groves.

Getting to know an island is getting to know the people, so before you set off, learn a few words of Spanish. The 'Gomeros' are a reserved people. However, if you do speak some Spanish, you will find them responsive and helpful. (It's not likely that you'll have time to master the other 'language' spoken on La Gomera — the *silbo,* the centuries-old 'whistling language' developed by the Guanches to communicate across the enormous ravines that slice down from the *cumbre*.)

## Walk 29: FROM VALLE GRAN REY TO ARURE

**Distance:** 8km/5mi; 3h15min

**Grade:** ● very strenuous, with an overall ascent of 800m/2600ft. You must be sure-footed. Red-white waymarked (GR132).

**Equipment:** walking boots, fleece, windproof, sunhat, raingear, picnic, plenty of water

**Refreshments:** bar, restaurants in Valle Gran Rey and Arure

**Access:** on foot or ⛐1 or 6 to La Calera; or ⛴ to Vueltas, then on foot to La Calera. Return on ⛐1 or 6 from Arure; journey time to Valle Gran Rey 35min

**Alternative walks:**

**1 Arure to Valle Gran Rey** (8km; 5mi; 2h25min). ● Moderate, with an overall ascent of 100m/330ft and descent of 800m/2600ft. You must be sure-footed. ⛐1 or 6 to the Bar-Restaurant El Jape (**❸**) in Arure; journey time from VGR 35min. Return on ⛐1 or 6 from

La Calera or ⛴ from Vueltas. See notes on page 131.

**2 La Mérica from Arure** (7km/4.3mi; 2h25min). ● Quite easy ascent/descent of 100m/330ft; equipment as above. Access: ⛐ or ⛐1 or 6 from Arure. The walk proper starts on the lane to the **Mirador Ermita del Santo** (**❼**), which turns west off a hairpin bend in the main road. By car, park opposite Casa Conchita (**❽**) in the centre (28° 8.129'N, 17° 19.074'W) and walk 500m downhill to the turn-off on your right. By bus, alight at the Bar-Restaurant El Jape (**❾**) and walk north along the road, past the Las Hayas turn-off, to the first turning left. This tarmac lane reverts to track after 200m. Use the map to follow the GR132 to the TRIG POINT on the **La Mérica** summit (**❺**); return the same way.

---

**T**his walk scales the precipitous rock walls that over-shadow La Calera and then heads north. The really fit will start out from Valle Gran Rey early in the morning and watch the sun creep slowly over the *barranco* below. Those who prefer a more leisurely approach can *descend* the well-graded route *from* Arure (Alternative walk 1). Climbing or descending, your views dip into every nook and cranny of the Gran Rey ravine and out over the desolate southwest.

**Start out** at the BUS STOP/TAXI RANK (**❍**) on the GM1 in **La Calera**, 100m north of the roundabout. Take the wide steps (CALLE EL CONTERO) at the left of the *ayunta-miento* (town hall, with flags), then the first steps on the right. At the top of the steps turn right along a narrow alley between houses, then turn left when you meet a road higher up (on a bend). Leave this road just beyond a small BRIDGE and above a large WATER TANK; a GR132 FINGERPOST marks the start of the walk proper (**❶**; 10min). Take the stone-laid steps left uphill beside the stepped *barranco* and swing left almost immediately to

cross it. This initial stretch of path, on well-graded zigzags, is paved in places, but sometimes very gravelly with loose grit and small stones. From here on ignore any turn-offs.

As you climb, banana planta-tions, a deep blue sea, and dark bluffs come into view below — followed by a glimpse of the small *barrios* (urban districts) occupying the highest corner of the valley, a shrill patch of greenery in these monochromatic surroundings.

A solid slog lasting well over an hour brings you to a RIDGE, from where you look straight down onto La Playa and Vueltas (Valle Gran Rey's port area). This setting

*Top: the Risco cliffs towering above La Calera; bottom: the Mirador de la Ermita del Santo overlooks Taguluche.*

is dramatised by the jagged ridges tumbling down alongside you (**Riscos de la Mérica**). Later you reach the CREST (**1h45min**), where goats graze on the remains of terracing. You pass a couple of paths off left to the edge of the Riscos — another fine viewpoint.

Ten minutes later you walk between a RUINED COW BARN on the left and huge circular ERA on the right (threshing floor; ❷; **1h55min**). Continue up the gently sloping terraces, to catch sight of Arure, set back in a shallow gully on the edge of the plateau. About 15 minutes past the *era* you pass to the left of the CISTERN and RUINED HOUSE/LIME KILN shown opposite (❸). Soon the country villages of Chipude, El Cercado and Las Hayas (from right to left) come into view.

Five minutes later (**2h15min**) you pass a few paths forking left to the summit of **La Mérica** (❹). You cross over a neck of ridge and now briefly catch a view northwest — a formidable landscape of bare rock, devoid of life and drained of colour … the perfect site for a rubbish tip! La Palma lies before you, two rounded peaks emerging above a cape of lingering cloud.

On reaching a TRACK (❺; **2h35min**), continue along it, ignoring the turn-off left to the RUBBISH TIP a few minutes later. Less than 20 minutes along the track, ignore a path on the left signposted to Taguluche. Just beyond the turn-off, you're gazing down onto Taguluche — a patchwork of gardens in a tremendously deep basin.

Having crossed the ridge a few times, you descend to a tarmac lane. Follow this for 100m, then turn left on a cobbled path to the **Mirador and Ermita del Santo**

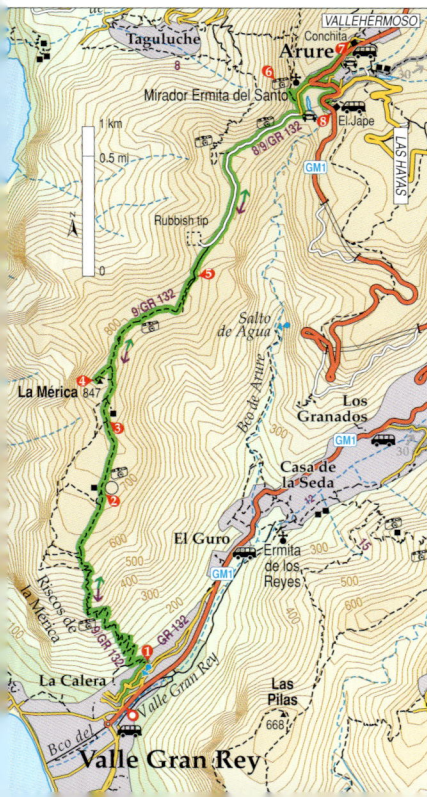

## La Mérica — not always so desolate

The trail so popular with walkers today has a very long history, as can be seen north of La Mérica, where there are caves once inhabited or used as burial tombs by the indigenous people.

And the trail was an important communication link for centuries: people on the heights went down to the sea with wine, firewood or fruit to sell; the seaside dwellers climbed up to sell their fish.

In addition, there was farming and industry on these heights — up until the 1940s. Centuries before, people kept cattle, then tried cultivating cereals. It was quite successful, the area was rich … and then it stopped raining. A reservoir was promised, but the pipes never reached La Mérica.

In the 1930s and 40s there was much unemployment on the island. But unlike most of the Canaries, La Gomera had limestone rock veins. So lime kilns were built on this hill, and near them were cisterns like the one shown at the left. The water was mixed with lime to make calcium hydroxide for industrial use. La Mérica's lime kilns were tasked with producing it for the building of the Arure–Valle Gran Rey road.

(**6**; **3h10min**), the magnificent viewpoint overlooking the Taguluche ravine shown opposite.

From the *mirador*, go back to the lane junction and turn left to the main road. Head left uphill to the restaurant CASA CONCHITA in **Arure** (**7**). Or walk downhill to the Bar-Restaurant EL JAPE (**8**). In either case you'll reach a BUS STOP (**3h15min**).

**From Arure to Valle Gran Rey**
**Start out** at either restaurant in **Arure** (**7** or **8**). Follow the GM1 north or south, then turn left to the **Mirador and Ermita del Santo** (**6**). From there go back to the junction and turn right along the road (then track), soon passing a path off right to Taguluche and, later, a track off right to a RUBBISH TIP. Some 250m past the rubbish tip track, turn right on a GR132-signposted path (**5**; **25min**).

This broad trail is easily followed. Turn right when you come to a path off right (**50min**) and climb to the TRIG POINT on **La Mérica** (**4**), then return to the main trail. Further south you first pass a cluster of rocks on the left with a RUINED HOUSE and a CISTERN (**3**), then a RUIN on the right and huge circular THRESHING FLOOR on the left (**2**; **1h15min**).

Ten minutes later, at a junction, ignore the path off right to the Riscos de la Mérica; keep left for the zigzagging descent — steep but not *too* hard on the knees and *not* vertiginous. Ignore all turn-offs. Eventually the trail emerges at GR132 FINGERPOSTS (**1**). Turn right and follow the lane for 250m; then, after a hairpin bend to the left, bear right down to a BUS STOP/TAXI RANK on the GM1 in **La Calera**. The BUS STATION is to the left of the roundabout (**2h25min**).

**Distance:** 9.4km/5.8mi; 3h
**Grade:** ● relatively easy, with an ascent of 200m/650ft and an overall descent of 750m/2460ft. But the descent on the cobbled trail between ❼ and ❽ *is very steep and tough on the knees.* Various waymarks, signposts, some cairns
**Equipment:** walking boots, walking pole(s), sunhat, fleece, windproof, raingear, picnic, water
**Refreshments:** available in Arure, Las Hayas and VGR

**Access:** 🚐1 or 6 to the El Jape Bar-Restaurant in Arure; journey time from VGR 35min. Return on the same bus from Los Granados; journey time 10min to VGR
**Short walk: From Las Hayas to Los Granados** (5.2km/3.2mi; 1h55min). ● Grade (descent) and equipment as above. Access: 🚐1, 4 or 6 to La Montaña Restaurant (❸) at Las Hayas; journey time 50min. Follow the main walk from the 1h05min-point to the end.

$F$ew walks on this island are without their ups and downs, and most have at least one vertiginous section. But this walk has no long uphill slog, and the vertiginous bits can be avoided. The gentle climb through a fragment of the laurel wood and the spectacular descent into Valle Gran Rey make this a superb, fairly easy hike — for those with strong knees!

**Start out** at the Bar-Restaurant EL JAPE ( ⭕ ): continue along the road towards **Arure**. But just around the bend in the road, fork right towards Las Hayas on another road. Arure is strung out along the far wall of the valley, while the floor of the *barranco* is crammed with vegetable gardens. A good five minutes uphill, leave the road just above a SMALL RESERVOIR: take the path down to and alongside the dam wall. Beyond the dam wall turn right at the fork. Once past the houses above the dam, follow the path up to the left (northeast) over a rocky ridge; small cairns mark the route. The ridge is covered in yellow-flowering *Tecina linifolia Gomerae*.

Crossing the crest, a view opens up over an elevated valley. The path, rich in mauve, pink, and terracotta hues, joins a track and curves to the right. Tarmac comes under foot at the first house, and the lane passes above a second reservoir (**Embalse de Arure;** ❶;

*Valle Gran Rey, from about the 1h30min-point in the walk*

30min). At the T-JUNCTION just past the reservoir (**35min**) turn right, and at the following Y-fork (with many signs) turn right again

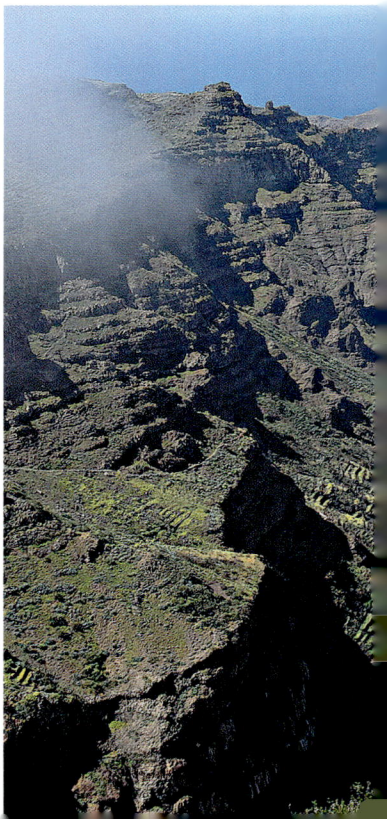

for 'LAS CRECES', climbing into a basin full of vineyards.

At the next fork, 300m further on, keep right for 'LAS HAYAS'. Follow the tarred lane uphill until it ends just above a stream bed (**40min**). Cross the *barranco* and ascend a path into a patch of laurel wood. Meeting another ROAD (**❷; 50min**), turn left. Keep to the crest of this ridge (**Cabezo de la Vizcaína**), ignoring all turn-offs. Soon Las Hayas comes into view, a small scattering of houses surrounded by heather and laurel woods. Approaching the village, a road joins from the right. Five minutes later, just before the main road in **Las Hayas**, go half left uphill on a track and then turn right on a lane, to emerge facing the MONTAÑA RESTAURANT (**❸; 1h05min**), where vegetarians will be in their element — and you can sample *gofio* (see panel overleaf).

From the restaurant, return to the main road, and immediately turn sharp left on a lane (GR131; red and white waymarks). This leads down into a valley of palm trees, crosses a *barranco* and then rises gently. Coming over a low crest, you meet a crossing road (**1h15min**): go straight over but, 25m further downhill, turn left on the GR131 (**❹**) and begin to descend into another valley of palms. Then, at a Y-fork 50m further on, *leave the GR:* turn right for 'LA VISCAINA' (**❺**; the GR131 continues ahead to El Cercado). Cross a track to continue into the valley and, on the far side, at a JUNCTION (**❻**) beyond another low crest, go right— to overlook an abyss, the **Barranco del Agua**, a tributary of the Barranco Valle Gran Rey.

From here you can make out the line of a path ascending the

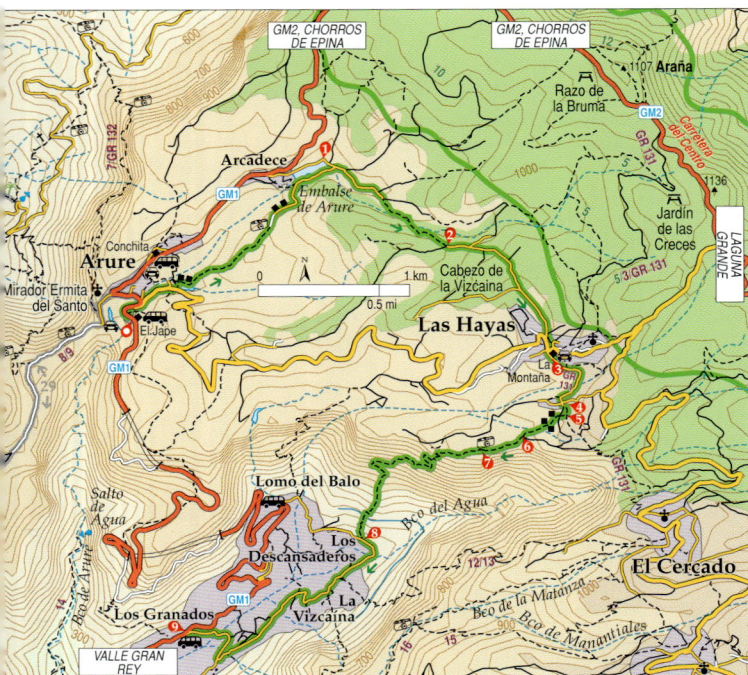

valley wall opposite; it climbs to El Cercado. La Fortaleza, a table-topped rock, sits in the background. Soon the striking

grandeur of Valle Gran Rey, a luxuriant tapestry of banana groves, cane and vegetable gardens, comes into view. A small *mirador* with a stone bench (**7**) makes a fine picnic spot.

Coming onto cobbles (**1h 30min**), you now begin a *very steep* descent down a zigzag path; it's a fine piece of workmanship, and not at all vertiginous. The whole length of the valley lies in view. Cross a small watercourse and keep left at a fork just beyond it, to step down to a road in **Los Descansaderos** (**8**; **2h30min**). Turn left down the palm-flooded valley floor. Keep to this road all the way to the Valle Gran Rey road, ignoring the side road forking to the left. When you reach the main road at **Los Granados** (**9**; **3h**), descend to the BUS STOP, just downhill to the left.

## Walk 31: BARRANCO DE SANTIAGO

**Distance**: 12km/7.4mi; 3h40min

**Grade:** ●✝ fairly easy descent of 1100m/3600ft. But the first half hour is steep, and pine needles underfoot make it slippery. You must be sure-footed and have a head for heights on a couple of short stretches. Don't attempt in wet weather. Good signposting

**Equipment:** walking boots, walking pole(s), sunhat, fleece, windproof, raingear, picnic, water

**Refreshments:** in Pastrana (el Mon) and Playa de Santiago

**Access:** 🚌1 to Roque de Agando; journey time from San Sebastián 35min. Return on 🚌3 from Playa de Santiago

***Shorter walk: From Roque de Agando to Pastrana*** (6.5km/ 4mi; 2h30min). ● Grade as main walk, but the descent is just 800m/ 2600ft. Equipment and access as main walk. Return by 🚌 taxi from Pastrana (pre-arrange or telephone a taxi on arrival: 34 629 234900).

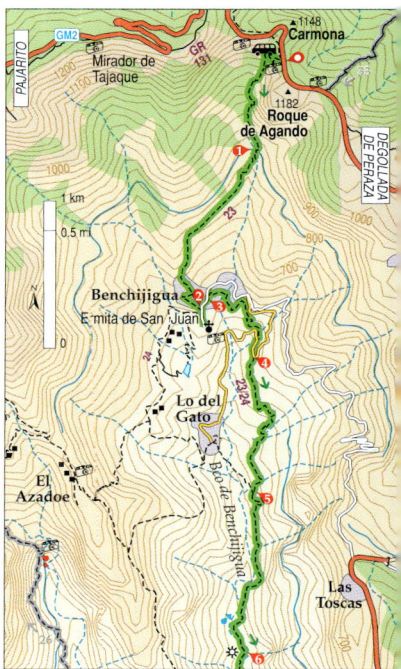

The Barranco de Santiago is not one of those 'love at first sight' ravines. But once beyond its stark and inhospitable façade, the most unexpected sight greets you — a boulder-strewn floor crammed with gardens and orchards. Small hamlets and pretty palms decorate the valley walls, while in winter a stream adds to the beauty.

From the *FOREST FIRE MEMORIAL* (**●**) at the foot of **Roque de Agando** take the cobbled trail signposted to '*BENCHIJIGUA*' (Trail 23). After passing below the foot of Roque de Agando, you cross a covered *canal* (**❶**) and then the stony bed of the **Barranco de Benchijigua** (30min).

When you reach **Benchijigua** — just a few houses, some burnt-out, others lived in (**❷**; **1h05min**), be sure to take a break at the **Ermita de San Juan**, to enjoy the view shown overleaf. Returning from the *ermita*, turn right along the motorable track, but after 50m

turn right down the green/white waymarked trail for '*PASTRANA*' (**❸**) — briefly descending a *barranco* bed and passing below some beflowered cottages. Cross another small *barranco* and ascend to a low crest. Turn left and descend to the *LO DEL GATO ROAD* below (**1h20min**).

Follow this road left uphill for about 120m, then pick up your ongoing trail on the right (**❹**). After about 20 minutes ignore the trail off right to Lo del Gato (**❺**). In another 20 minutes you pass two *WATER TANKS*, then drop into the stream bed and find an old, but

135

*View north to Roque de Agando, from near the Ermita de San Juan in Benchijigua (1h30min)*

still functional, GOFIO MILL on the right (**6**).

The trail climbs up left from the stream bed and rises to **Pastrana** (**7**; **2h30min**) and the end of a road coming from Playa de Santiago. Follow the road for 120m, then turn right at a fingerpost with *yellow/white* waymarking: 'EL RUMBAZO/PLAYA DE SANTIAGO'; **8**). This path drops you down to a lower road beside the **Barranco de Santiago**, which you follow via **Taco** for just over 5km down to **Playa de Santiago** (**9**; **3h40min**).

### Gofio

*Gofio* is a popular local flour made from toasted grains (barley, beans, wheat, maize, etc). It was a staple food of the Guanches, and in times of famine it was even made from the roots of ferns. Toasting the grain before milling kills any mold toxins due to poor storage.

*Gofio* is made into a thick paste and mixed with stews and soups or with honey, almonds, bananas, even cheese. The savouries are an acquired taste, the sweets addictive! Freshly-ground *gofio* is highly aromatic.

If you have lunch at La Montaña in Las Hayas (Walk 30), you may be served maize-based *gofio escaldado* — *gofio* paste with big onion slices on top, used to 'spoon' it into your mouth. If you find *golfio* too bland, you can add some red *mojo picón* — the sauce described on page 39.

## Walk 32: EL CEDRO CIRCUIT FROM LAS MIMBRERAS

**Distance:** 6 8km/4.2mi; 2h30min

**Grade:** ● Fairly easy, but with a steep and slippery 15 minute descent to El Cedro and beyond, to the waterfall view. Over-all ascents/descents of 300m/1000ft. You must be sure-footed.

**Equipment:** walking boots, walking pole(s), fleece, windproof, raingear, picnic, water; *torch for the tunnel (optional)*

**Refreshments:** bar/restaurant La Vista in El Cedro

**Access:** 🚌 to Las Mimbreras (28° 7.460'N, 17° 13.402'W). To get there, turn down the El Cedro road at Reventón Oscuro and take the first left turn (after 1.5km): this forestry track is signposted 'Arroyo de El Cedro'. The Las Mimbreras parking area is 1.8km further on.

**D**on't be surprised if you're completely enveloped by mist on this walk — an ideal way to cool down on a hot day. Swathes of lichen hanging from the trees testify to the moisture in the air here. El Cedro has double the average annual precipitation for the island and four times that of coastal areas! So it is one of the most important places on the island for water collection, and you can see a *galería* similar to the ones described on page 119.

**Start out** at **Las Mimbreras** (○) by continuing along the track signposted towards *LOS ACEVIÑOS*. (*Mimbreras* is Spanish for willows. The willows in this area were used for basket-making, having first been soaked in the Barranco del Cedro to make them more pliable. Baskets were needed to transport the produce grown in the valley.) The track climbs gently before levelling out after about 20 minutes, affording glimpses through the lichen-festooned trees towards Hermigua, the Barranco del Cedro and the sea.

A few metres before the track heads off to the left, turn right on a path signposted '*CASERIO EL CEDRO*' (**35min**). Five minutes later, this path meets another path at a T-junction, where you turn sharp right (**❶; 40min**). Zigzag steadily downhill for about 15 minutes, to a TARRED LANE (**❷**). Go straight across, then bear right on a skiddy path to descend a ridge between terraces. At the bottom, turn left on the road, cross the car park and head into restaurant LA VISTA at **El Cedro** (**❸; 1h**).

After perhaps taking a break, descend steps from the restaurant terrace down to a paved trail (**❹**).

137

**Nuestra Señora de Lourdes**
*The chapel was founded by an Englishwoman, known to the local people as Doña Florencia — governess to the children of a wealthy industrialist. She built the chapel when she retired, and among the hundreds of people at the inauguration in 1935 was 'the patriarch of El Cedro', a local character with a very long beard who lived in the forest and fed himself on gofio made from fern roots (see the panel on page 136).*

*The celebrations held here on the last Sunday in August were the most important on the island until 1984, when they were suspended due to a huge fire in the area. Today they are much more low-key, but the iconic dance of the tambourine is still performed.*

Your ongoing path is to the right, but first take time to see the island's highest waterfall. Turn left on the trail, ignoring a path right down to the river and coming in a few minutes to an ELECTRICITY PYLON marking a a PASS at the top end of the valley leading down to Hermigua. Here you get your first view of the Roque de San Pedro pointing straight up out of the wall of the Barranco de Monteforte. (There are in fact *two* rocks there, and they are often called 'Los Gemelos', The Twins — or 'Los Enamorados', The Lovers.)

The steep cobbled trail winds down in tight curves and steps, to a *mirador* (**5**; **1h25min**) on the right with a brilliant view to the 150m/490ft-high waterfall in the **Boca del Chorro**. Unfortunately, it will only be at its best if there has been heavy rain. But the view north is worth the trip in any case — you overlook the whole Hermigua basin, beyond the small Embalse de los Tilos, the old power station and 'The Twins'.

Return to the fork at **4** and now carry on straight ahead along the trail. After 250m, you might like to peek into the WATER TUNNEL (**6**; **2h**) a few metres to the left. If you venture into it at all, be sure to use a strong torch; it's pitch black and 550m long. The tunnel emerges near a hairpin bend (with parking space) on the road between Reventón Oscuro and the GM1. If you don't suffer from claustrophobia, you could make a circuit via the tunnel referring to the map on the previous page.

Just past the tunnel entrance, turn left up a road, then turn right at the first junction for 'LAS MIMBRERAS' (**7**). After the second house on the left, turn left, climbing a wide stone-laid PATH WITH STEPS. Ascending the valley wall, you pass several side paths; keep to the widest and clearest all the way, passing some houses and coming to a sign at the boundary of the National Park ('PARQUE NACIONAL GARAJONAY'; **8**).

A shady path with tall spindly moss-coated laurels leads you steadily up to a small rustic chapel, **Nuestra Señora de Lourdes** (**9**; **2h20min**), with picnic tables, benches and a piped spring (coming out of a tree). Beyond the chapel, a small wooden bridge takes you over the stream and deeper into the forest. Cross another bridge and climb back to the forestry track where you parked. Turn right and, after some 50m, you're back at **Las Mimbreras** (**2h30min**).

## Walk 33: CIRCUIT FROM THE DEGOLLADA DE PERAZA

**Distance:** 8km/5mi; 3h15min
**Grade:** ●: strenuous, with overall ascents/descents of 650m/2130ft. The initial descent of 450m/1475ft is steep. You must be sure-footed and have a head for heights. Don't attempt in wet or windy weather. Good trails (PR LG 17, GR131)
**Equipment:** walking boots, walking pole(s), sunhat, fleece, windproof, raingear, picnic, water

**Refreshments:** at the Degollada de Peraza; shop off route in La Laja
**Transport:** 🚌 or 🚐 1, 3 or 7 to/ from the Degollada de Peraza; journey time from San Sebastián 20min, from Playa de Santiago 1h. By car park at the bar/restaurant (28° 5.916'N, 17° 10.989'W) if you plan to eat there; otherwise park by the Ermita de las Nieves (28° 6.062'N, 17° 12.117'W) and start there.

The Barranco de Las Lajas, the setting for this walk, is a picturesque valley with a number of reservoirs and, higher up, cascading streams and pine-wooded slopes. This classic hike makes a short steep descent down towards the rustic village of La Laja, followed by a short steep climb back up to the crest, from where you overlook a number of curiously-shaped volcanic chimneys — Los Roques.

**The walk starts** at the **Mirador de La Laja** at the **Degollada de Peraza** (⊙). Descend the signed PR LG 17 at the right of the viewpoint balcony. This superbly cobbled path leads down the hillside all the way to La Laja (still in hiding far down to the left). Initially you overlook a valley of tumbling ridges. Crossing the first ridge, the Roques appear higher

### Los Roques

Like Roque Nublo (Walk 15), Los Roques are volcanic plugs which once filled volcanic chimneys. So they were not caused by eruptions: magma was *not* released, instead it cooled and hardened. When the surrounding vents (chimneys) were eroded over millions of years, the 'plug', a rock tower, was revealed.

Five Roques form this Natural Monument: Agando, the most impressive, Ojila, Zarcita, Carmona and Las Lajas. And as with Roque Nublo, these rocks were sacred to the indigenous peoples. Sacrificial shrines were found on the summit of Agando, but looted in the 1980s.

up in the valley: La Zarcita (left) and Ojila (right) — smooth conical volcanic plugs. Thick, fleshy-leafed aloes proliferate on these barren inclines. Some 35 minutes down from the pass, charming La Laja comes into view (❶) — a small strung-out village. Ten minutes later, from the crest of a sharp ridge, you find the ideal VIEWPOINT over this peaceful little haven (❷; **45min**).

At this viewpoint, *leave* the main path, and follow the left-hand fork along the steep hillside at the edge of the pine woods, passing *above* the village of **La Laja**. Take care: the pine needles are very slippery underfoot. A bubbling stream and the green *barranco* bed below enhance the freshness of the valley floor. Five minutes later, the other path rejoins from the right. Continue above the village for another couple of minutes, then come to another fork.

This next fork, signed 'ROQUE DE AGANDO' (❸; **1h**), marks the beginning of your ascent: keep left here. A steep climb through pines follows. Ignore any minor paths to the left or right. The trail crosses four stream beds on wooden bridges or planks. Higher up you reach an enchanting old ramshackle SHELTER with a veranda at the **Degollada del Tanque** (❹; CASA DEL MANCO; **1h45min**), on a crest at the edge of the wood. From here three volcanic chimneys are in view, the product of lava that solidified inside volcanic vents. On the left is Carmona, and the other two you identified earlier in the

*Chejelipes, a short way east of La Laja, is an oasis of greenery and palm groves — with no fewer than three reservoirs!*

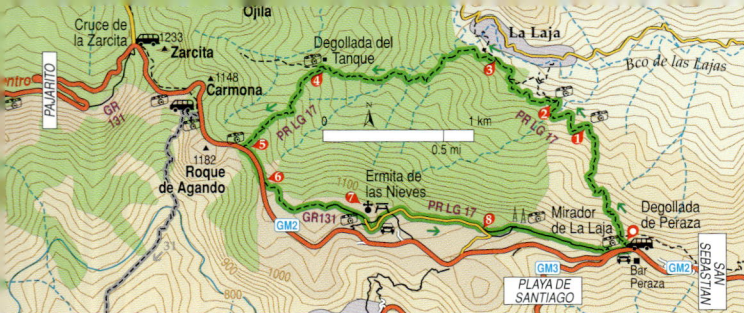

hike. Roque de Agando rises behind the crest to the left.

To make for the main road near Roque de Agando, take the path at the left of the shelter, to continue up the spine of the ridge (*not* the path behind the shelter). On the ascent, a wonderful panorama

unfolds over the faded-green valleys below. Tenerife sits in the background, clearly outlined. Eventually you reach the main road just below and to the east of **Roque de Agando** (**5**; **2h20min**). Turn left on the road to continue the walk (or first follow the road to the *right* for a few minutes, to a forest fire memorial and *mirador,* for a fine view down into the Barranco de Benchijigua and the route of Walk 31). Some 240m along, turn left uphill with the GR131 (**6**; *'DEGOLLADA DE PERAZA'*). After 10 minutes or so the trail descends to a track, which takes you down to the **Ermita de las Nieves** (**7**; **2h40min**). Picnic facilities have been set up here, to take advantage of the fine views.

From the chapel follow the lane downhill. After 10 minutes, 80m before the lane turns sharp right downhill to the main road, head left uphill on a track (**8**; still the GR131). Another track joins from the right and you pass two masts. Don't miss the magnificent views down into the Barranco de Las Lajas from the edge of the escarpment here, but be careful if it's windy! When the track fizzles out after 10 minutes, continue on the cobbled trail, which almost at once begins to drop steeply to the main road below, 100m west of the **Mirador de La Laja** (**3h10min**).

*Casa del Manco at the Degollada del Tanque, dwarfed by Roque de Ojila, and the trail up to Roque de Agando*

## Walk 34: BARRANCO DE GUARIMIAR CIRCUIT

**Distance:** 11.7km/7.3mi; 4h30min
**Grade:** ● ❗ very strenuous, with
overall ascents/descents of some
1000m/3300ft. You must be sure-
footed, with a head for heights.
Don't attempt in wet or windy
weather. Well signposted trails.
**Equipment:** walking boots,
walking pole(s), fleece, windproof,
sunhat, raingear, picnic, water
**Refreshments:** available at Alajeró
**Transport:** 🚐 to/from a lay-by
with walkers' signboard at the El
Rumbazo turn-off (28° 3.578'N,
17° 12.812'W). Nearest 🚌 access is
the Targa turn-off on the main
road (pick up the walk at ❸)

**Alternative walk: Barranco de
Guarimiar from Pajarito**
(10.5km/6.5mi; 3h20min). ● ❗
Moderate linear route, with a
descent of about 1300m/4265ft.
Some gravelly, slippery paths,
otherwise grade/equipment as
main walk. Refreshments available
in Imada. Transport: 🚌 1 from
San Sebastián to the Pajarito
junction; journey time about
35min. Return by pre-arranged 🚕
taxi from the El Rumbazo turn-off
(allow plenty of time to finish the
hike). Or walk from there down to
Playa de Santiago (4km/2.5mi;
1h) to catch a bus or boat.

**Start out** at **Pajarito** (●): from
the car park on the southeast side
of the roundabout follow the track
signposted 'LOS ROQUES'. After
250m (**4min**) fork left up a path
(❶; the GR131). This trail rises to
the main road at a wide, signposted junction (**20min**). Turn
sharp right here on the forestry
track signed for 'IMADA'. (The GR
continues ahead, after just 50m
passing a tiny concrete hut with
antennas (❷) that has given this
area its local name — the CASETA
DE LOS NORUEGOS or CASA OLSEN.)
Your track descends through

laurel woods ravaged by fire
several years ago. Slowly
regenerating, the slopes reverted
first to heather, with splashes of
pine and eucalyptus. The massive
**Barranco de Benchijigua**,
plunging away on the left, attracts
your attention, while monolithic
Roque de Agando bulges up out of
the landscape on the far side of the
*barranco*.

Where the track swings right,
you reach a small PARKING BAY/
VIEWPOINT (**50min**) overlooking
Benchijigua far below. From here
take the trail straight ahead. Overgrown vineyards lie almost
unnoticed on the rock-rose- and
broom-clad valley walls. A good
15 minutes down, ignore the left
fork to Azadoe (❸), cross the
**Barranco de Azadoe** above a
small seasonal cascade, and then
keep right for Imada.

The path now runs along the
edge of a vertical escarpment,
where you'll need a head for
heights. Rounding the nose of the
ridge, you look straight down onto
Imada, a biggish farming village
sheltering high in the Barranco de
Guarimiar. Looking down the
*barranco*, you can trace the continuation of your route below the
village.

Descending to a road at the
upper end of **Imada** (❹;
**1h20min**), continue downhill,
forking right past BAR ARCILIA.
After 350m, just past the walled-in
SPORTS GROUND (❺) on the left,
descend steps to a lower road and
continue in the same direction,
passing a CHAPEL below on your
left. Some 200m further on, watch
for a fingerpost on the left, 'EL
RUMBAZO, PLAYA DE SANTIAGO'.
You have joined the main walk at
(❻; pick up the notes overleaf
just past the 2h40min-point.

143

The Barranco de Guarimiar is one of the top walks on Gomera. In the depths of this sheer-sided *barranco,* a great cliff-hanging but well secured path will leave you in awe. And the path up to Targa is one of the most impressive in the Canaries, still in immaculate condition. I like to start the walk at El Rumbazo to do my climbing early on, but you could start at Targa, Alajeró or Imada. Those travelling by bus, or who just prefer to avoid *all* the climbing, can do the linear Alternative walk from Pajarito and descend into the *barranco* from the island's wooded heights — and even continue down to Playa de Santiago.

**Start out** from the PARKING BAY WITH WALKERS' SIGNBOARD (⦿) at the turn-off to **El Rumbazo.** Climb the steep road to the hamlet and, at the end of the road, turn sharp right up a trail passing in front of the houses. You look out across the **Barranco de Guarimiar,** teeming with palms. The village set along a hillside shelf over on the right, in the Barranco de Benchijigua, is Pastrana. The prominent finger of rock at the far end of the *barranco* is Roque de

*The beautifully engineered path up to Targa at times seems to hang in mid air.*

jutting pieces of cliff, with a breathtaking outlook.

Crossing a *PASS*, you suddenly re-enter civilisation: the pretty little village of **Targa** lies before you when you meet a road (❸; **1h25min**). Follow the road to the right for 300m; then, just past the bend, turn right up a signposted trail ('ALAJERÓ'). In a little over 10 minutes this joins a narrow road. Go left for 75m, then pick up the trail again on the right, now wide and cobbled. Go right at the T-junction, past a threshing floor on the right. On the left is the Calvario, with the island of El Hierro in the background.

When the trail meets the busy main road in **Alajeró** (**1h45min**), follow it to the right, past a *BUS STOP*. Keep to this road for a little over 1km (15 minutes), passing the *BUS STATION* up to the right. Then, just as the road curves left, go right up a trail with a *FINGER-POST* for Trail 20 ('IMADA'; ❹). In a good 10 minutes you meet the *IMADA ACCESS ROAD* (❺) on the ridge. Head right, cutting off the hairpin bends on narrow paths/ steps where there's a break in the roadside barrier. Meeting the access road for the third time, follow it downhill for 200m, to the next break in the barrier. This path leads to a narrower road in the lower part of **Imada**, by fingerposts and a *BREEZE-BLOCK GARAGE* on the left (**2h40min**). Follow this down-hill, curving left. Then, just before the road bends right below a large white building, go right down concrete steps (❻; fingerpost 'EL RUMBAZO/PLAYA DE SANTIAGO').

The path descends a bouldery slope in the **Barranco de Guarimiar**. Terracing covers the slopes all the way up to the rocky crags that line this valley. By the

Agando, and the hamlet set on the ridge separating the two valleys is El Cabezo.

After a couple of minutes ignore the fork down to a house. Crags of all shapes and sizes rise out of the valley walls above you. Gardens burgeoning with produce line the valley floor, although much of the hillside terracing is abandoned. When you reach a junction by a couple of *STONE BUILDINGS* (❶; **15min**), turn left uphill (the way ahead leads to Imada). As you climb, looking straight up towards towering over-head cliffs, you'll wonder where on earth your cobbled path goes. On reaching a signposted *JUNCTION* (❷; **55min**), turn left; you will return on the path to the right.

From here the path will be vertiginous in places, although amply wide. You cross a *canal* spectacularly engineered in the sheer valley walls. The path winds up from ledge to ledge, clinging to

**Date palms** *(Phoenix canariensis)*
Unlike the true date palm from North Africa to which they are related *(P dactylifera)*, the fruits of the Canarian palm are skimpy and tasteless. But their graceful beauty has made them synonymous with sun and holidays throughout the world — a tourist board's dream.

Forget Haría's valley of 1000 palms (page 45) or Fuerteventura's Vega de Río Palmas (pages 74-76). With some 100,000 individual trees, La Gomera is *the* palm island of the Canaries *par excellence* — and the only island using the sap of the trees 'industrially': it's tapped to produce 'palm honey' *(miel de palma)* as a sweetener.

time the *barranco* has folded into a narrow passageway of rock, you reach a rock balcony VIEWPOINT (❼; **3h10min**). A hamlet lies far below, in a valley liberally sprinkled with palms.

From the end of this rocky ledge keep down to the right, to descend the sheer nose of the ridge below you. The path seems to disappear off the end of the ridge, but in fact is built into its side. Stepping down, and very close to the edge, you discover the onward path — a narrow ledge hanging out high above the valley floor, well protected with a handrail. No need to worry about turn-offs on this stretch! Heart-beat back to normal, you cross a wide *canal* built into the valley wall (**3h30min**).

146

Some 20 minutes later you come to some houses in the lush and verdant lower part of **Guarimiar** (❽; **3h50min**). Before the first house, a trail heads left to the road. Ignore this; keep straight ahead, at the left of the first house. Continue along the right-hand side of the *barranco*, briefly joining the village road. After 330m (five minutes), keep right at a fork (❾; TRAIL 20/'TARGA'), soon passing a hillside buttress with a fantastic view down over the valley. At the next junction, you rejoin your OUTGOING ROUTE (❷; **4h10min**), and under 10 minutes later, you walk above the first house of **El Rumbazo**. The rest of them, a tight cluster, perch on the hillside. Join the road and descend back to the PARKING BAY (**4h30min**).

## Walk 35: CIRCUIT FROM AGULO TO THE JUEGO DE BOLAS AND THE MIRADOR DE ABRANTE

**Distance:** 12km/7.5mi 4h05min
**Grade**: ● ● fairly strenuous, with ascents/descents of 600m/2970ft overall. You must be sure-footed and have a head for heights. Don't attempt in wet or windy weather. Well signposted trails
**Equipment:** walking boots, walking pole(s), sunhat, fleece, wind/rainproofs, long trousers, picnic, plenty of water
**Refreshments:** bar-restaurants in Agulo, Juego de Bolas, Mirador de Abrante
**Transport:** 🚌2 or 🚗 to/from the

Agulo bus stop on the GM1 at the edge of the village; journey time from San Sebastián 50min. Park by the bus stop (28° 11.155'N, 17° 11.663'W).

**Short walk: Mirador de Abrante**
(3.5km/2mi; 55min). ● Fairly easy, with a descent/ascent of 100m/330ft. Trainers will suffice. Access by 🚗: park at the Centro de Visitantes (28° 10.669'N, 17° 12.859'W). Use notes from the 2h-point in the main walk at 4; return the same way.
*Note: The Garajonay Park Visitors' Centre (Juego de Bolas) is open daily from 09.30-16.30.*

Agulo is the most spectacularly sited village on the island, and this walk is one long *mirador*. It takes you up to two viewpoints from where you can appreciate the village setting, before returning to Agulo above the pretty Barranco de las Rosas. Midway, you can call at the Visitors' Centre for enlightenment and at a potentially terrifying *mirador*.

**Start the walk** in **Agulo**, from the BUS STOP (●) follow the main road towards Vallehermoso, past the POST OFFICE. A minute along, just past the PHARMACY, turn right up stone steps (fingerpost: 'ROUTES 34, 35; MIRADOR DE ABRANTE, CENTRO DE VISITANTES', and more).
Rise through terracing, cross a lane and, a minute later, cross the main road. The trail heads steeply up towards the base of the cliffs and then, without respite, climbs in zigzags to a pass at the **Mirador de Agulo** (①; 45min), from where you can marvel at the village setting, the terracing, banana plantations, the tunnel under its sugarloaf guardian ... and El Teide on Tenerife.
From here the route swings right, away from the Barranco de Lepe, to ascend above the **Embalse de Agulo**. On reaching a tarred lane, follow it up the valley; two minutes later, just above the

Casas del Chorro holiday complex, turn left on a road which later becomes a track.
Fifteen minute from the dam, the track crosses to the left-hand side of the stream; five minutes later ignore a short-cut to the Visitors' Centre via a bridge on the right (②; Trail 34). From here the way is tarred, then stone-laid. Two-three minutes from the short-cut you cross a small ravine. Some 550m further on — 50m past a turning place — turn right uphill. At a junction three minutes up, turn right and climb to the **San Isidro** chapel and PICNIC SITE at **La Palmita** (③; **1h40min**). From here follow this lane up right to the main road and then head right to the excellent Garajonay Visitors' Centre (**Juego de Bolas**; ④; **2h**).
Leaving, take the road between the centre and now-closed Bar-Restaurant Tambor (RED/WHITE WAYMARKING; GR132). After

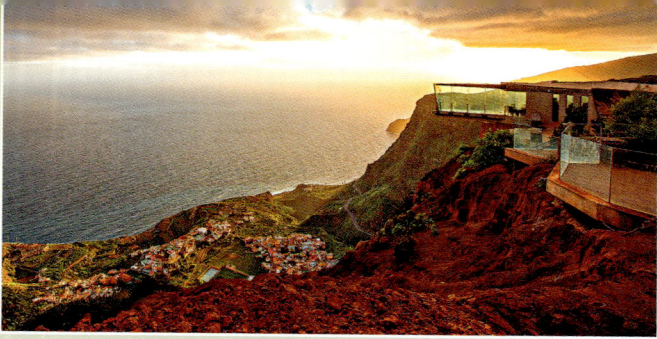

**Agulo's skywalk: the Mirador de Abrante**

The viewpoint sits atop the Risco (Cliffs) of Abrante — named for a Gomeran beauty in love with a handsome young man called Zula. Handsome, but poor — so her mother forbade them to meet. Abrante fled her home and climbed the cliffs to meet Zula, but slipped, fell and died.

Zula, mad with grief, wanted revenge against Abrante's mother. A witch had the answer: if Zula would jump from the cliffs, a new height would rise that would leave her in perpetual darkness.

The legend is far, far more complicated than that, but … he jumped, and you are standing on the cliff that arose thanks to witchcraft.

100m, continue straight ahead on a washed-out red earthen track. About 15 minutes from the Visitors' Centre, past a small pine wood, turn half left up a minor track at a Y-FORK (**5**). Just 125m further on, at another Y-FORK (**6**), is your ongoing route (left) back to Agulo. But first, go straight ahead down the crest to the **Mirador de Abrante** (**7**; **2h25min**) — a spectacular viewpoint with a SKYWALK and a welcoming bar-café. You *really* need to be vertigo-free to brave its GLASS FLOOR, hanging out 625m/2050ft above Agulo!

Back at the turn-off for Agulo, head right; the path follows a greyish erosion gully. Soon you're on a cobbled trail, with fine views over the Barranco de Las Rosas. When the trail forks above a CHARMING OLD HOUSE (**8**), go right with the GR132. When you eventually meet the main road, follow it to the right for 50m, then turn left back onto the trail. Rounding a nose of rock, you descend to the village CEMETERY (**9**), from where a cobbled road leads back to the BUS STOP at **Agulo** (**4h05min**).

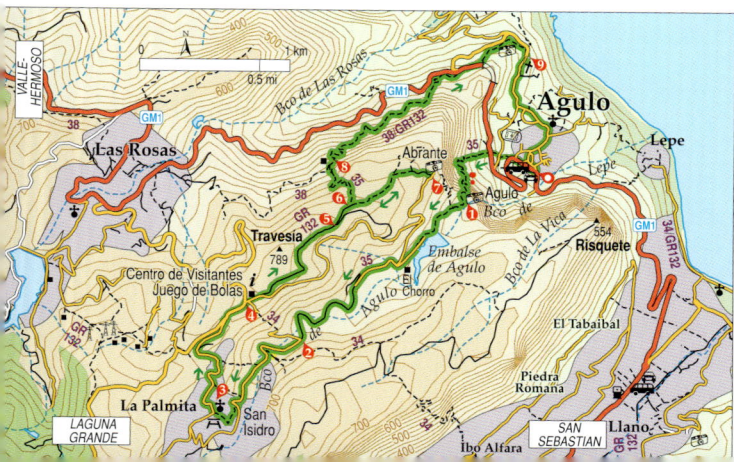

## Walks on
# La Palma

### La Palma
AREA: 708/km² (273sq mi)*
LENGTH OF COAST: 166km (103mi)*
HIGH POINT: Roque de los Muchachos (2423m/7949ft)
POPULATION: 85,840 (2020)
POPULATION DENSITY: 117/km² (302/sq mi)
CAPITAL: Santa Cruz de La Palma (pop ±16,000 (2020))
PROVINCE: Santa Cruz de Tenerife

In natural beauty, La Palma rivals all the other islands put together. Its immense, abyss-like crater, the Caldera de Taburiente (Walk 39), which geologists now refer to as an enormous landslide, is one of the largest of its kind in the world. Deep within its pine-speckled, towering walls is a year-round abundance of water — gushing streams, boisterous cascades, and a plummeting waterfall.

---

*These figures, taken from Wikipedia early in 2022, are not final. The land area and coastline have grown from the eruptions during 2021, but no official statistics hd been released by press date.

## LA PALMA

Garafía
Gallegos
Barlovento

N

0 — 5km
3mi

Llano Negro
**41**
Los Tilos *i*
Los Sauces
Las Tricias
Puntagorda
**36**

**37**

Observatory *i*

**CALDERA DE TABURIENTE**

Puntallana

Tijarafe
**39**
**42**

Los Llanos de Aridane

**Santa Cruz de La Palma**

Visitors' *i* Centre

Tazacorte
El Paso

Site of 2021 eruptions

Mazo

Puerto Naos
★
**CUMBRE VIEJA**

**38**

Los Canarios (Fuencaliente)
**40**

*Salinas de Fuencaliente*

Outside the crater, high on the cloud-catching hillsides, two million-year-old laurel forests grow as dense as jungle (Walk 37). In the southern half of the island, hills pitted with volcanic craters (Walk 38), and mini-deserts of black *lapilli* speak of the island's volcanic past … *and present!* This stark, striking landscape, all the more dramatic for its stabs of volcanic reds, oranges, and yellows, is far removed from the lush and verdant, tree-clad north.

La Palma isn't as well know to walkers as is its easterly neighbour, Tenerife, but as this book goes to press, the island is certainly attracting the attention that may well bring it to prominence as a great hiking destination.

**Distance/time:** see Walks a and b
**Grade:** ● ⚡ easy-moderate, but
with a possibility of vertigo
**Equipment:** walking boots or
stout shoes, raingear, jacket,
trousers, picnic, water, *torch*
**Refreshments:** at Los Tilos
**Transport:** 🚗 to Los Tilos: either
park at the Interpretation Centre
(28° 47.388'N, 17° 48.130'W) or, if you
are just doing Walk a, park by the
first track on the left (28° 47.487'N,
17° 47.977'W), 500m short of the
Centre (**1**). Or 🚌10) from Santa
Cruz to/from the 'Restaurante Los
Nacientes' bus stop just before the
bridge over the Barranco del Agua;
journey 35min ( +55min *each way*)

### *Walk a: Mirador Espigón*
**Atravesado** (6.6km/4mi; 1h50min
*from the visitors' centre*, 5km/3mi;
1h30min from the lower car park).
● ⚡ Mostly on track, with an
ascent/descent of 320m/1050ft
overall; the final path to the view-

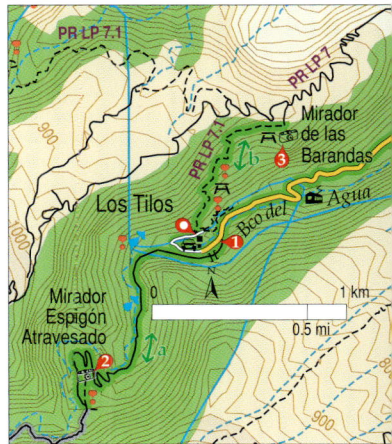

point is vertiginous but protected.

### *Walk b: Mirador de las Barandas*
(2.4km/1.5mi; 1h). ● ⚡ Ascent/
descent of about 250m/820ft
overall, on a *steep*, somewhat
vertiginous path. Take care on the
return: the descent is slippery!

---

Both of these short walks are ideal leg-stretchers during a
car tour. Each focuses on the magnificent Barranco del
Agua at the heart of the biosphere reserve — Walk a overlooks it from the south, Walk b from the north. Do both!

**Start Walk a** from the INTERPRETA-
TION CENTRE (**O**): follow the road
back the way you arrived for some
500m/yds, until you come to the
lower parking area. Take the track
signposted 'MONTE EL CANAL Y LOS
TILOS' (**1**) into the forest, the
yellow/white-waymarked PR LP
6. In about five minutes you go
through a 100m/yd-long TUNNEL,
emerging in a primeval *laurisilva*
where the sun hardly penetrates.
Just below to the right you can
hear the tinkle of water in the *canal*
mentioned in the panel at the right.

   Beyond a STONE BUILDING (**30-
40min**), the track climbs a bit
more steeply. Eventually you come
to a WIDE JUNCTION with an
information board (**50min-1h**),

from where Walk 37 continues
ahead. Just below it, take the path
and steps sharp left along a very
narrow ledge (with protective
railings). This excitement lasts for
about five minutes, until you come
to the precarious and vertiginous —
but brilliant! — **Mirador Espigón**

### Giant ferns at Los Tilos
*Most impressive at Los Tilos are the
gigantic* Woodwardia radicans
*(see photo on pages 4-5). It's
worth visiting the* canal *here:
you'll find it two minutes below
the Interpretation Centre/picnic
area: follow it to the left. The path
is vertiginous, but there are
railings. You'll see a lovely waterfall streaming down over ferns.*

**151**

**Atravesado**, a tiny fenced-in viewpoint looking out north over the ravine (**❷**; **1h-1h20min**).

Return the same way to the Interpretation Centre — or first follow the track to where it ends at an old goods hoist, to take in even more of this green jungle.

**Start Walk b** behind the *INTER-PRETATION CENTRE* (**❍**): climb the steep yellow/white waymarked path (PR LP 7.1) ascending the hillside from the car park to the **Mirador de las Barandas** (**❸**; **35min**), shown below, from where you look straight down into the Barranco del Agua and as it twists and winds into the *laurisilva* of the central massif. Los Tilos lies below, in the V of the *barranco*. Tables and benches, a tap and a shelter invite you to pause before retracing steps.

## Walk 37: CASA DEL MONTE • NACIENTES DE MARCOS • NACIENTES DE CORDERO • LOS TILOS

**Distance/time:** 12.7km/7.9mi; 4h15min

**Grade:** ●❓ very strenuous, with an ascent of about 180m/590ft and drawn-out descent of over 1000m/3300ft. You must be sure-footed and have a head for heights: for about 1h20min the walk follows a *canal* cut into the sheer *barranco* wall. Only attempt this walk during a spell of fine, stable weather, and turn back *immediately* if the weather deteriorates. *Do not attempt the walk just after bad weather: there is a danger of rockfall and landslides* (the walk may be closed due to rockfall). *There are also 13 tunnels, some narrow: not recommended for those who suffer from claustrophobia!* Yellow/white PR waymarks on most of the route, as well as white/green poles from the Casa del Monte up to the springs of Cordero.

**Equipment:** walking boots, raingear, jacket, trousers, picnic, water, *plus torch, large waterproof covering, extra pair of socks* (tunnel 12 is as wet as a power shower: cover yourself and your rucksack!)

**Refreshments:** at Los Tilos
**Transport:** 🚗 to Los Tilos: park at the foot of the first track on the left, 2km up the Los Tilos road (500m short of the visitors' centre; 28° 47.487'N, 17° 47.977'W). Or 🚌100 from Santa Cruz to/from the Restaurante Los Nacientes bus stop just before the bridge over the Barranco del Agua; journey time 35min. (Allow an extra 55min *each way* from the bus stop by the bridge to the track where the walk begins and back down to the main road.) From the kiosk at this track 🚕 4x4 taxi to the Casa del Monte to start the walk — an exhilarating drive of some 50min on a dirt track. Taxis are available every day: either call and make an appointment with Toño (629-213435), Luis (616-418847) or Pepe (649-945481) — they all speak a bit of English — or just show up at Los Tilos on the day: a taxi will be on duty. In general the drivers arrive at Los Tilos between 09.00-09.30 and try to fill their taxis, so there may be a short wait. Cost about €18 per person at press date.

This walk can be summed up in three words: exhilarating, breathtaking (in more ways than one), and tiring. You start the walk high up in an isolated valley, following an irrigation *canal* with 13 tunnels — a marvel of workmanship. It's my favourite walk on the island, even though cliff-hanging watercourses give me the jitters. Your reward is water splashing down out of the hillsides once you reach the *nacientes* (springs) of Marcos and Cordero. This is followed by a scramble over rocks and boulders through an impressive *barranco,* similar to the one in the Caldera de Taburiente (Walk 39). until you eventually reach a good but long, drawn-out descent path through a 'jungle' of laurel woods.

**Begin the walk** at the drop-off point near the **Casa del Monte** (●), at a height of 1330m/4360ft, where a gushing open *canal* meets the track. There are some large boards here, with information about the trail. Follow the *canal* to the left through the laurel forest. You will be walking along this watercourse for about an hour and

20 minutes — sometimes you will need to scramble up onto the edge of it but, in general, the path runs alongside it.

After five minutes the views open up and an immense *barranco* lies at your feet, with drops of several hundred meters. A rickety railing offers some psychological protection, but *don't lean on it!* There are also many steep and narrow sections still without railings, so *please watch where you're walking* **all the time**. *To appreciate the magnificent scenery, stop walking, then look!*

Some 10 minutes along the FIRST OF THE 13 TUNNELS presents itself; at the outset it seems straightforward — wide and high — but, just 10m in, this changes drastically into a narrow passage with steps leading down into the dark. The floor is probably covered in puddles, so if you haven't worn waterproof walking boots, it's too late now! The THIRD AND LONGEST TUNNEL (❶; 350m) is a narrow affair and quite a squeeze, very romantic … especially when you meet a group of 20 other sweaty hikers halfway through!

Continue winding your way around the steep hillside, taking in the tremendous drops and the game of clouds filling in the canyon from time to time.

After tackling the NINTH TUNNEL (**55min**) you get a grand view of what is still in store for you. To the right, strain to see your ongoing path to the springs of Cordero through a gap in the inaccessible-looking cliff face.

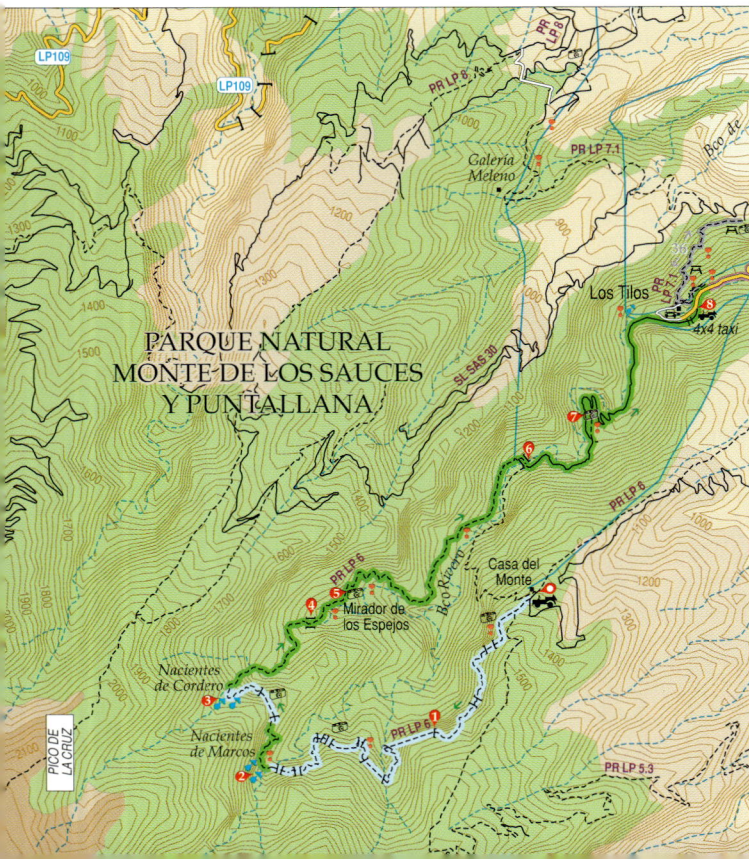

Straight ahead is a dark vertical wall pierced with holes, where you'll encounter the (in)famous 12TH TUNNEL, where you'll have your 'power shower'. All the while, the sound of water gets stronger. Put all your cameras and other delicate equipment away and deploy your waterproof cover-up to tackle this 'amusement park tunnel', with water coming out of the walls from all angles and a small river at your feet.

When you emerge in the sunshine at the other end, probably drenched, you reach the first springs en route, the **Nacientes de Marcos (❷; 1h10min)**, where water spouts out of the mountainside in small cascades.

Now haul yourself up the steep path alongside the raging stream until you reach a higher *canal*. One more TUNNEL awaits you before you reach the second springs, the **Nacientes de Cordero (❸; 1h30min)**.

Leave the springs and head into the canyon by taking the clear path to the right of the springs. After five minutes you enter the riverbed and cross it. Some enormous boulders may appear to block your way, but waymarking guides you round them. Then follow the path on the left-hand side of the *barranco,* only to cross back to the other side after a few minutes.

Stay on this path for 10 minutes and cross again to the left side of the riverbed (**1h50min**). When you regain the barranco bed after a good five minutes, follow it

down to the left, scrambling (occasionally on all fours) over rocks, boulders and tree trunks, avoiding small puddles and wet walls dripping with beautiful colonies of giant prehistoric ferns, the *Woodwardia radicans* (see panels on pages 125 and 151). Little light penetrates this dark fissure.

After 20 minutes in the *barranco* bed, you come to a SIGNPOST and a path on the right, which takes you across a *WOODEN BRIDGE* (❹; **2h25min**). The torture is over, and you are now on a good but drawn-out path that will take you all the way down to Los Tilos. *But don't let your guard down:* in some places the path narrows, with steep drops. Eventually the valley opens up ahead and you come to the **Mirador de los Espejos** (❺), where more fencing protects you as you peer down into the *barranco.*

But then you enter the laurel forest once more and, the further down you go, the more the path is shaded with dense foliage. After an hour down this path you cross the deep **Barranco Rivero** on another *WOODEN BRIDGE* (❻; **3h25min**), this one more imposing (but *don't* lean on the handrail!). Climb up to

the main Los Tilos track and follow it down to the left, again passing enormous colonies of ferns.

Ten minutes later, at a junction of paths and an INFORMATION BOARD, turn right up a narrow and vertiginous path to the **Mirador Espigón Atravesado** (**7**; **3h40min**), a brilliant viewpoint overlooking the dense jungle of Los Tilos. *(Walk 4a comes up to this point from Los Tilos, then returns the same way).* Then, ignoring all side paths, follow the main track down to the PARKING AREA below **Los Tilos** (**8**; **4h15min**).

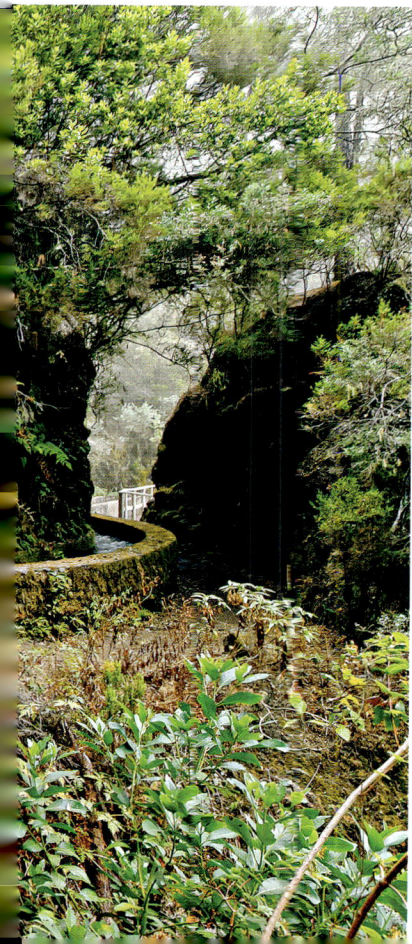

## Water through the centuries

The collection, storage and distribution of water in the Canaries has varied over the centuries.

The indigenous population, not large, could depend on rainwater collected in basins or springs on the hillsides.

With the coming of the Spanish conquerors, much more water was needed, both for the populace and for agriculture.

From the late 1800s to the mid-1900s most of this precious resource was in private hands: it was needed for the sugar cane planations and the other mills — as well as for crops like bananas and tomatoes being grown for export. Water was linked to the land: if land was sold, the water rights went with the sale.

These years saw the introduction of the *galerías* (see page 119), reservoirs (see page 97) and the *acequías* (watercourses) like the one shown at the left, to carry water from mountain springs to the lowlands.

These watercourses are like trees: the main channel is the trunk, while branches off the main trunk get are ever more narrow. Controlled by sluice gates, water is diverted to each proprietor by *acequieros*, who also carry out maintenance work.

By the turn of the 21st century, especially in view of climate change, new methods of collection are needed. Piping is one answer, desalination another. A fairer method of distribution has been put in place, but some people are worried that the great heritage of these beautiful island reservoirs and open-air *acequías* will be lost forever.

## Walk 38: RUTA DE LOS VOLCANES

*Important: At press date, this walk was not possible because of the eruptions on Cumbre Vieja in the last months of 2021.* So we have been unable to rewalk it for this edition and report on any changes — or describe any of the 'sights' that will have come about as the result of the upheavals. But we've kept the hike in this book because it is one of the *classics;* like Walk 39, it simply *has* to be in any 'top' selection of La Palma walks.

**Map begins below, ends overleaf**
**Distance/time:** 18km/11.3mi; 6h10min

**Grade:** ●: strenuous, with an ascent of 700m/2300ft and descent of 1400m/4600ft. The walk is also very long, and much of it crosses volcanic gravel. Recommended only in fine weather: when the Cumbre Vieja is under cloud or mist, it's very easy to stray off the path, and *this could be dangerous.*

Can be cold and very windy. You must be sure-footed and have a head for heights. Red and white GR131 waymarking; some green and white SL waymarking
**Equipment:** walking boots, sunhat, sunglasses, suncream, raingear, fleece, windcheat, picnic, plenty of water
**Refreshments:** snacks at the Refugio El Pilar, bar/restaurants in Los Canarios
**Transport:** 🚕 taxi or with friends to the Refugio El Pilar (28° 36.845'N, 17° 50.191'W). Return on 🚌201 from Los Canarios to Santa Cruz; journey time 45min or 🚌210 to Los Llanos; journey time 30min
***Shorter walk: El Pilar — Volcán Deseada — El Pilar*** (●: 13km/ 8.1mi; 3h50min). Grade, equipment and access as main walk. Follow the main walk to ❺ (the 2h15min-point) and return the same way.

Here's a walk to rival Tenerife's Cañadas or Lanzarote's Timanfaya. You go from one volcano to another, and each is more impressive than the last. Magnificent views lure you on, surround you, and trail behind you. By the time you reach Los Canarios, you'll have seen enough volcanoes to last a lifetime.

**The walk starts** by the VISITORS' CENTRE in the **Refugio El Pilar** picnic area (●). Some 50m/yds beyond (south of) this building, turn right on a path opposite a WATER TANK (signpost: 'LOS CANARIOS, GR131'). A steep ascent up through a pine wood follows.

Under 10 minutes uphill, at a fork, keep right. Soon you're following a well-manicured path around the steep slopes of a volcano. Leaving the pines, a fine panorama unfolds at a *mirador* with a signboard (❶; **15min**): the hillsides slide down into the pine-studded basin

*Climbing above the Refugio El Pilar at the start of the walk*

cradling the Llano del Table. Beyond these dark sands lie grassy fields, below the walls of the crater and the *cumbre*. El Paso spreads around the tail of a lava tongue, and Los Llanos is swallowed up amidst banana plantations.

Walk round the hillside, ignoring any paths ascending to the left. Descend to a TRACK (**45min**; SIGNPOST). Turn left uphill, ignoring some minor tracks and paths. Then, after 15 minutes, turn right on a wide path (initially flanked by stone walls: SIGNPOST), into a 'rock garden' of *cedeso (Adeno-carpus)* and chrysanthemums.

Cross a WOODEN BRIDGE (**❷**; **1h20min**) and, a good five minutes later, ignore two signposted paths to the left. After another 10 minutes' climbing, you reach a jagged-edged crater on the right — **Hoyo Negro** (**❸**; 'black hollow'), looking exactly like its name. Ten minutes later, you're peering down into a lava lake, the **Cráter del Duraznero** (**❹**; **1h55min**). Descend to the right of this cone and, after a few minutes, at a fork, turn left uphill. (You will rejoin the right-hand fork further on.)

Just below the edge of the brilliantly-coloured **Volcán Deseada** (**❺**; **2h15min**), the path forks to encircle it. Take the right fork. A minute later the crater tumbles away below you. Stay on the higher path halfway round the crater. A twin crater, to the left of the main one, emanates equally striking pastel hues — orange, pink, yellow and cream. (*The Shorter walk returns from here.*)

Leaving Deseada, you mount a neck of ridge, and ascend to yet another crater (**2h35min**). There are several paths to the rim of the crater — any one will do. This crater offers a spectacular view

along the volcanic spine of its dark naked slopes. Swifts by the score whistle past. Bearing round to the right, you pass a CONCRETE POST. Just below the post, you rejoin the path that forked right just beyond El Duraznero. Continue straight downhill here. Leaving a shallow basin (SIGNPOST), you cross a low crest. At a signposted crossroads of paths (WATER TAP 20m to the right; **❶**) carry straight on. Entering a long shallow valley (**3h10min**), head across the sand and continue straight downhill (SIGNPOST); the odd survey post and stones intermittently line the path.

Soon (**3h45min**) the best views of the hike unfold by an INFORMATION BOARD. The sea appears just over the edge of the sandy volcanic slopes, with the reddish-pink cone of Volcán Martín stealing the show. Luminous green pines dot the immediate hillsides. Within 10 minutes, at a major fork on the slopes of **Volcán Martín** (**❻**; **4h**; SIGNPOST), turn left. Turn left again at the fork that follows immediately. A minute downhill you're looking straight down into Volcán Martín, its rim ablaze with hues of mauve, cream and orange. Opposite, you can see a spring in a cave beside the crater floor. This is your last volcano, I promise.

Return to the forks and take the second left. (Or, if you're a glutton for punishment, take the first left, to ascend the crater rim and take in the extravaganza of volcanic shades shown overleaf — as well as a fine view over the southern tip of the island. Allow an extra 15 minutes for this.) Continuing, just head straight down, ploughing through the fine gravel — great fun.

Just below Volcán Martín turn right at a fork, *leaving* the main

GR131 path for the well-trodden SL LP 111 path with green and white waymarking (**7**; signpost: 'FUENTE DEL TIÓN'). When you reach a TRACK (**4h35min**), cross it (signpost: 'LOS CANARIOS POR PISTA'). Then descend for a few minutes, to a junction (SIGNPOST).

**The Cumbre Vieja eruption**
As we were putting this book together in September 2021, Cumbre Vieja began erupting, a catastrophe lasting just two months. This has turned out to be the most costly eruption in the recorded history of the islands — despite the fact that Lanzarote's 18th century eruptions lasted on and off for six years.

Although no lives were lost, some 3000 buildings were destroyed and 7000 people displaced — 8% of the population. Perhaps even worse are the livelihoods interrupted: the LP2 main road has been cut and won't be ready for repairs for about a year (until the lava cools down), cutting off convenient tourist access to the island's best beaches, and over 3000 acres of the island's most fertile banana fields have been buried.

*Photo: the extravaganza of volcanic hues on the rim of Volcán Martín*

Take the track opposite and, from now on, just follow the signs for 'LOS CANARIOS' — going right at a fork after about 30 minutes (signpost: 'LOS ARREBOLES, FUENCALIENTE'). (After about 55 minutes the track crosses the original GR131 footpath to Los Canarios. If you decide to take this short-cut (**b**), turn right here. After three minutes cross another footpath and after another few minutes cross the track, to continue along the path, rejoining the main walk.)

Attention is needed around an hour down the main track (**5h40min**), when you are circling to the right of a vineyard. Just before it, ignore a minor turn-off left. After a few minutes a track joins you from the left. Ignore the signposted path to the right, and continue on the track towards Los Canarios. A few minutes later, keep an eye out for a WATER TANK on the right. Some 30m past the tank, turn left on a path (**8**; signpost: 'GR131') and follow it straight downhill, picking up red and white waymarking again.

On reaching a road, follow it to the left (SIGNPOST). Soon you pass a basin with pines and see a sports field in the distance. When the road veers right, take the path to the left (SIGNPOST). Los Canarios comes into sight just below, through the trees. On meeting the road again, cross it and continue on the path (SIGNPOST). Emerging on a street in **Los Canarios** (**6h05min**), follow it 100m downhill to the MAIN ROAD. Turn left and walk past Bar Parada (where Walk 40 begins). The BUS STOP is just three minutes further on; a bus shelter is opposite (**9**; **6h10min**).

**Distance/time:** 12.5km/7.8mi; 5h
**Grade:** ⬤❗ long and quite strenuous — basically a descent of 850m/2790ft. Accessible to all fit walkers who are sure-footed and have a head for heights. *Don't attempt in bad or windy weather, or after heavy rain:* conditions change every year in the *barranco* after heavy rain, with a danger of rockfall or (very rarely) flash flooding. The going also depends on how much water is in the *barranco*, making the walk easier (usually in summer) or more difficult (usually in winter). Other hints: It can be very cool: be prepared! And don't lean on any handrails: they may be loose. PR LP13 signposting; yellow/white waymarking
*Important notes:* (a) This walk may be closed if wind brings toxic air from Cumbre Vieja's eruption. (b) Permission is needed from the Parques Nacionales if you wish to stay in the national park overnight (obtain this at the Visitors' Centre on the LP3, book online at www.reservasparquesnacionales.es), or

telephone 922-922280. You may camp *only* at the designated site. (c) *Please do not follow the watercourses in this crater, as suggested in some books: they are too dangerous.*
**Equipment:** walking boots, sunhat, sunglasses, suncream, raingear, long-sleeved shirt, long trousers, fleece, warm jacket, gloves, swimwear, picnic, water, walking pole(s). It's a good idea to leave a dry pair of shoes, socks and trousers in your car or backpack, especially in the winter, in case you slip while crossing the river!
**Refreshments:** nothing en route; take a picnic and high-energy food!
**Transport:** 🚌 car or taxi to/from the parking area in the floor of the Barranco de las Angustias (28° 41.137'N, 17° 54.586'W), then 🚍 jeep taxi to Los Brecitos (they wait here for walkers; shared cost is about €15 per person). The taxis only operate from 08.00-13.00 in summer, 08.00-12.00 in winter.
**Detour: Cascada de los Colores** (from ❼; this adds 30min return; see page 168.

---

The Caldera de Taburiente *is* La Palma. If you don't spend at least a day in it, you haven't really seen the island. Streams tumble down from every *barranco*; indeed, these streams formed the *caldera* (cauldron), which at first was thought to be volcanic. Some nine kilometres (six miles) across at its widest point, and 2000 metres (over a mile) deep, Taburiente is one of the largest craters in the world to be formed by erosion. Recent studies, however, shy away from the volcanic crater theory, claiming it to be a massive landslide instead. It's one of La Palma's three natural wonders — the other two being the Ruta de los Volcanes (Walk 38) and Los Tilos (Walk 36).

**The walk starts** at the car park in **Los Brecitos** (⬤); descend the path by a large NATIONAL PARK SIGNBOARD, pass through a turnstile, and head down into the *caldera*. Follow the path signposted 'ZONA DE ACAMPADA',

ignoring all turn-offs. Hillsides tumble away below, and the rocky crater walls tower overhead, with pines clinging to the sheer slopes. *The pine needles can be very slippery underfoot!* You cross a number of small *barrancos*, some with

163

streams. The prominent peak rising out of the *caldera* wall opposite is Pico Bejenado.

A large boulder marks your crossing of the **Barranco de las Traves** (**❶**; **35min**). More boulders begin appearing on the hillsides. The next ravine, the **Barranco de las Piedras Redondas** ('ravine of round rocks'), is well-named. The **Mirador del Lomo de Tagasaste** (**❷**), from where you have a good view into the centre of the crater, follows. The deeply-gouged ravine of the **Barranco de Bombas de Agua** (**❸**; **1h15min**) will either impress you or terrify you, or both, as you continue along the path! Erosion here eats away at least a couple of feet from the *barranco* walls every year.

You finally arrive at the floor of the **Río Taburiente** at a wide basin known as **Playa de Taburiente** (**❹**; **1h25min**). Here you're enveloped by grand scenery. Small clumps of cool, shady Canary willow (*Salix canariensis*) stretch along the wide stony *playa*, where you can paddle in smaller or larger pools with crystal-clear water.

To continue to the camping site, cross the river, hopping over boulders and stones, and look out for a gap in the willows on your right approximately 50m/yds downstream (*SIGNPOST; WAYMARK*), to locate the path that ascends the eastern bank of the river to the *CAMPSITE* above (**❺**; **1h30min**). There is an attractive stone-built services centre here (information and toilets).

Keep to the left of the buildings (*SIGNPOST*); follow a wide path over to the edge of a cliff with a wonderful view straight down to the Río Taburiente. The path continues over a col and soon

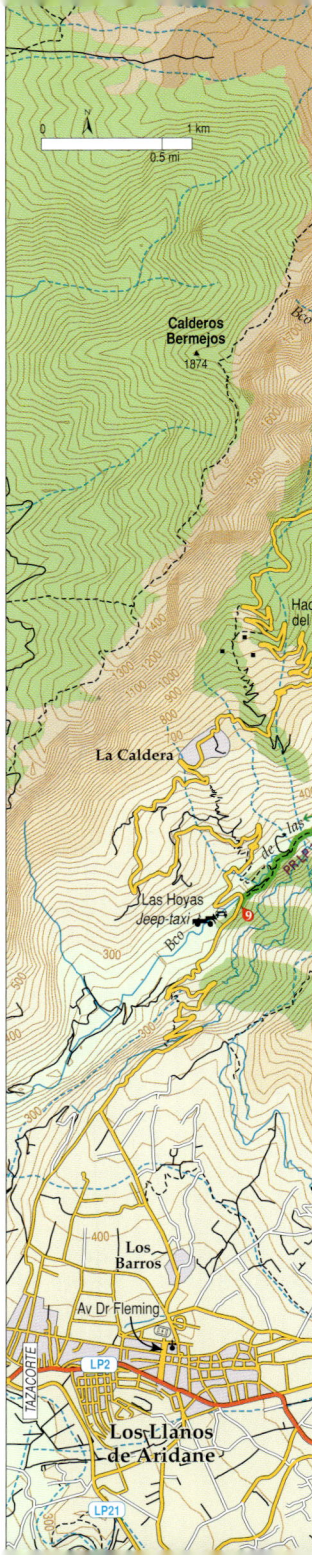

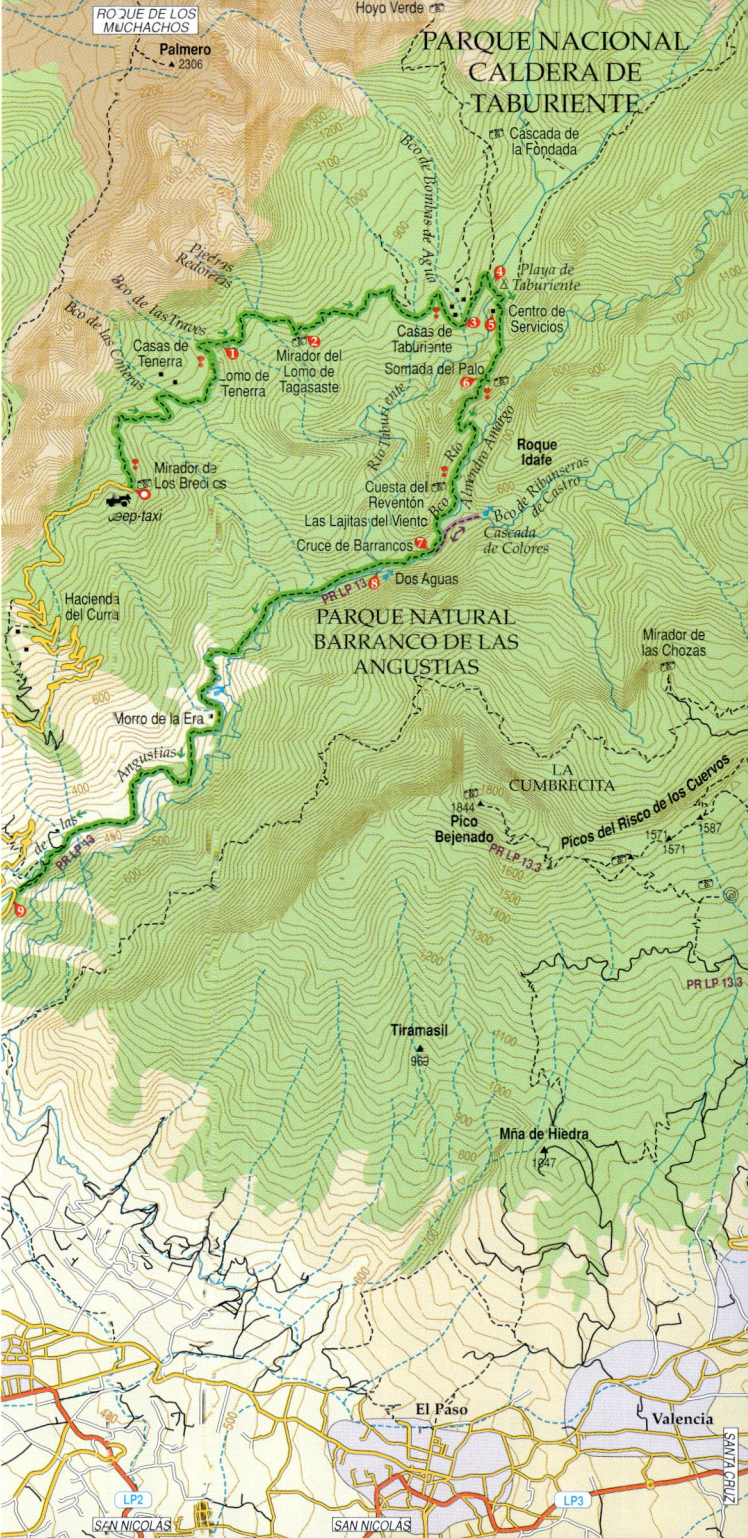

ROQUE DE LOS MUCHACHOS

Hoyo Verde

Palmero
▲ 2306

PARQUE NACIONAL
CALDERA DE
TABURIENTE

Cascada de
la Fondada

Piedras
Redondas

Bco. de Bombas de Agua

Bco. de las Traves

Bco. de las Cuevas

Playa de
Taburiente **4**

Casas de Tenerra

Mirador del
Lomo de
Tagasaste

Lomo de
Tenerra

**1**

**2**

Casas de
Taburiente

**3** **5**

Centro de
Servicios

Somada del Palo

**6**

Mirador de
Los Brecitos

Roque
Idafe

Ría Taburiente

Río

Bco. Almendro Amargo

jeep-taxi

Cuesta del
Reventón

Las Lajitas del Viento

Cruce de Barrancos **7**

Bco. de Ribanceras de Castro

Cascada
de Colores

Hacienda
del Cura

PR LP 13

**8** Dos Aguas

PARQUE NATURAL
BARRANCO DE LAS
ANGUSTIAS

Mirador de
las Chozas

Morro de la Era

Angustias

LA
CUMBRECITA

1800

1844
Pico
Bejenado

PR LP 13.3

Picos del Risco de los Cuervos

1571
1587
1571

PR LP 13

600

500

400

1600

1500

1400

1300

1200

PR LP 13.3

Tiramasil
▲ 969

1100

1000

800

Mña de Hiedra
▲ 1247

El Paso

Valencia

SANTA CRUZ

LP2

LP3

SAN NICOLÁS

SAN NICOLÁS

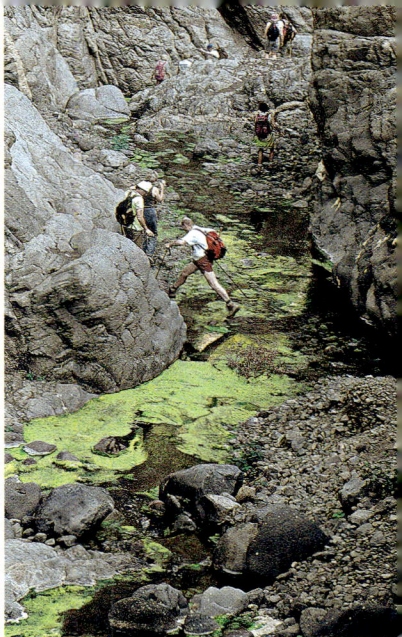

*Right: boulder-hopping in the Barranco de las Angustias, not far from Morro de la Era; left: not far below Dos Aguas*

Roque Idafe comes into sight, a prominent finger of rock balancing on the end of a ridge.

The **Somada del Palo** (**6**; **1h45min**), a signposted viewpoint on a nose of hillside jutting out into the plunging **Barranco del Río Almendro Amargo** ('bitter almond'), provides a fine perch over the river and equally good views back up to the heights of the crater. After about 30 minutes' descent on the partly-cobbled, winding path, look back up the *barranco* for a good view of a wall spanning the ravine. At the fork that follows five minutes later, keep right. A few minutes later the path that branched off to the left rejoins your route at **Las Lajitas del Viento**. Continue downhill.

Another signpost (**7**; 'LAS ANGUSTIAS/ZONA DE ACAMPADA'; **2h25min**), marks the confluence of two streams, the **Cruce de Barrancos**. *(The detour heads into the river here, to the 'Cascada de Colores'; see overleaf.)* The main walk keeps right; continue along the path, reaching the river bed in five minutes. There is usually a fair amount of water here all year round, as no water is collected at this point. Hop across as best you can, hoping to keep dry!

Soon you arrive at **Dos Aguas** (**8**; **2h40min**), the confluence of the Almendro Amargo and Taburiente gorges. There is a giant grate on the left here, to collect debris from the river where it flows into a *canal*. Cross the **Río Taburiente**, then pick up the continuing path (at the left of a low concrete wall built across the **Barranco de las Angustias**; signpost: 'BARRANCO DE LAS

ANGUSTIAS, SALIDA'). Continue downstream along this *barranco*.

The time spent in the *barranco* greatly depends on your agility, as you scramble over rocks and jump across the river. Depending on the amount of water the river carries, you may have to leave the stream bed several times. All seven diversions are signposted with green boards, but the signs are rather high up the ravine walls and easily missed. The first detour, to the left, is just after a large pipe crosses the *barranco* above your head (at about **3h10min**). The second comes up about five minutes later, also on the left-hand wall. The third is also on the left. The fourth is on the *right-hand* wall. (Of course it is usually possible to stay in the bed of the *barranco*, getting your feet wet!)

Eventually you arrive at **Morro de la Era**, a derelict stone building (**3h50min**). After returning to the *barranco* for five minutes, there's another detour up the left wall, then you descend once more to the

167

### The Cascada de Colores

The orange-yellow rocks at the Cascada de Colores owe their colour to the iron content in the river (clearly visible in the photo below). But the green algae and mosses contribute to the overall effect, as does the black of the volcanic rock. The intensity of the colour is seasonal: it depends on the amount of water!

To get there, keep left in the Barranco de Ribanseras. You will have to cross this stream several times on loose, slippery rocks; the last two minutes are especially awkward and need care. Remember that conditions in the *barranco* change every winter, and you may have to paddle or clamber over landslides to get to the waterfall.

In 15 minutes you should arrive at the 'coloured falls', a brilliant sight. Then return to the Cruce de Barrancos.

*barranco* bed (**4h15min**). Before crossing the stream again from here, head *upstream* for two minutes, to a delightful pool and cascade hidden in a rocky corridor under a natural rock arch — most hikers miss this spot. After a sixth detour up the right wall, continue in the stream bed, which eventually dries up (in summer). A seventh detour is to the left just before the car park, but it is not usually necessary to follow this one. When you arrive at the main track your car will be in the PARKING AREA a couple of minutes along to the left (**9**; **5h**).

*Looking up the Barranco de Ribanseras del Castro from just below its confluence with the Río Almendro Amargo — the Cruce de Barrancos*

**Distance/time**: 8km/5mi; 1h50min
(16km/10mi; 4h20min if you
return the same way)
**Grade**: ◉ moderate, with a
descent of 700m/2300ft on gravel
slopes (steep and stony in places).
You must be sure-footed and have
a head for heights, but this walk is
*recommended for everyone* (there is
only one very short stretch that
might prove unnerving for those
who suffer from vertigo). It is
usually very windy here, especially
around the volcanoes. *Do not try to
ascend to the rim of the Volcán de
Teneguía in strong winds!* (when
the authorities will close the path
in any case). Red and white GR131
waymarking for most of the way
*Note:* There is a pay booth at the
Volcán de San Antonio, €5 entry
fee per person; some walkers avoid
this by going straight onto the
signposted path on the right,
100m before the pay booth. If you
avoid the pay booth, you will not
be able to ascend to the crater rim.
**Equipment**: walking boots,
walking pole(s), sunhat, sunglasses,
suncream, long trousers, fleece,
windcheat, raingear, swimwear,
picnic, plenty of water

**Refreshments**: restaurants in Los
Canarios and at the Faro
**Transport**: 🚐210 from Los
Llanos to the 'Fuencaliente' bus
stop in Los Canarios; journey time
30min or 🚐200 or 201 from
Santa Cruz; journey time 45min.
Return on 🚐23 from El Faro to
Los Canarios; journey time
30min, then change to 🚐210 to
Los Llanos or 🚐200 or 201 to
Santa Cruz as above
**Shorter walk**: *Volcán de San
Antonio — Roque Teneguía —
Volcán de Teneguía — Volcán de
San Antonio* (6km/3.5mi;
1h40min). ● Easy, but there is a
stiff climb of 200m/650ft at the
end. Equipment as above, but
stout shoes will suffice. Access by
🚗: park at the Volcán de San
Antonio. To get there, leave Los
Canarios on the Las Indias road
and, just past the last houses, turn
left on a gravel track to the car
park (28° 29.222'N, 17° 50.904'W),
where a fee is payable. Follow the
main walk from ❶ (the pay booth
just before the 10min-point) to the
1h05min-point at the edge of the
Volcán de Teneguía (❺), then
return the same way.

**T**he Volcán de Teneguía is one of the most colourful
volcanoes on La Palma, and the combination of striking
coastal scenery and intriguing volcanic landscape make this
a 'not to be missed' hike. The walk ends at Faro de Fuencaliente, a working fishing hamlet with a popular restaurant.

**Begin the walk** at **Bar Parada** in
**Los Canarios** (◯), 200m/yds west
of the 'Fuencaliente' *BUS STOP* on
the main LP2 road. Walk down the
narrow street opposite the bar. Go
through a junction and reach the
*LAS INDIAS ROAD*. Follow this to
the right downhill and, after 100m
fork right on a road, the *CALLE DE*

*LOS VOLCANES*. You pass a housing
estate on the right. Descending,
you look straight onto the dark,
flat-topped Volcán de San Antonio.
Cross the Las Indias road again
and head straight on for the crater.
There is a *PAY BOOTH* (❶); the
entry fee allows you to walk on the
rim of the crater and visit the

*Above: descending to the lighthouse; left: at the beach*

centre with a film about the Volcán San Antonio and Teneguía's eruption in 1971. There is also a good exhibition about vulcanism world-wide, so it's well worth a visit. (*The Short walk starts here.*)

Go through the VISITORS' CENTRE and onto the path at the right-hand side of the volcano (**10min**). A spectacular view opens up across hillside vineyards to Las Indias on your right; the sheer slopes of the western escarpment fill the backdrop, and you can see Puerto Naos, a handful of buildings backing onto what was once a sea-flat of banana plantations, and now is buried in lava (see the panel on page 162). The crater rim is narrow in places, and some people may find a short stretch vertiginous. Roque Teneguía is the yellow rock jutting out of the hillside below. The southern coast unfolds, with El Faro sitting near the southernmost tip, by glaring-white salt pans. But it's the magically-coloured Volcán de Teneguía that

holds your gaze. It used to be possible to circle the whole of the **Volcán de San Antonio** CRATER (❷) on this path, but today it has been closed off halfway round for conservation reasons, so you will have to retrace your steps.

Return to the VISITORS' CENTRE, pass the pay booth and after 100m turn left on a path (❸; signpost: 'FARO DE FUENCALIENTE, GR131'). A steep, gravelly and dusty descent brings you down to a track: turn left. Rounding the slopes, you look down on Roque Teneguía. Banana plantations and greenhouses vie to smother the coastal flat. Barely five minutes along the track, fork right on a clear path down to **Roque Teneguía** (❹; **50min**). Although not large, this hunk of rock is a prominent landmark and a good viewpoint. While you are here, look out for petroglyphs; there are several of them on the sloping side of the rock, but they are quite faded. A barrier prevents visitors from clambering over this fragile

171

*Photo: Roque Teneguía*

rock and damaging the petroglyphs even more.

To continue, take the stone-marked path opposite the rock for less than a minute, climb down into a gully and walk down until you reach the *canal*. Turn left along the *canal*. Shiny-leafed *vinagrera* (of the dock family) flourishes here. After a few minutes, descend to a track seen below (at the left of a large WATER TANK) and follow it to the left, to where it joins the end of a track by a residents' parking area. Then take a path off right, to the EDGE OF THE **Volcán de Teneguía** (**5**; **1h05min**).

(A path ascends to the left-hand RIM (**a**) of this spectacularly coloured crater. It's a stupendous climb, *but narrow, vertiginous and very dangerous in a strong wind*. If it's calm and you make this ascent, add 20 minutes. Inside the crater, holes in the left-hand wall emit hot gases.)

The main walk continues by going back towards the parking area but, shortly before it, fork right on the continuing GR131, down into the lava. Keep between Teneguía and its offspring (a baby volcano) on the left. A clear stone-lined path soon leads you to a junction, where you turn right. Within minutes, at another junction, turn right again on a cleared path through an intriguing lava stream. The twisted and jagged rock here is spellbinding.

Out of the lava stream, your path crosses smooth rolling slopes. As you mount a crest, the pink-tinted salt pans and the lighthouse appear not far below. On arriving at the ROAD TO THE LIGHTHOUSE (**6**; **1h35min**; SIGNPOST), turn right for 100m, then pick up the continuation of your path on the left (SIGNPOST). A few minutes later cross the road again (SIGNPOST). Close to the edge of the cliffs, you look out over Playa Nueva, embraced by a lava flow.

Cross the road once more and descend to the tiny fishing hamlet of **Faro de Fuencaliente** (**7**; **1h50min**). It's a desolate yet striking spot. Parched, windswept and covered in dust, you're just in the mood for a dip, then a cool beer and a reviving meal in the themed restaurant 'Jardin de la sal' right in the middle of the salt pans. There's a small but interesting MARINE RESERVE VISITORS' CENTRE here, too, in the old lighthouse (€2 entry fee at time of writing). There's a bus back to the village and a sign with the local taxi telephone number. Or allow 2h45min to return on foot.

**Distance:** 8km/5mi: 2h35min (2h05min for motorists)
**Grade:** 🔴🔵 relatively easy, with a descent of 400m/1300ft and ascent of 300m/1000ft. You must be sure-footed and have a head for heights. Not recommended in wet weather. Red/white GR130 waymarking, also some local signposts
**Equipment:** walking boots, sun-hat, sunglasses, suncream, fleece, picnic, plenty of water

**Refreshments:** café in Las Tricias
**Transport:** 🚌120 from Barlo-vento to the 'Las Rosas' bus stop at the turn-off for the El Fayal *zona recreativa* just before Puntagorda; journey time 1h25min or 🚌110 from Los Llanos to the El Fayal turn-off; journey time 55min. Return on 🚌120 from Las Tricias to Barlovento or Puntagorda. Or 🚗 to Las Tricias (28° 46.827'N, 17° 57.780'W).

L as Tricias is known for two groups of residents — arboreal (the unique assembly of dragon trees) and human (the transient 'alternative life-stylers'). Both have become note-worthy curiosities in themselves, attracting tourists in droves. To avoid the crush, finish this walk before midday, and you'll be able to share the sights with just a few other people.

**Begin the walk** from the 'Las Rosas' BUS STOP at the turn-off for El Fayal (🔴): continue northeast along the road towards Las Tricias. The surrounding slopes are wooded in Canary pines. Three minutes along, you'll see an INFORMATION BOARD and GR signposting for SANTO DOMINGO at the side of the road and a small white SHRINE below you, on the edge of the Barranco de Izcagua. Take the path down past the shrine and into the *barranco* (sign: 'LAS TRICIAS'). The path sidles down the sheer escarpment, where some guard rails lend psychological support *(but don't lean on them!)*. A stand of pine trees fills the valley floor. Ten minutes down, the way swings left and enters the bed of the **Barranco de Izcagua**. Five metres further on, the path leaves it again, to ascend the right-hand bank.

Mount the crest, greeted by a grove of almond trees. Continuing along the edge of the *barranco*, pass through a gate (please leave it as you find it) and ignore a few

entrances to fields on the right (**25min**). A minute later, on joining a concrete lane, turn left (signpost: 'EL FAYAL, PUNTAGORDA, GR130, CAMINO REAL DE LA COSTA'). Some 20m/yds downhill, turn right on a track (**❶**; signpost: 'LAS BURACAS, ST DOMINGO'). When this track ends, the old path becomes your way again, lined at the left by small country dwellings. Crossing a small *barranco*, you gain a first view of some large dragon trees on the hillside above. This scattered little quarter of **Las Tricias** retains much of its original character. As you pass between some old homes with traditional high windows, chickens and cats scatter in all directions.

Emerging from the houses, you descend to the *LAS TRICIAS ROAD* (**❷**; *SIGNPOST*; **40min**), below the village centre. Cross a smaller road going left here and make your way down the main road to the right. Some 400m (a little over five minutes) down the road, just before it curves to the right, take the first cobbled trail on the left

173

(signpost: LAS BURACAS). It passes between two houses, and you come onto a track. Two minutes down the track, you pass through an intersection, and asphalt comes under foot. Just past the first house on the right, take the cobbled path descending to the right (signpost: 'RT TRAVIESA'). A minute down, opposite a house named LA CASA BLANCA, rejoin the road and follow it downhill for about 80m. At this point, just after the road bends right, turn left on a track running along the edge of Barranco de Izcagua, *ignoring* for the present the signposted GR path (❸) at the very beginning of this track (it is the return route). The track quickly peters out into a narrow path. Keeping straight down, pass rustic cottages set amidst colourful gardens and fruit trees. Although the hillsides are cultivated, they have a dishevelled appearance. More dragon trees appear.

Reach the ROAD (❹) and turn left, making for an old windmill standing on the hilltop ahead, by following the road to the left, then ascending a chained-off track on the right. The WINDMILL (❺; **1h05min**) has an adjacent museum dedicated to *gofio*, which certainly merits a visit (see panel on page 136). A good vista awaits you as well: the ridges flatten out on their descent before finally dropping into the sea. The ridge to the north is the refuge for the island's biggest concentration of dragon trees. Humble cottages lean up against the rocky ridge.

From here return the short way to the road junction where you turned left to visit the mill (❹).

*The windmill and museum at Las Tricias, where you can learn about* gofio *and its importance to the Canarian diet*

Turn left and follow this road for some 200m, to regain the cobbled GR path (❻; SIGNPOST). Turn left, cross a track in a couple of minutes, and descend past some superb dragon trees. Follow the beautifully cobbled path as it descends the crest of the ridge and takes you past more dragon trees.

Your next stop is the Buracas Caves, soon to be seen in the far wall of the *barranco* to the right. A good ten minutes down the ridge on this manicured path (ignoring turn-offs), you pass some low cottage rooftops on your left. At a T-JUNCTION (❼) 50m further on (signpost: 'BIO CAFÉ FINCA ALOE'), turn right and round the wall of the *barranco*. At the next junction, near this café-bar (which offers lovely light refreshments and health food), go right again.

In a few minutes you're standing in front of the **Cuevas de Buracas** (❽; **1h30min**). The main cave is really just an overhang of rock. It's not much to look at, but a short way up the path beyond it there are a few more (equally

unspectacular) caves, and some rocks marked with petroglyphs.

Now return to the ridge and ascend it, keeping to the crest. In 25 minutes you reach a track (SIGN-POST). Cross it (and the adjacent *canal*) and continue up a cobbled path. You cross a road a minute later — back at ⑥ (SIGNPOST). Heading up through almond trees,

you walk under a massive dragon tree. Joining another track, turn 3m left to the road and follow this back up to LA CASA BLANCA, now on your right.

Ascend the cobbled path opposite, and return along your outward route. Once back on the LAS TRICIAS ROAD (**2h15min**), follow it uphill for five minutes

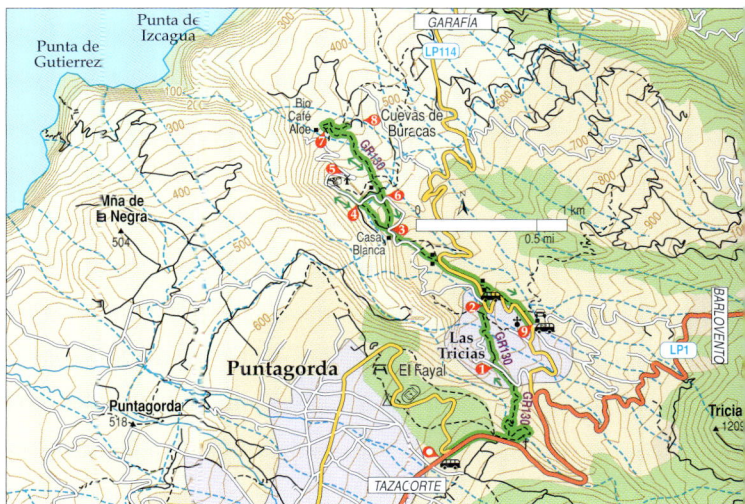

**Dragon tree (Dracaena draco)**

The dragon trees at Las Tricias comprise the greatest concentration of this almost extinct Macronesian endemic in the Canaries.

Because they don't have growth rings, their age is generally judged from their flowering periods (every 14 to 15 years): this is when new branches are formed. But this method of dating seems quite haphazard; the most famous *draco* in the Canaries, the so-called 'millennial' dragon tree at Icod de los Vinos on Tenerife, has been judged to be anywhere between 400 and 1000 years old…

The tree takes its name from mythology, from the Greek *drakón* (dragon or snake). Indeed, there are a host of myths and legends associated with the dragon tree.

What is *known* is that the Guanches used the wood, bark and leaves. But they prized it most for the 'magical' properties of its blood-red sap, which they even used to mumify their dead.

The Spanish conquerors learned from the Guanches of the sap's many medicinal uses, and it became a prized remedy through-out Europe. So it is possible that all the 'bleeding' of these already-scarce trees for their resin — making deep cuts which allowed insect lavae to infest the wood — contributed to their further decline. They are protected today.

(300m), until you see a concrete lane ascending between two houses on your left (the house on the right is called 'Casa de Café'). At this point you are 100m short of where you first joined the main road at ❷. Just ahead is a bus stop called 'Entrada Buracas'. But I prefer to catch the bus up by the church and shop (where motorists will have left their cars). To get there, climb this concrete lane and rejoin the road. Some 100m up the road, turn left up another concrete lane, possibly with a couple of crabby little dogs at your heels. Then follow the main road to the left for 180m, up to the church, shop/bar and BUS STOP (❾; **2h35min**) in **Las Tricias**.

## Walk 42: FROM PICO DE LA NIEVE TO THE NATIONAL PARK VISITORS' CENTRE

**Distance/time:** 16.5km/10.2mi; 5h45min

**Grade:** ●● moderate but long, with an initial ascent of 350m/1150ft and a descent of 1400m/4600ft. Accessible to all sturdy hill walkers who are sure-footed and have a head for heights, but only suitable in fine weather. Avoid on very windy days. At times the path may be overgrown with *codeso*. Both yellow/white (PR LP 3) and red/white (GR131) waymarking

*Important: Weather conditions can change rapidly; be prepared! If cloud descends, utmost care is needed, as the walk edges the rim of the crater for much of the way.*

**Equipment:** walking boots, sunhat (and something to tie it on with!), sunglasses, suncream, long-sleeved shirt, long trousers, fleece, warm jacket, gloves, raingear, picnic, plenty of water

**Refreshments:** none en route — pack a picnic/high-energy snacks

**Transport:** 🚖 taxi to the Pico de la Nieve turn-off on the LP4; journey time 35min from Santa Cruz. Return on 🚌 300 from the National Park Visitors' Centre — to Santa Cruz or Los Llanos.

**Short walk: Pico de la Nieve**
(4.7km/3mi; 2h). ● Easy-moderate ascent of 350m/1150ft. Equipment and access as main walk or 🚙 *(4x4 only!)* to a parking area at the end of the track to Pico de la Nieve (28° 43.974'N, 17° 49.739'W) — saves 100m/330ft; 20min of climbing). Follow the main walk from ❶ to the 1h15min-point (❺), then turn left. Ten minutes later rejoin your outgoing path at ❷ and turn right downhill, back to ❶.

**Alternative walk 1: Refugio de la Punta de los Roques from the Ermita de la Virgen del Pino**
(17km/10.5mi; 6h10min). ●● Very strenuous, with an ascent of 1150m/3770ft. Only suitable in fine weather. Equipment as main walk. Access by 🚗: park at the Ermita Virgen del Pino, north of the Visitors' Centre (28° 39.773'N, 17° 50.506W). Or 🚌 300 to/from the National Park Visitors' Centre; journey time from Santa Cruz 25min; add 30min *each way*). Referring to the map on page 183, follow the main walk in reverse to ❼; return the same way.

**Alternative walk 2:** see page 185 and the map on page 186.

---

I consider this one of the top walks in the Canaries. Circling the Caldera de Taburiente, often on its very rim, spectacular views unfold. On the descent, your outlook sweeps across the plain of Los Llanos, over the volcanoes of El Pilar, and along the *cumbre*. If you're reasonably fit, this is *one walk you've got to do!* And the good news is that a taxi or friends with a hired car will do most of the climbing for you.

**Start out** at the PICO DE LA NIEVE TURN-OFF on the LP4 (●). Walk up the road for 10m/yds, then take the hillside path on the left (sign-post: 'PICO LA NIEVE, PR LP 3'). After a couple of minutes, the path swings back left, then climbs a gentle slope and widens out. Cairns mark the way through a typical Canary pine forest — spacious and with a floor clear of scrub. The path takes you to a CAR PARK (*where the Short walk can begin and end;* ❶; **20min**) and continues uphill for another 15 minutes; here you turn right on the path to the

177

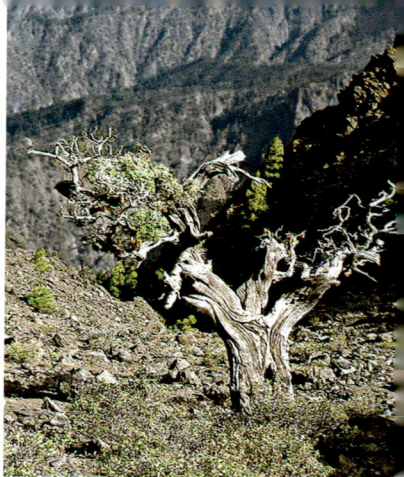

summit (**2**; *SIGNPOST*). Your view stretches across the forested shoulders of the *cumbre* — on clear days to Tenerife and La Gomera in the distance. Santa Cruz sits far below.

Approaching the edge of the crater, turn right uphill on the GR131 (**3**; signpost: '*ROQUE DE*

LOS MUCHACHOS'). (Ignore signposting for the Refugio del Pilar to the left.) At the next fork, keep left (the right-hand fork leads to Roque de los Muchachos). From the *SUMMIT OF* **Pico de la Nieve** (**4**; **1h**) a breathtaking view opens before you, of a deep cauldron lined by sheer ridges. The white buildings peeping over the crater walls on the right belong to the observatory.

Return to the first Roque de los Muchachos junction and turn right; turn right again at the next fork (**3**; signpost: *REFUGIO DEL PILAR*). Along this stretch, several short paths branch off right to viewpoints on the edge of the *caldera*. When a path joins from the left (**5**; **1h15min**); follow it to the right. (*But for the Short walk, turn left.*) After a few minutes, you cross the pass of **Degollada del Barranco de la Madera**. Here you'll notice some very colourful rocky outcrops rising out of the crater wall.

A few minutes later you encounter a signposted turn-off left to some petroglyphs (**a**; signpost: '*PETROGLIFO TAGOROR PICO DE LA SABINA*') and, above and to the right, a sign indicating some old corrals. Some 200m

*Striding along the* cumbre *on the descent to the Reventón Pass*

further on the petroglyph detour path rejoins, then you pass a bald gravel mound in hues of mauve, pink, smoky blue, and rusty brown.

The next section of the hike is the most striking. A zig-zag descent leads you down and across another pass—the **Degollada del Río** (**6**; **2h05min**). The ridge here is narrow and slides away on either side of the path. The huge valley to the left is the Barranco de la Hortelana, while to the right the crater just opens into a bottomless abyss. A steep climb follows, up the side of a precipitous jagged crag. Back on the inside of the crater, you pass by the eye-catching weather-beaten *cedro* shown on page 178. Ahead is a magnificent viewpoint. In the depths of this cataclysm of rock, you can see the floor of the Barranco de Taburiente and a corner of the Playa de

Taburiente. Then you round a bend and arrive at the **Refugio de la Punta de los Roques** (**7**; **2h35min**).

Although there is no heating, and fires are prohibited, the shelter may be welcome nonetheless. There are wooden bunks where you can lay out a sleeping bag, and water is available in bottles. The slope falling from the refuge overlooks the extensive open valleys of El Paso and Los Llanos. The big hump of a mountain bordering the *caldera* on the south side is Bejenado, with Cumbre Vieja in the background.

Continuing, pick up the path below the refuge. The route descends the *cumbre*, never straying far from the crest. Ignore a path to the left 10 minutes past **Pico Corralejo** (PR LP 2) and another path five minutes past the sign for **Pico Ovejas** (PR LP 2.1). The western side of the *cumbre* opens up, affording another fine view over Santa Cruz.

The path finally drops down onto the **Pista Cumbre Nueva**. Continue ahead on this wide forestry track. Some 20 minutes later you arrive at **Reventón Pass** (**8**; **4h25min**), where there is a WATER TAP (but outside winter and spring it may well be dry). Fork right downhill here on the PR LP 1 (signpost: 'ERMITA DE LA VIRGEN DEL PINO').

A beautiful old cobbled path leads you down the steep slope, below trees festooned with lichen and beside moss-covered rocks. A basin of small fields lies below. Five minutes down, a path joins from the right. Some 30 minutes down, you descend a splendid 'avenue' of regal Canary pines, some reputedly 400 to 500 years old. A signposted path from La Cumbrecita joins

### Ermita de la Virgen del Pino

Legend has it that during the Conquest, a Spanish soldier found an image of the Virgin in the pine tree shown here. A chapel was built beside it, at a pass where weary travellers on the Camino Real de la Cumbre often chose to rest.

The current chapel dates from 1927. Every three years a festival takes place on the first Sunday in September, when the image is taken down to the town of El Paso.

Although it doesn't look it in the photo, this pine is one of the grandest in the archipelago — 32m/100ft high, with a radius of 120cm/4ft. It is believed to be between 600-800 years old. On its side (not shown here) is a large niche, 2m/6ft high and 50cm/20in wide, in which the original image is thought to have been sheltered.

---

from the right here. Five minutes later you join a faint track leading to the **Ermita de la Virgen del Pino** (**9**; **5h15min**).

The National Park Visitors' Centre is just under half an hour away: follow the road from the chapel and, after 15 minutes, at a junction, turn left. On reaching the LP3, turn left again to the **Visitors' Centre** (**5h45min**). The Santa Cruz bus stops opposite.

### Alternative walk 2: From the Cruce del Refugio to the Visitors' Centre

(16.5km/10mi; 5h20min). ● Strenuous, with an ascent of 620m/2035ft. Equipment as main walk. Access by 🚐 to Cruce del Refugio (Línea 300); journey time from Santa Cruz 25min.

From the junction where you leave the bus at **Cruce del Refugio** (**O**), walk north along the main road for 50m/yds, then turn left on a country road. Referring to the map, follow roads to the

**Map labels:**

LP3021
Aula de la Naturaleza
PR LP 1
Reventón
Pista Reventón
LP302
Barrial
Ermita de la Virgen del Pino
PR LP 1.1
1435
Reventón
GR131
Cumbre
Lomo de los Mestres
SANTA CRUZ
Valencia
Centro de Visitantes
PR LP 1.1
EL PASO LOS LLANOS
PR LP 14
LP3
Cruce del Refugio
CUMBRE NUEVA
Cumbre Nueva
N
0   1 km
0.5 mi
LP301
SL LP 100
SL LP 101
Mña de Enrique
1251
SL LP 102
Mña Quemada
1366
PARQUE NATURAL CUMBRE VIEJA
GR131
Cumbre Nueva
Pista Cumbre
La Pared Vieja
SAN ISIDRO
Llano del Jable
SL LP 103
PR LP 18
1505
LP301
SL LP 103
PR LP 14
LP301
1512
SL LP 104
Refugio El Pilar
3
GR131

---

**Ermita de la Virgen del Pino** (❶; 40min) and then ascend to the **Reventón Pass** (❷; 1h55min). There is a WATER TAP here, but outside winter and spring it may be dry.

Turn right at the pass on the **Pista Cumbre Nueva** and follow the red/white waymarked GR131 either along this track or the path beside it. You look straight across to Pico Birigoyo. PR LP 18 comes in from the left just before the path rejoins the wide track, and you reach the LP301 road. Turning right, you soon come to the **Refugio El Pilar** (❸; 3h35min).

To end the walk, use the map above. Highlights on the descent are the Llano del Jable and Montaña Quemada, before you come to the BUS STOP opposite the **National Park Visitors' Centre** (❹; 5h20min).

182

## Walks on
# El Hierro

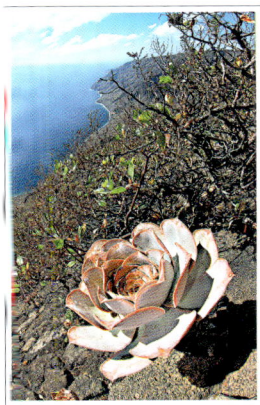

**El Hierro**
AREA: 269/km² (104sq mi)
LENGTH OF COAST: 110km (68mi)
HIGH POINT: Pico de Malpaso (1501m/4925ft)
POPULATION: 11,338 (2020)
POPULATION DENSITY: 41/km² (106/sq mi)
CAPITAL: Valverde (pop ±11,000, 2020)
PROVINCE: Santa Cruz de Tenerife

Landing on El Hierro by boat many years ago, Noel wondered what he had let himself in for. He wrote 'Before me rose a dried-up, sprawling mountain of rock, climbing straight out of the sea, treeless and barren. Tired stone walls stretched half-heartedly across steep sea slopes … the only hint of civilization.

But day by day the island's charms revealed themselves to me: dramatic cliff top views, highland pastures shrouded in mist, a countryside littered with volcanic cones, a maze of stone walls, turquoise-green rock pools, delightful rustic villages, venerable Canary pines and wizened junipers…'

183

# EL HIERRO

These are but a few of the island's unpublicised treasures. Still untouched by mass tourism, there are no high rises, no English pubs or German beer gardens, no sandy beaches, and hardly any hotels. You can swim in natural sea pools and stay in one of a handful of hotels, the four-star *parador,* a villa or an apartment. The island authorities have limited construction to less than half of El Hierro's total land surface and buildings to two storeys.

At the far southwest of the Canaries, this island was the 'edge of the world' — the furthest land to the west known to Europeans before the discovery of the Azores. Under Louis XIII, France declared Puerto de Orchilla the site of the prime meridian, and it remained so for over 200 years — before it was transferred to the Royal Observatory in Greenwich in 1844. There is a monument to this near the lighthouse at Orchilla … and, to tell the truth, El Hierro still seems a million miles from nowhere.

Noel also wrote to us, 'And where else would your taxi driver buy *you* lunch? El Hierro is by far the friendliest place in the Canaries.' Long may it remain so.

**Distance:** 4.5km/2.8mi; 1h10min *by car;* 9.5km/6mi; 2h20min *by bus*
**Grade:** ● easy, flat; *recommended for everyone.* The path is far enough away from the waves to be safe, but spray (especially from blowholes) may reach the path on a rough day *care with children!* And *do not leave the path:* the coastline itself is crumbly and unstable.
**Equipment:** walking shoes, jersey, water

**Refreshments:** only in Pozo de la Salud or Sabinosa
**Transport:** 🚌 to/from the signposted 'Arenas Blancas' parking area on the HI500 (27° 45.964'N, 18° 7.573'W); at times this low-lying road is closed after storms. Or 🚐12 to/from Pozo de la Salud and walk along the very quiet road to the Arenas Blancas parking area (allow an extra 2.5km/35min *each way*)

T his spectacular coastal path is really for everyone! Impressive lava formations, coastal arches, blow holes and weird rocks accompany you on the first leg of the walk; steep cliffs and a view of El Golfo fill the backdrop on the second part.

**Start off** at the signposted *PARKING AREA FOR ARENAS BLANCAS* (●) by following the clear track towards the coast. On the right is the small beach of **Arenas Blancas** with golden yellow sand. In the distance is the arc of El Golfo and nearby, on the black and bleak coastline the spa

hotel of Pozo de la Salud. At a first fork, keep right; then, 50m/yds further on, keep left. The track now loops back to the left, and a clear stone-lined coastal path runs forward along the rocky cliffs. (This path will eventually form part of a GR coastal route round the island, but at time of writing is

*Halophytic vegetation at the start of the walk — saltwort* (Schizogyne sericea), *sea fennel* (Astydamia latifolia; *see page 29*) *and sea lavender* (Limonium pectinatum). *Ice plants are halophytes* par excellence; *see page 30.*

*Arco de la Tosca*

your left. A lovely *mirador* on a cliff, overlooking a large sea-arch, the **Arco de la Tosca**, is on your right (**3**; **45min**). Here a track meets you from the left. Follow it down to the Playa del Verodal road (HI500), and turn left.

Walk back along this quiet road to the BLANCAS PARKING AREA (**1h10min**) — or continue on to **Pozo de la Salud** (**a**; **1h45min**) for your bus.

neither signposted nor waymarked.)

Follow this path to the left. After a few minutes you pass a first, large BLOW HOLE on the right (**1**; **10min**). Then the path moves inland for a while, to round a beautiful inlet. Another inlet follows (**20min**). Then you come to an elevated LAVA STREAM (**2**; **25min**), where path rises and falls a little, crossing this tremendous lava flow. Ten minutes later you pass through a *kipuka* (**35min**) — a patch spared by the lava, where an abundance of the original vegetation shown on page 185 flourishes.

After another 10 minutes you pass some stone-lined fields on

### Halophytic plants

*Near the coast, plants have to also be salt-tolerant (halophytic) in order to survive. They have to make do with very little water, as there's hardly ever any rain. Halophytes are perfectly adapted to this milieu and the salty air.*

*Salinization is a worldwide problem, increasing every day due to scanty rainfall, poor irrigation systems and water contamination. All this affects crop productivity: a significant proportion of cultivated land is salt-affected.*

*At present only about 2% of plants are halophytes. But study of their genetic properties can be used to modulate plant physiology according to salt stress and widen the agricultural base.*

## Walk 44: FROM FRONTERA UP TO THE MIRADOR DE JINAMA AND ON TO SAN ANDRÉS

**Distance/time:** 8km/5mi; 2h50min
**Grade:** ●● strenuous, with an ascent of 900m/3000ft and descent of 600m/1970ft. You must be sure-footed and have a head for heights. Take care crossing any loose gravel, whether on the path itself or as the result of a landslide. Don't attempt after heavy rain (danger of rockfall). *Only worth the effort on fine days!* It can be very windy and cold on the *cumbre*. Yellow/white waymarking (PR EH 8)

**Equipment:** walking boots, sunhat (tied on!), sunglasses, suncream, long-sleeved shirt, long trousers, walking pole(s), fleece, windcheat, raingear, picnic, water
**Refreshments:** available in Frontera and San Andrés
**Transport:** 🚐 taxi or with friends to Frontera (27° 45.313'N, 18° 0.078'W) — or 🚌 4 to Frontera bus station and then walk or 🚌 3 to 'Plaza Candelaria'. Return from San Andrés by 🚌 2 or 5, or taxi.

The first half of this walk follows the beautiful Camino de Jinama shown overleaf — an old transhumance trail, once used by shepherds twice a year. After the tough but beautiful ascent, during the second half of the walk you can stride out across the Nisdafe plateau to San Andrés, the island's highest village.

**Start the walk** in the tiny village of **Frontera** (⭕): take the small road between the two bars opposite the CHURCH. At the fork 10m/yds uphill, keep left for 'JINAMA'. A steep narrow road takes you up a hillside stepped with vineyards. An amphitheatre of precipitous walls encircling the entire bay rises up before you. Your path will climb this very wall! A couple of minutes after passing a parking area with a couple of benches, the road bends sharp right (**①**; **10min**). Turn left here, up a wide cobbled path (SIGN-POST). This fine centuries-old trail will take you up to the *mirador*. On reaching the road again, go left for 20m, then rejoin your path. Thick stone walls flank the *camino*. Cross the road one last time, by a sign, 'CAMINO DE JINAMA' (**20min**).

Above the vineyards the route dives into shady laurel woods and crosses the **Barranco las Esquinas**. The higher you climb, the more striking the views. The distant splash of white, high up the

mountain wall near the end of the *cumbre,* is Sabinosa. The path, a work of art, ascends in a string of tortuous Zs. The precipitous cliffs are home to some rare endemics: *Bencomia sphaerocarpa, Crambe strigosa* and *Sideritis canariensis,* as well as the more common *Echium strictum* and *Aeonium holochrysum*.

A BALCONY VIEWPOINT (**②**; 'Miradero'; **1h20min**) makes makes a good rest stop, looking across the coastal plain of *malpaís*. Pineapples are cultivated in the numerous greenhouses spread across it. The surrounding vegetation drips with moss and lichen. After ignoring a minor fork to the left, as you near the summit, a couple of stone tables and benches at a hillside *mirador* (**③**; **1h50min**) provide a superb view over the gulf, framed by the *cumbre*.

You will know you are finally approaching the top of the climb when you pass a DYKE and look ahead to the view overleaf: the path passes under an 'ARCHED'

187

*Almost there! We are just below the arched juniper, at the top of the trail.*

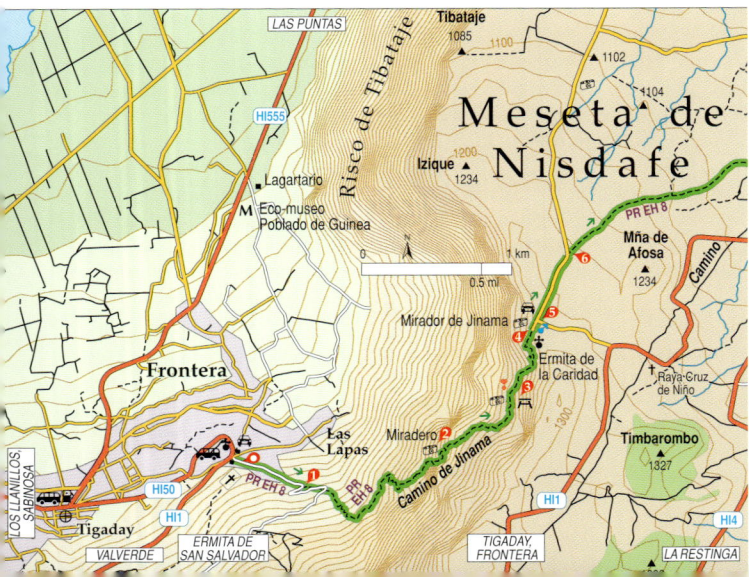

JUNIPER, with a MIRADOR to the left. There's a fountain and chapel at the **Mirador de Jinama** (**4**; **2h05min** — and a glorious view over El Golfo.

Follow the road away from the *mirador*. When it swings right towards the main road, continue straight on (**5**) along a country road. After seven minutes (500m), turn right on a wide, yellow/white waymarked path (**6**; 'PR EH 8, SAN ANDRÉS'). Some 30 minutes from the road, shortly after the path has widened to a track, turn right at a fork. Two minutes later, when a track joins from the right, follow it to the left (**7**; 'GR131, TIÑOR–VALVERDE, CAMINO DE LA VIRGEN').

This is the famous cross-island pilgrims' trail from the Ermita Virgen de los Reyes to Valverde, but you soon leave it. Just around the bend, turn right on another track. Minutes later, you cross the Guarazoca road and enter **San Andrés**, passing the SCHOOL and CHURCH. The BUS STOP (**8**; **2h 50min**) is outside the shop on the left, where you meet the main HI1.

### El Golfo

*Mega-landslides are arguably the most spectacular phenomena in nature — as can be seen on the neighbouring island of La Palma's Caldera de Taburiente.*

*The crater known today as El Golfo was formed by two giant overlapping landslides, 'only' a few thousand years apart, which devastated the El Golfo volcano on the north side of the island about 80,000 years ago. The underwater remains of the landslides lead geologists to reckon that these mega-slides were 1.5km/1mi long and 300m/1000ft high, submerging no less than 40% of the island! The result is a crater 15km/9mi wide, with walls 1000m/3300ft high.*

*It is not thought that there was any catastrophic tsunami associated with these landslides because they did not occur all at once, but as multiple events over time. As we were putting this book together, it was a great relief that the eruptions on La Palma did not result in a mega-landslide.*

*A work of art — the Camino de Jinama, an old camino real*

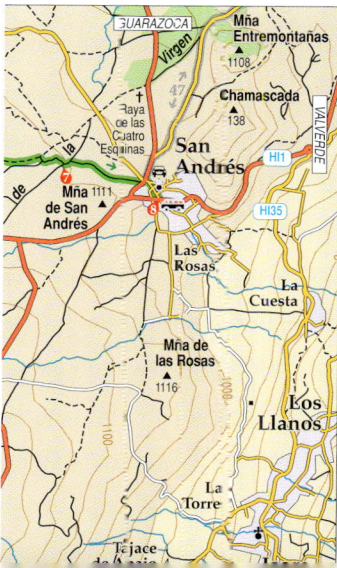

# Walk 45: FROM THE PISTA AL DERRABADO TO SABINOSA

**Distance/time:** 6.5km/4mi; 2h05min

**Grade:** ●● quite easy, with a descent of 600m/2000ft. You must be sure-footed and have a head for heights on some short sections. Don't attempt in wet weather. It can be very windy and cold on this walk, and the *cumbre* is often covered in cloud. White/yellow PR EH 1 waymarking much of the way

**Equipment:** stout walking shoes, sunhat, sunglasses, suncream, long-sleeved shirt, long trousers, jacket, windcheat, raingear, picnic, water

**Refreshments:** available at Sabinosa

**Transport:** 🚗 taxi or with friends to the Pista al Derrabado (27° 44.356'N, 18° 2.883'W). Return on 🚐7 from Sabinosa or telephone to Tigaday for a taxi from the bar in Sabinosa

**Alternative walk: Pista al Derrabado — Fuente de Mencáfete — Pista al Derrabado** (10km/6.3mi; 3h30min). ● Moderate, with an overall ascent/descent of about 340m/1115ft. Gentle track walk, but the final path to the *fuente* is steep and slippery. Access by 🚗 as above; wear walking boots. Follow the main walk to ❸, at which point stay on the track. This climbs in wide bends. Ignore the PR EH 1.2 joining from the right (🅐) and continuing uphill about 100m further on — it's easier to avoid as much of this steep path as possible. After about 25 minutes the track ends and a steep, narrow signposted path continues another 80m/260ft up to the **Fuente de Mencáfete** (🅑; **1h45min**) — two small round basins high in the valley.

This walk, on a lovely forestry track above the Golfo crater, is ideal for beginners. It takes you into the Reserva Natural de Mencáfete, home to fine examples of *fayal-brezal* and *laurisilva*. In fact the laurels up at the Fuente de Mencáfete (Alternative walk) are some of the most beautiful on the island — but that involves a tricky path.

**Start the walk** at the junction with a track, the **Pista al Derrabado** (🔴; signpost: 'FUENTE DE MENCAFETE'). From here you have a splendid view across the banana and pineapple plantations of El Golfo to the rocky islets of Salmor. Set off by following this track: it gradually descends around the sheer face of the escarpment, into the **El Golfo** crater. The hills are thickly wooded in laurel. The western part of the crater is bare of life save for the veins of stone walls that cross it. A spa, the Pozo de la Salud, is marked by a prominent hotel standing above the sea.

At one point (**35min**) you have an uninterrupted view through a gap in the vegetation over the

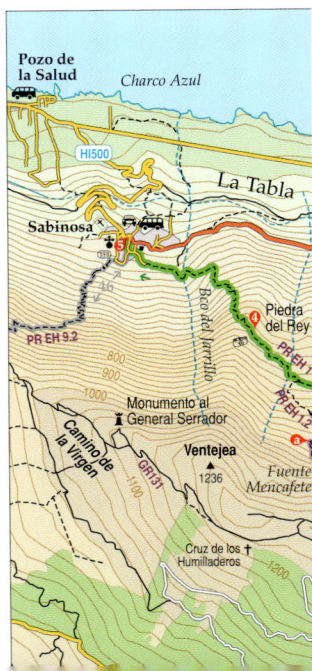

western wing of the crater. Pass through farmland set on shelves high in the wall of the *cumbre*. A good 20 minutes later, a path (the PR EH 1) joins you from the left (**1**). Some 200m/yds further on, where an asphalt road goes right, go left for 'FUENTE MENCAFETE' (**2**).

Around five minutes uphill, an ENCLOSED PROPERTY sits off the track to the right (**1b**). Just beyond it, be sure to leave the track, taking a grassy, perhaps overgrown path downhill (**3**); signpost: 'SABINOSA, PR EH 1'). Five minutes later, ignore a steep path left up to Fuente de Mencáfete. You round a steep hillside and will keep to this path all the way to Sabinosa: ignore any minor paths turning off.

A stone bench with a sign, 'KING'S STONE' (**Piedra del Rey**; (**4**; **1h20min**) makes a good rest stop. Just past it, as you round a bend, a bird's-eye view unfolds down onto the picturesque but rather severe looking Sabinosa, atop a volcanic mound that protrudes from the crater wall.

**The *fayal-brezal* zone**
While in northern Europe we're used to seeing heather coming up to our knees, in Macronesia we talk about *tree* heath — and in fact heather can grown up to about 15-20m/45-60ft high.

In Spanish the name for erica (heather) is *brezo*. Together with the wax myrtle or bayberry tree *(faya* in Spanish), they make up the *fayal-brezal* zone, common in the western Canary Islands between 500m and 1200m. They create a transition between the *laurisilva* and the higher pine forests. The *fayal-brezal* is at its best in spring, when the tree heather has tiny white bell flowers.

The dark volcanic slopes that surround it are patched in vineyards. The descent of these gravel slopes may prove slightly unnerving for some.

When you reach a street in **Sabinosa** (**2h**) keep straight ahead to Camino la Dehesa. Then go right downhill on Calle Hoya del Moral. The bus leaves from the *plaza* (**❺**; **2h05min**); the local bar is to the right.

*View to Sabinosa on the descent*

# Walk 46: THE ERMITA DE LOS REYES AND EL SABINAR

**Distance/time:** 9km/5.6mi; 2h35min

**Grade:** ● quite easy, with overall descents/ascents of about 200m/650ft on very lightly trafficked roads and tracks with one path section. But it can be very windy and cold, and the *cumbre* is often covered in cloud. GR 131 red/white waymarking on the path section; some yellow/white PR EH 9a waymarking

**Equipment:** trainers, sunhat, sunglasses, suncream, long-sleeved shirt, long trousers, jacket, wind-cheat, raingear, picnic, water

**Refreshments:** only in Sabinosa

**Transport:** 🚗 private transport to/from the Ermita de los Reyes (27° 43.801'N, 18° 7.259'W)

**Alternative walk:** *Ermita de la Virgen de los Reyes and El Sabinar from Sabinosa* **Distance/time:** 14.2km/8.8mi; 5h25min

**Grade:** ●: very strenuous; overall ascent/descent of about 900m/2300ft. You must be sure-footed and have a head for heights. Don't attempt in wet weather. It can be very windy and cold, and the *cumbre* is often covered in cloud. White/yellow PR waymarking throughout, also some red/white GR waymarking. Refreshments and equipment as main walk, but walking boots recommended. Access by 🚌 12 or 🚗 to/from Sabinosa; motorists should park near the *plaza* (27° 44.861'N, 18° 5.887'W). Notes on page 194.

La Dehesa, the island's pastoral highland, is an enchanting landscape, often enveloped in teasing fog and mist. This walk visits several highland beauty spots. It can be an easy, mostly track walk, if you base it on the *ermita*, or you can climb from the pristine village of Sabinosa (Alternative walk), if you are bursting with energy.

**Start the walk** from the **Ermita de la Virgen de los Reyes** (**○**): continue towards El Sabinar on the HI506/PR EH 9. The road quickly reverts to motor track and you come to a signposted junction by the **Piedra de los Regidores** (**❶**). The 'Bajada de la Virgin' (see

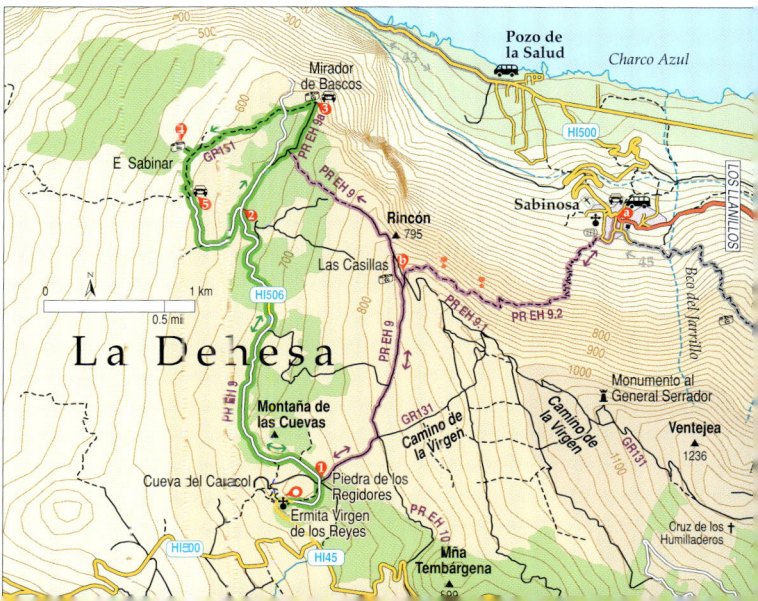

**El Sabinar**

*Above Sabinosa, in the Deshesa uplands, buffeted by northeast trade winds, are remnants of Canary junipers (Juniperus turbinata canariensis) — some so bent by the wind that their crowns touch the soil.*

*Once there were substantial juniper groves in the western Canaries. Like the laurels, these trees have been cut down for building or land clearance or have been the victims of fire.*

*The Sabinar is a magical place — especially in mist.*

the panel opposite) begins here at dawn. Turn left and pass through a GATE as you round the richly red **Montaña de las Cuevas**.

Undulating pastures criss-crossed with stone walls stretch back up to the hills. Remaining on the main motor track, take the first turn-off right some 2km along (**2**), walking through fragments of pine woods — a picturesque corner. At a fork about 400m along, head right. The **Mirador de Bascos** (**3**; **1h05min**) sits high on the very edge of the escarpment that encircles El Golfo. What a view! You look straight down on Sabinosa and the Pozo de la Salud and, if it's not in cloud, the view extends over the whole El Golfo basin to Las Puntas. The Alternative walk climbs to El Sabinar via this viewpoint.

From the car park here at the *mirador* turn half right downhill with the signposted PR EH 9. You

194

cross a motorable track and 15 minutes later pass a *VIEWPOINT* (**4**) at the right of the trail, on the far side of a wall. Already you can see the wind-buckled junipers *(sabinas)* below at El Sabinar. Now the trail descends beside the wall to the **Sabinar** CAR PARK (**5**; **1h25min**). This is a magnificent refuge for scatterings of centuries-old, twisted and gnarled *sabinas* (native junipers) — the result of the harsh unrelenting winds that batter this corner of the island. The track ends just in front of the island's most famous and most photographed specimen (shown at the left). An interesting information board explains the origin of these weird, 'arthritic' trees — unique in the archipelago. The surrounding vegetation here is thickly covered in moss and lichen. Please note that this is a protected area.

Leaving El Sabinar, follow the track out: in 15 minutes it rejoins the track from the Bascos viewpoint. Turn right, and retrace your steps to the **Ermita de la Virgen de los Reyes** (**2h35min**).

### Alternative walk: Ermita de la Virgen de los Reyes and El Sabinar from Sabinosa

**Start the walk** at the WALKERS' INFO BOARD and SIGNPOSTS by the *plaza* in **Sabinosa** (**1**): walk up Calle Hoya del Moral on the yellow/white waymarked PR EH 1. At a fork 100m/yds along, keep right. Then, just where this lane begins to descend, turn left uphill on a well-maintained path for 'CAMINO A LA DEHESA' (the yellow/white waymarked PR EH 9.2).

A steep zigzagging climb past vineyards and then heather follows, with no turn-offs to worry about. Dark green junipers dot the lower inclines. Don't forget to enjoy the views behind you. On reaching the *fayal-brezal* zone (see

**Ermita de la Virgen de los Reyes**

This dazzling white, isolated refuge is the sanctuary of the island's patron saint. Every four years, on the first weekend in July, a very popular pilgrimage (the 'Bajada de la Virgen') begins here, and an image of the Madonna crosses the island to Valverde

The island's most famous walk, the 28km-long 'Camino de la Virgen', follows this pilgrimage route, and our walks use the trail from time to time. The fiesta continues for almost a month. As you can imagine, many legends are associated with the Virgin.

---

panel on page 191), you may well be enveloped in cloud, surrounded by rocks and tree trunks thick with moss. Nearing the *cumbre* the way is slightly vertiginous. This is where you feel the full brunt of the wind, too.

Just over the CREST, by a SIGNPOST, you meet the end of a track on the edge of the **Dehesa** highland at a place called **Las Casillas** ( ⓗ ; **1h45min**). You overlook a pastoral landscape here, littered with old lichen-clad stone walls. Some 40m further on, at a fork, turn sharp right downhill on another trail, the PR EH 9 at the edge of the El Colfo crater.

The trail moves away from the edge of the basin, and after 10 minutes or so you go through a GATE. You leave the pasture walls behind as you walk to the left of a small pine wood making a half-hearted attempt to forest this uneven basin. But these pines are

out of the wind and, with luck, in the sun — as idyllic a spot as you'll find on the island. Ten minutes from the gate you meet a crossing track: turn right here, to the **Mirador de Bascos** (❸; **2h25min**).

From here follow the main walk from ❸ to **El Sabinar** (❺; **2h45**). Then just take the HI506 motor track past the **Piedra de los Regidores** (❶) to the **Ermita de la Virgen de los Reyes** (❍; **3h35min**). From the *ermita* retrace your steps to the Piedra de los Regidores, then take the signposted 'CAMINO DE LA VIRGEN'; it's waymarked yellow/white for the PR EH 9 and red/white for the GR131. In 10 minutes you come to a crossroads, where you turn left with the PR EH 9 on another motor track. Keeping straight ahead, in some 20 minutes you'll be back at **Las Casillas** ( ⓗ ; **4h15min**). Now retrace your steps down the zigzag path to **Sabinosa** (**5h35min**).

## Walk 47: FROM SAN ANDRÉS TO THE ARBOL GAROÉ

**Distance/time:** 7km/4.3mi; 1h50min

**Grade:** ● easy, with an ascent of under 100m/330ft; easily followed (some yellow/white PR and red/white GR signposting). Note that these highlands can often disappear under cloud and mists, and it can be cold and windy; the walk is best kept for fine, cloudless days.

**Equipment:** comfortable walking shoes or boots, fleece, jacket, long trousers, warm hat, raingear, water

**Refreshments:** available in San Andrés

**Transport:** 🚌2 or 5 to/from San Andrés. By 🚗: park in San Andrés (27° 46.239'N, 17° 57.293'W)

*Alternative walk: San Andrés — Arbol Garoé — Tiñor* (7.3km/ 4.4mi; 1h50min). ● Grade/ equipment/refreshments/access as above (🚌2 or 5 to San Andrés; 🚌2 back from Tiñor. See notes overleaf.

A visit to the Arbol Garoé (or Arbol Santo — El Hierro's 'Holy Tree') is a must. There is a very interesting interpretation centre where you can learn about 'horizontal rain', but the tree itself is mystical — an ideal place to meditate.

**Start the walk** by leaving **San Andrés** from the BUS STOP/CAR PARKING (○): walk past the CHURCH on your right and the school to the HI10 road, where you at first follow the yellow/white-waymarked PR EH 7/11 to the right. After 150m, turn right on a wide track (SIGNPOST), soon passing a row of volcanic cones on the right. After just under 1km along the track, you come to a junction where you meet the cross-island **Camino de la Virgen** (❶): keep right (signpost: 'GR131, PR EH7, TIÑOR, VALVERDE, EL GAROE, EL MOCANAL, LA CALCOSA').

A little over five minutes later, fork left uphill on asphalt (❷; **20min**; sign: 'ARBOL SANTO'). *(The Alternative walk leaves from this junction after visiting the tree.)* The way is tarred only for the first few minutes, then the beautiful earthen track shown on page 12 becomes your way. A basin of stone walls lies below to the right, and on the left volcanic mounds grow out of a tilting plateau. After 20 minutes, at the next fork, go left downhill (❸; signpost: 'ARBOL SANTO/GAROE'). A tarred road leads you down to a PARKING AREA/VISITORS' CENTRE (❹; open daily from 10.00-19.00, small entry fee) — a fascinating

### The Arbol Garoé

Chronicles dating from the Spanish Conquest refer to this tree ('Garoé') being venerated by the native Bimbaches. It was an enormous *til* (an indigenous laurel), with a trunk 1.5m in diameter, standing at an altitude of 1000m, where there is the greatest concentration of mists and rainfall from the trade winds. Its leaves were said to be plentiful enough to condense water to fill the cisterns and satisfy the needs of this small group of people. It is also known that in 1610 a strong hurricane tore the tree down. A new *til*, the one shown here, was not planted until 1949. It will take hundreds of years for it to achieve the girth of the original.

El Garoé is also the subject of many legends — one of which tells of a Bimbache maiden, Guarazoca, who fell in love with a Spanish soldier and revealed to him the source of their water. The tribe had been keeping the tree's location secret in the hope that the soldiers would leave the island because of its lack of water. For this betrayal she was punished with death.

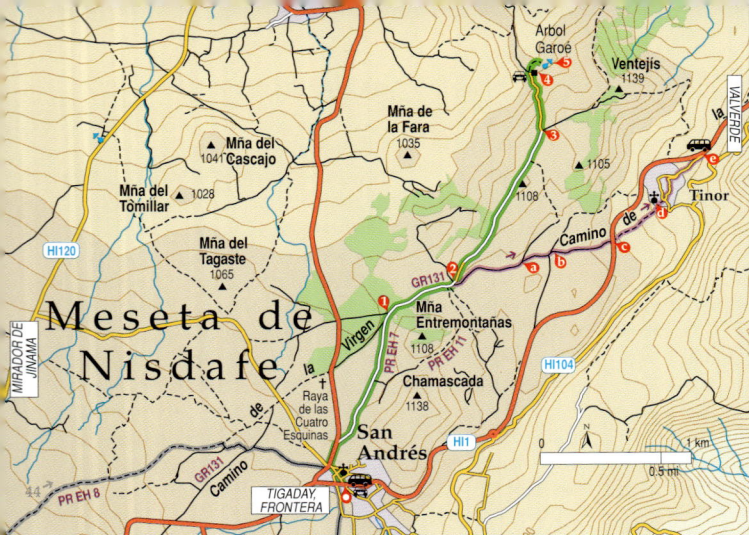

*One of the old cisterns near the Arbol Garoé*

place, where you can learn about the legends surrounding the tree but also about the phenomenon of 'horizonal rain'.

From the visitors' centre a well-trodden path heads right, round the hillside to **El Garoé**, the site of the original 'holy tree' (**5**; **Arbol Santo**; **55min**). From here retrace your steps to **San Andrés** (**1h50min**).

### Alternative walk: San Andrés — Arbol Santo — Tiñor

Follow the main walk to the Arbol Garoé, then return to the fork first encountered at the 20min-point (**2**; less than 30 minutes back; **1h20min**; signpost: 'GR131, TIÑOR, VALVERDE'). Turn sharp left here, across a sheltered basin. After a good five minutes, ignore a faint track to the left (**a**). Continue ahead for about another 200m and, at a staggered junction, first turn left and then, at the fork that follows 20m further on, keep right along a COBBLED TRAIL (**b**).

Above lie fields of *tagasaste*

(broom); its branches are cut for animal fodder. Soon you cross the MAIN HI1 ROAD (**c**) and descend to **Tiñor**, a quiet hamlet tucked away in a concealed valley. Entering the village, pass the CHURCH (**d**) and cross a road, to continue straight ahead on a signposted path, which descends to a driveway. Follow the drive back to the road, then keep straight on (right) for a couple of minutes, to regain the HI1 main road. There is a BUS STOP (**e**; **1h50min**) just here, or pick up your taxi.

# Index

Geographical names comprise the only entries in this index; for other subjects, see Contents, page 3. A page number in *italic type* indicates a map; **bold type** refers to a photograph: both may be in addition to a text reference on the same page.